W9-BCL-333

MILTON STUDIES
XXXI

MILTON STUDIES

XXXI ❧ *Edited by*

Albert C. Labriola

UNIVERSITY OF PITTSBURGH PRESS
Pittsburgh and London

MILTON STUDIES

is published annually by the University of Pittsburgh Press as a forum for Milton scholarship and criticism. Articles submitted for publication may be biographical; they may interpret some aspect of Milton's writings; or they may define literary, intellectual, or historical contexts—by studying the work of his contemporaries, the traditions which affected his thought and art, contemporary political and religious movements, his influence on other writers, or the history of critical response to his work.

Manuscripts should be upwards of 3,000 words in length and should conform to the old *MLA Style Sheet*. Manuscripts and editorial correspondence should be addressed to Albert C. Labriola, Department of English, Duquesne University, Pittsburgh, Pa., 15282-1703. Manuscripts should be accompanied by a self-addressed envelope and sufficient unattached postage.

Milton Studies does not review books.

Within the United States, *Milton Studies* may be ordered from the University of Pittsburgh Press, Pittsburgh, Pa. 15260.

Library of Congress Catalog Card Number 69-12335

ISBN 0-8229-3861-8

A CIP catalogue record for this book is available from the British Library

US ISSN 0076-8820

Published by the University of Pittsburgh Press, Pittsburgh, Pa. 15260

Manufactured in the United States of America

Printed on acid-free paper

Eurospan, London

CONTENTS

MILTON STUDIES
XXXI

SPIN CONTROLLING APOCALYPSE IN
SAMSON AGONISTES

Mark Houlahan

D URING JANUARY 1991 an evangelical cable television station
was soliciting donations for New Testaments to be sent to the American
soldiers then stationed in Saudi Arabia. This *Prayer Warrior's Pocket New
Testament* was designed to be easily carried into battle; an extra donation
would secure for the prayer warrior of your choice *The Prayer Warrior's
Pocket Guide to the New Testament.* The whole venture was called Operation Divine Shield. Much could be made of the complicity assumed here
between divine and American aspirations in the Persian Gulf. Presumably
just as Operation Desert Shield was being supported by Operation Divine
Shield, so too the Desert Storm which rained down on Iraq was assisted by
or perhaps was merely part of a Divine Storm through which Jehovah on
behalf of his chosen nation had once again put the pagans to rout. That at
least was the official American spin on the war: the forces of good had once
again triumphed over the forces of evil. But my purpose is not to question
that contemporary politico-biblical spin. It is rather historical: for such
martial formats of the good news are old news; and the *Prayer Warrior's
Pocket New Testament* was but the latest in a series of Protestant Scriptures
designed specifically for the use of soldiers in battle. The first such scripture
was published in August 1643 during the First English Civil War, on behalf
of the Parliamentarian Army.[1] This was a sixteen page octavo pamphlet
designed to "supply the want of the whole Bible; which a Souldier cannot
conveniently carry about him."[2] It consists mostly of passages from the Old
Testament showing a "fit Souldier" how "to fight the Lords battels." One of
the Lord's soldiers—or prayer warriors—chosen as an example is of course
Samson, under the heading "A Souldier must pray before he goe to fight."
The pamphlet cites Judges xvi, 28, just before Samson pulls down the
temple of the Philistines: "Then *Sampson* called unto the Lord, and said, O
Lord God, I pray thee thinke upon me, O God, I beseech thee strengthen
me at this time, &c."[3]

The *Souldiers Pocket Bible* used the 1560 Geneva translation, cherished by Protestant readers for its voluminous marginal commentary. Like

3

Edmund Calamy, the editor of the *The Souldiers Pocket Bible*, the Geneva translators and annotators were certain that Samson "shulde be separate from the worlde and dedicate to God," the better to prosecute his task which was to "begin to save Israel out of the hands of the Philistims [sic]."[4] Just as the Pocket Bible does, moreover, the Geneva Bible encouraged its readers actively to emulate Samson as deliverer. The marginal commentary in the Geneva Judges narrative mostly discusses Samson in the third person, as a historical example. At the climax of Samson's story, however, as he stands between the pillars, immediately prior to pulling them down upon himself and the Philistines, the commentary shifts into the first person, offering the interpretive gloss of the subject of the story. Thus in the text we read Samson praying "strengthen me at this time onely, that I may be at once avenged of the Philistims" before shifting to note *n* which reads "According to my vocation, which is to execute Gods judgements on the wicked."[5] "My vocation" ascribes a motive to Samson while offering one to readers, a point where they can imaginatively enter the story, becoming themselves part of God's plans. And this same verse is the one Calamy chose to encourage soldiers in his pocket Bible. His "&c." works similarly. Geneva's Judges xvi, 28 continues "strengthen me . . . that I maye at once be avenged of the Philistims." Presumably Calamy expected his readers to remember (or recite) this conclusion to the verse and act accordingly.

Judges xvi, 28 thus functions as a seventeenth century proof text for understanding Samson as a divinely inspired warrior and by extension as a "culture hero" for the soldiers of the New Model Army and its supporters.[6] Milton knew the Geneva text of Samson[7] and quite possibly the *Pocket Bible* as well, for he knew Calamy, compiler of the *Pocket Bible*, as part of the acronymic Smectymnuus group, whose attacks on Bishop Hall he had defended in 1641 and 1642. This familiarity with Calamy's earlier writings increases the likelihood that Milton would have known and sympathized with the Bible of 1643.[8] It is not so much a question of the *Pocket Bible* and Geneva "Samsons" being sources for *Samson Agonistes;* rather a matter of all three advancing a martial, Protestant version of Samson's story. As Joseph Wittreich has exhaustively shown, Milton was certainly aware of diverse critical readings of Samson available in the Renaissance; despite this, like Geneva's and Calamy's Samson, Milton's Samson thinks of his vocation as being that of a prayer warrior also. He begins the play lamenting his lapse from that vocation: "Promise was that I / Should *Israel* from *Philistian* yoke deliver; / Ask for this great Deliverer now" (38–40). Even in his torment he seems attuned to the phrasing of the Genevan commentary; and he leaves the stage vowing to commit "some great act" (1389).[9] In so doing Samson practices a form of biblical or Renaissance spin control, interpreting his story for his auditors, just as, for example, the Pentagon "spun" the story of the action in the Persian Gulf for the benefit of the international media, who took the role played in *Samson Agonistes* by the Messenger, their mutual task to narrate and interpret events their audience could never themselves see. Like those messengers, moreover, Samson spins interpretation not only to control what his auditors within the play will think and say of him but also to shape his future reputation. Stanley Fish has commented on Samson's fear of being a spectacle merely, reduced and constructed, in a Mulveyesque manner, by those who gaze upon him.[10] Samson seems rather more productively conscious of his status than Fish allows for, acutely aware of being gazed on and talked about, and anxious therefore to control both his contemporary and posthumous reputation. It is as if he were conscious, for example, of the Genevan Protestant reading sketched above; or the use that would be made of that reading in Milton's text—one of many plays and operas on the same subject; as well as the multiple readings by critics of seemingly every persuasion since the first publication of *Samson Agonistes* in 1671. "Am I not sung and proverb'd for a Fool / In every street" (203–04), Samson asks of the Chorus, anticipating the complex ways he has become part of Samsonite entertainments as well as an enduring folk hero. In his last scene Samson's anxious fear of being derided has been allayed, and he speaks of his renewed vocation (and concomitant fame) with prophetic grandeur:

> I begin to feel
> Some rousing motions in me which dispose
> To something extraordinary in my thoughts
> . . . .
> If there be aught of presage in the mind,
> This day will be remarkable in my life
> By some great act, or of my days the last. (1381–83; 1387–89)

For Samson narrating and interpreting his selves, backsliding and then returning to grace, is an integral part of realizing his vocation, at least within the confines of the Greek tragic form Milton self-consciously uses, in which Samson, the Chorus, and their visitors have little to do but discuss and report events unfolding elsewhere. The play was intended for an imaginary audience, to be heard and read, not seen. Yet it is not by any means a monodrama, for it is constructed, like the closet dramas of Milton's contemporary Margaret Cavendish, as a multiplicity of voices.[11] Each of the scenes in *Samson Agonistes*, in which there is nothing much to see though much to hear, takes the form of a debate, a contest as it were of speculators. Like Samson himself each of these speculators practices spin control, each convinced that his or her version of Samson is the truth. These speculations, furthermore, are placed in dialogic relation to each other, so that the play exfoliates these varying views rather than pronouncing on the absolute rightness of any one of them. The characters all speak with Miltonic accent, but he has exercised on this occasion the dramatist's privilege of removing himself from the spectacle of his characters' interpretations.

These Samsons are established in relation to the book of Revelation. The play's Hebrew characters each place Samson as prayer warrior in some kind of violent apocalyptic drama: these competing apocalypses are the subject of this essay. I shall first demonstrate the apocalyptic cast of the play's events, depicted as scenes in a universal, catastrophic theatre. Then I shall show how Samson, Manoa, the Chorus, Dalila, and the Messenger seek both to comprehend the apocalypse and, at the same time, to control future understandings of these events. Both Hebrews and Philistines demonstrate a theatrical grasp of Apocalypse. The events described in the temple, which pit Hebrew against Philistine, can be seen as a contest of theatrical spectacles, through which both spiritual and nationalist supremacy is sought. Those final spectacles may then be placed in relation to the history of Milton's attempts to understand and describe the promises of Apocalypse.

Spectacle in *Samson Agonistes* has been canvased by three recent commentators on the play: my discussion owes something to each of them. In both his recent "Spectacle and Evidence" and his earlier "Question and Answer in *Samson Agonistes*,"[12] Fish has highlighted the play's dialogic, interrogative form, noting especially the way key questions as to Samson's inspiration and motives remain unanswered in the play. Nothing, in Fish's terms, finally comes of anything here. The problem with this outlook is that not having found everything he sought—full disclosure of Samson or God—Fish refuses to find anything at all: "God and Samson unite only in being inaccessible, objects alike of an interpretive activity that finds no corroboration in the visible world."[13] Despite its witty subtlety, Fish's reading makes an almost perversely comprehensive demand of Milton's drama. When was the last time God unequivocally and irrefutably showed himself forth? There being no answer to *that* question, I have focused instead on the dramatic nature of the play's action, which puts several versions of Samson into play. Since each version is that of a particular and limited character, none holds out ultimate wisdom. The metaphor of spin control seems useful as a way of describing this process of shaping a particular version of events and then acting upon it. The play may indeed be as bitterly emptied of significance as Fish claims, but that is not what any voice in the play maintains. Moreover the Geneva/Calamy glosses demonstrate the possibility at least of a positive, activist Samson such as that bloodthirstily imagined by Manoa and the Chorus.

The *Samson Agonistes* presented here is thus much more akin to that advanced by David Loewenstein. He argues that we should take seriously Milton's appetite for regenerative violence, saving destruction in history, and, consequently, that *Samson Agonistes* "dramatizes a turbulent side of Milton that was deep in his writings from at least the early revolutionary tracts."[14] The case argued here supports Loewenstein's general argument for turbulence by paying closer attention to the play's immersion in Revelation itself, so that it becomes more specifically apocalyptic rather than iconoclastic. Loewenstein demonstrates the continuity between *Samson Agonistes* and Milton's prose works. This emphasizes the theatricality of the play's rhetoric, but flattens its dramatic texture, since it makes the drama seem coterminous with Milton's opinions. Fish's "Question and Answer" is a useful corrective to this kind of monologic tendency.

Finally, Laura Lunger Knoppers has presented not the spectacle of evidence or iconoclasm but the spectacle of the martyred and /or treasonous bodies of the regicides, which were displayed in London in October 1660.[15] Knoppers usefully underlines Samson's awareness of his status as a spectacle, the righteous potential of violence in the play, and the likelihood of it having been composed after 1660. My approach assumes likewise that this dating is correct. In the sequence of Milton's apocalypses, *Samson Agonistes* makes sense as a Restoration text—a point to which I will return in my conclusion. Until Parker's arguments to the contrary are convincingly extended, it seems best left there.

Milton's *Samson Agonistes*—the play as well as its chief character—was conceived in fire. In the Trinity College Notebook there is a list of forty-two possible scenarios for a tragic drama. The Samsons sketched here are "Samson Pursophorus" (Firebringer) or "Hybristes" (the Proud); "Samson Marrying"; and finally "Dagonalia."[16] Elements from all these scenarios have survived into the final play: either despairing or triumphant Samson is conspicuously proud of his special relation to God; the central scene of the play explores the anguish of Samson's marriage to Dalila; and the play unfolds on a festival day dedicated to Dagon, though the celebrations do not proceed quite as the Philistines had planned. These scenarios are thus part of the play's early archaeology, in much the same way that the drafts of Satan's speeches for the play *Adam Unparadis'd* emerge twenty years later in *Paradise Lost.*[17]

For our present purposes "Samson Pursophorus" is the most intriguing of these proto-Samsons. Merritt Y. Hughes notes that this suggests a
play based around the "arsonist Samson who drove three hundred foxes
with torches on their tails into the standing corn of the Philistines,"[18] an
incident not referred to in the 1671 text. Samson's status as a divine
arsonist, a bearer of God's flame and hence as an agent of apocalypse, is
however made very clear. Samson's birth was foretold by an angel which
"in flames ascended / From off the Altar . . . / As in a fiery column char-
ioting / His Godlike presence" (25–28). The Chorus heralds Samson's
departure for the temple by recalling this same angel (1431–35). Samson's
own recollections of his violent career are "Toucht with the flame: on thir
whole Host I flew / Unarm'd" (262–23). His final triumph of course occurs
at the "blaze of noon" (81); this leads the Semichorus into their inflamma-
tory praise of Samson's "fiery virtue" comparing him to an Evening Dragon, an Eagle bolting thunder on Philistine heads, and finally to the Phoenix, reviving from its ashy womb, signaling the "beginning of a new age."[19]
In their rhetoric the Chorus increasingly transforms Samson's individual
feats into those of a cosmic force: they are the keenest proponents of
Apocalypse in the play.

Just such forces, it was thought, would be required to dispense with
the old heaven and earth and, as Revelation promises, issue in their new
replacements. Ten years after *Samson Agonistes* was first published, for
example, Thomas Burnet proposed his *Theory of the Sacred Earth* (1681)
which postulates that the forces required to transform the earth from what
it was before the Fall to what it now is and shall be after the final deluge
could only be volcanic. *Paradise Lost* depicts comparable scenes of cosmic
upheaval during Michael's narrative in Books XI (822–35) and XII (545–
51). For Milton's generation Samson is of course a historical figure, so his
actions in ancient Israel cannot directly portend the Apocalypse to come.
Rather the play's strategy is to describe these actions as if they were
apocalyptic, as a way of evoking their extent and force. The Chorus thus
hopes that Samson's execution of his "errand on the wicked" (1285) will be
"Swift as the lightning glance" (1284) which anticipates their posthumous
troping of Samson as a force of nature. They revel too in the images the
offstage sounds of Samson's destruction evoke for them of "universal
groan" (1511); and even temperate Manoa says of the shout of Philistine
triumph that it "tore the Sky" (1472). The Messenger confirms these
catastrophic speculations. His eyewitness account depicts Samson's actions in global terms as a terrene and aerial upheaval. He seems well-
versed in Revelation's vision of such transformations, borrowing from it

transforming winds and waves, convulsing mountains, and of course apocalyptic thunder:

> straining all his nerves he bow'd;
> As with the force of winds and waters pent
> When Mountains tremble, those two massy Pillars
> With horrible convulsion to and fro
> He tugg'd, he shook, till down they came, and drew
> The whole roof after them with burst of thunder. (1646–51)

The play presents us unflinchingly with reports of this "so horrid spectacle" (1542) which the Messenger tries to flee but yet which in fleeing he is forced to confront again through having to describe.

How to read this "horrid" apocalypse is open to debate. As Wittreich's *Interpreting "Samson Agonistes"* documents, Samson's story has always been a site of contest, always already open to strategic misprision. *Samson Agonistes* is of course a play for several voices, so the claims for Samson's apocalypse begin to be made during the play, on the festival day itself. In the final stages of the play Manoa, the Messenger, and the Chorus come to sound rather like Old Testament media experts forced to pronounce instantly on a series of events only one of them has witnessed and the significance of which is far from clear.

Samson himself initiates these obsessive readings of his actions. Having been God's "nursling once and choice delight, / His destin'd from the womb" (633–34), he is uncertain whether he is still to be Israel's deliverer from the Philistines or whether that role has passed him by as a result of his apostasy. He reveals these confusions in his opening soliloquy and first exchange with the Chorus. He enunciates to them the despairing, quietist reading of his situation: "Myself my Sepulcher, a moving Grave" (102). Later he announces to them (or at least hints at) his restoration to divine favor. He leaves the stage buoyed up by "rousing motions in me which dispose / To something extraordinary my thoughts" (1382–83). It is never made clear whether at the pillars Samson acts opportunistically in a situation he had not foreseen or whether the "something extraordinary" in his thoughts includes the pillar scenario, rather than a more general desire to enact God's vengeance.

What is clear is that Samson's recovery of his status as prayer warrior means that he returns also to his former violent career. Samson, Manoa remarks, "hath quit himself / Like *Samson*" (1709–10), like someone who is proud of his martial skills and proud too to reclaim them. As his combative spirit is replenished during his confrontations with Dalila, Harapha, and

the Philistine officer, so too his urge to commit further acts of violence in
God's name returns. The first return occurs toward the end of his exchange
with Dalila when he repels her with the most terrible of all his threats: "Not
for thy life, lest fierce remembrance wake / My sudden rage to tear thee
joint by joint" (952–53). This is followed by his Tamburlainean instruction
to Harapha:

> Go baffl'd coward, lest I run upon thee,
> Though in these chains, bulk without spirit vast,
> And with one buffet lay thy structure low,
> Or swing thee in the Air, then dash thee down
> To the hazard of thy brains and shatter'd sides.   (1237–41)[20]

His relish for the task of delivering Israel is palpable. As Harapha leaves
the stage Samson has clearly recovered the strength necessary to "blank
[Dagon's] Worshippers" (471). Blank is usually glossed as meaning to
confound, but *O.E.D.* gives also a sixteenth-century usage "to strip off the
skin" which sounds more like what Samson has in mind.[21] Through this
capacity for violence what thus sounds like another vainglorious, Marlo-
vian boast, as Samson prepares to leave the state, that "this day will be
remarkable in my life" turns out to be blunt, cataclysmic fact. The unleashing of that cataclysm means that quitting "himself / Like Samson" (1709–
10) involves rewriting himself back into an approximation of Revelation's
scenario of cosmic vengeance and upheaval, on which, as we have seen,
the play so eloquently draws.

     After the Messenger has finished his narrative, Manoa and the Cho-
rus enthusiastically begin revising for their own purposes Samson's "catastrophe," his "conclusion or final event," his "calamitous fate."[22] Manoa
alternates between the zeal he feels on behalf of Israel's cause and Samson's role in prosecuting it and his more private concern for his son's
physical and spiritual welfare. When he had first visited Samson earlier he
tried to rouse his son from torpor by reminding him of the duties his gifts
impose on him (577–78). Manoa's efforts to stir Samson fail at that point.
When he returns he is preoccupied with Samson's private future, anxious
that at the least the Philistines will allow his son the untroubled "old age
obscure" (572) Samson sketched as his retirement plan earlier in the play;
and so it seems that Manoa's parental ambitions for his son as a national,
martial Messiah have been put to one side. His desire for filial glory
rekindles though, together with his nationalism, when he hears from the
Messenger of the Philistine defeat: "*Gaza* yet stands, but all her Sons are
fall'n, / All in a moment overwhelm'd and fall'n" (1558–59); to which

Manoa replies "Sad, but thou knowest to *Israelites* not saddest / The desolation of a Hostile City" (1560–61).

Here momentary compassion is outweighed by toughminded nationalism, an acceptance of fate tinged with joy at the Hebrew triumph. This leads further to a reconsideration of his son's having now "Fully reveng'd" (1712) himself. His paternal satisfaction in that full vengeance is partly temporal: his son has amply fulfilled his violent potential, leaving his enemies "years of mourning" (1712), as Manoa with some relish puts it. Partly too the satisfaction is spiritual. Manoa assumes that Samson's actions were divinely assisted, that finally God was not "parted" (1719) from Samson, but rather "favoring and assisting to the end" (1720). Manoa's apocalypse, then, combines personal, national, and spiritual concerns. His first question to the Messenger alludes to Revelation: "How died he? death to life is crown or shame" (1579). The Messenger's reply convinces Manoa that Samson must have triumphantly albeit proleptically fulfilled the contract offered the church of Smyrna in Revelation ii, 10: "be thou faithful unto death, and I will give thee a crown of life."

Confident that such a crown must now be Samson's reward, Manoa can begin planning his son's funeral, drastically revising his son's previous gloomy grave talk. Funeral rites will be Manoa's major means of influencing the posthumous spinning of Samson's reputation as a prayer warrior. The body will be prepared for burial as that of a fallen hero; Manoa's imagery recalls that of the apostrophes to the broken body of Hippolytus, borne over the stage at the end of Euripides' *Hippolytus* and Seneca's *Phaedra*. Manoa's anticipated actions demonstrate his grief and love for his son, at once tender and grotesque:

> Let us go find the body where it lies
> Soak't in his enemies' blood, and from the stream
> With lavers pure and cleansing herbs wash off
> The clotted gore.   (1725–28)

The subsequent ceremony will be a civic funeral with "silent obsequy and funeral train" (1732); the planned tomb sounds like that of a Renaissance noble, a harmonious edifice to replace the broken monument beneath which Samson lies buried here in Gaza. It combines Roman and Judeo-Christian elements, surrounded by laurel, signaling Samson's martial triumph; and palm, signaling Christian triumph and victory in death. It will itself become a kind of temple, visited on feastful days with Hebrew ceremonies to perpetuate the obliteration of Dagon's feast. By itself such a tomb might be sufficient to point the Hebrew moral; in seventeenth-century fashion it will also be inscribed with the record of Samson's "Acts enroll'd / In copious Legend, or sweet Lyric Song" (1736–37): it sounds rather as if Manoa has not yet made up his mind as to which genre might aptly commemorate Samson. In his choices Manoa reaches through the time in which he is ostensibly placed to anticipate Samson's continuing resonance for Judeo-Christian culture and, more particularly, the generic forms within which Milton has here spun him. "Copious legend" evokes a narrative text, like the Judges narrative or the Messenger's speech here; "sweet lyric song" suggests something like the song of Deborah, praising Samson as the "patron of national liberation"[23] or the psalmic songs of triumph with which the Chorus concludes the play.

The planned tomb would thus function as rather more than a vehicle for private, paternal grief. Reading its inscribed "copious legend" or "lyric song" would be to encourage a textual empathy, a subjective identification with Samson analogous to that encouraged in the Geneva and *Pocket Bible* texts. Such sublimation of readers to biblical exemplars (which is yet a fulfillment of each individual reader) is of course a well-studied part of the Reformation, made possible through the use of the printing press as an agent of change, as Elizabeth Eisenstein puts it. Vernacular Bibles and silent reading made such individual spiritual renewal widely practiced.[24] Bunyan's *Grace Abounding to the Chief of Sinners* is the most resonant example we have of this process at work in the life of a historical figure. Part of the power of *Samson Agonistes* as a dramatic fiction arises out of the immersion of its various spin controllers in a similar project.

Like Manoa, for example, the Chorus is well-versed in Old and New Testament prophecy: they know exactly what to expect of their prayer warrior's deliverance. After Harapha's exit they speculate that Samson may be numbered among heaven's patient saints and earn the crown Manoa also anticipates by "trial of . . . fortitude" (1288). This patient fate is an alternative to the more active one, where Samson "swift as the lightning glance" (1284) would execute "His errand on the wicked" (1285). Their glorying in Samson's subsequent prosecution of that errand suggests that this was all along their preferred alternative. Of all the play's spin controllers they seem most immersed in Revelation's fantasy ("extravagant or visionary fancy"[25]) of revenge. They assume that, like Babylon, the Philistines are "drunk with the wine of the blood of the saints" (Rev. xvii, 6). This accusation is first leveled by Manoa, scorning "th'Idolatrous rout amidst their wine" (443). The Messenger provides eyewitness proof of the connection between Philistine Dagonolatry, blood, and liquor: "Sacrifice / Had fill'd their hearts with mirth, high cheer, and wine, / When to thir sports they turn'd" (1612–14). He confirms what the Chorus had been led to expect, hence their transformation of his report into taunt-song, gloating over the defeat of those "Drunk with Idolatry, drunk with Wine" (1670). The satisfaction of knowing that the Philistines were finally as vilely pagan as they previously had seemed to be fuels the Chorus' glee at their destruction, the "dearly bought revenge, yet glorious!" (1660).

"Dearly bought" signals their awareness of the human cost of Samson's victory. Unlike Manoa they dwell for a moment only on Samson's death, moving quickly to consider instead the universal theatre of death Samson has brought into being. Their rhetoric here again recalls Revelation's universal scene. They are quick to expand on the scale, for example, of the noise Manoa hears before the Messenger's arrival, emphasizing the extremity of an apocalyptic event marked by "universal groan," the "whole inhabitation perish'd," "destruction at the utmost point" (1511–1512, 1514). They gleefully list the signs of an Apocalypse on a scale they envisage: "Blood, death, and deathful deeds" (1513). They assure Manoa of Samson's centrality to their fantasy: "Thy Son is rather slaying them" (1517) and envision that even as they speak Samson may "now be dealing dole among his foes, / And over heaps of slaughter'd walk his way" (1529–30). Samson here is endowed with an ultimate degree of destructive power: he sounds like some invincible automaton programmed like a Terminator or Spenser's Talus for compulsive destruction. Though cruelly inaccurate, since crushed beneath the temple "walk his way" is the last thing Samson could at this point be capable of, their vision has a grim and tactile vividness; like John of Patmos the Chorus is steeped in the rhetoric of gore.

To this journalistic hyperbole (this is what must be happening now) the Chorus adds the characteristic desire felt in the play to spin those events in order to control what this particular apocalypse will mean in the future. Manoa claims Samson's actual body for burial, leaving the Chorus to offer a series of epitaphs, commencing the accretion of Samsonite texts to which Manoa will contribute in turn the promised tomb inscriptions. The Chorus' elegies disclose the obverse of their certainty that the Babylonian Philistines have been justly and comprehensively routed, which they take as proof that God has borne "witness gloriously" (1752) to Samson now returned to "*Silo* his bright Sanctuary" (1674). They seek adequate formulation for Samson's actions, moving through the sequence Evening Dragon, Jovian Eagle before settling on the Arabian Phoenix, whose self-immolation guarantees its certain resurrection; promising then earthly fame for Samson, and anticipating also the heavenly crown which they are certain must now be his. Like Manoa's tomb plans, these epitaphs are as much a part of the seventeenth century as they are of the Old Testament; both evoke a commemorative "art [which] both describes the past life of the deceased and establishes the person's future reputation."²⁶ Like Geneva's or Calamy's Samson, moreover, they encourage emulation by their readers and hearers, whose future task will be to complete the vanquishing of God's enemies Samson has initiated.

We are not of course offered Philistine epitaphs for Samson's final hour. It seems likely that Dalila, Harapha, and the Officer, the play's Philistine spokespersons, perished in the temple, since only "The vulgar . . . scap'd who stood without" (1659). They do however provide us with alternative perspectives, pro-Philistine, anti-Hebrew, on Samson as a successful prayer warrior. In his confrontation with Dalila in particular we see Samson "agonistes" (just a champion or athlete) wrestling with an opponent who refuses to be cowed: from her perspective their scene might well be called "Dalila Triumphantes."

Samson and the Chorus seek to forestall any such Dalilan triumph by warning themselves against her powers. For them her attributes are pagan, Babylonian, Antichristian as well as those traditionally associated with the "seductress" who seeks power over men; in all these attributes Dalila's literary descent can be traced in part from Cleopatra, the "old Serpent of the Nile." Dalila too is a "pois'nous bosom snake" (763) possessed with "Adder's wisdom" (936), a "viper" (1001), a "manifest Serpent" (997), a "specious Monster" (230). In their choice of Dalilan epithets Samson and the Chorus speak with one voice, each encouraging the other in their scale of abuse. The snake of course suggests Lucifer or the Antichrist in one aspect; the sea imagery offers another. Dalila

> bedeckt, ornate, and gay,
> Comes this way sailing
> Like a stately Ship
> Of *Tarsus*, bound for th'Isles
> Of *Javan* or *Gadire*
> With all her bravery on, and tackle trim.   (712–17)

Since Dalila is here like a ship of Tarsus or "Tartessus in Southern Spain" we may think of her also as partly Spanish and Catholic²⁷; this returns us again to Revelation where Babylon standing in for Rome (for Patmos pagan, for Milton papal) is similarly "bedeckt": "And the woman was arrayed in purple and scarlet colour, and bedeckt with gold and precious stones and pearls" (Rev. xvii, 4). Like Babylon and like Circe also Dalila is a cunning "sorceress" (819) deploying a "fair enchanted cup" (934), like Babylon's "golden cup full of abominations and filthiness of her fornication" (Rev. xvii, 4); and her "warbling charms" (934) are like those of the Sirens: Samson seeks to evade her "fair fallacious looks, venereal trains" (533) by promiscuously comparing her to a series of female avatars. His desperate attempts to do so attest to the force of Dalila's power. Not only are her looks sexually diseased and compromising, for example, but her "gins and toils" render her capable of committing a wide range of felonies: "Murderer . . . Traitor, Parricide, / Incestuous, Sacrilegious" (832–33). Like Babylon herself "THE MOTHER OF HARLOTS AND ABOMINATIONS OF THE EARTH" (Rev. xvii, 5) there is seemingly no abomination of which Dalila might not be capable. That at least is the official Hebrew version, somewhere between a propagandist broadsheet and a press release, exonerating Samson for his submission to her. Her powers must indeed be as they claim: how else could the "invincible *Samson*" (341) have been vanquished?

But it takes two to sustain a holy war: Dalila's Philistine version of the events of her marriage is necessarily somewhat different. Her narrative self-fashioning contradicts the claims of Hebrew propagandists. She encounters Samson's rhetoric with a powerful voice of her own, making their scene the most dramatic of the play's encounters; she offers images of violence to equal his; and like Samson she too anticipates her posthumous reputation aware, again like Shakespeare's Cleopatra also, of the way her story will be enacted and narrated for future generations.

Dalila does not see herself as a "Traitress" (725); she has after all done her state some service, cajoled to do so "by all the bonds of civil Duty / And of Religion" (853–54) eventually sacrificing the claims of her marriage bond to those of "Virtue . . . truth, duty" (870). Her reluctance to become a Philistine heroine testifies to her feeling for Samson, and she begins their scene attempting to reclaim those affections; when Samson recoils from those advances she reverts to her role as patriotic heroine. The dignity and eloquence which so conspicuously mark Dalila here are not to be found in the Judges narrative; they are rather akin to traits of her literary ancestors, Cleopatra and Babylon: "for she saith in her heart, I sit a queen, and am no widow, and shall see no sorrow" (Rev. xviii, 7).

Her attempts at reconciliation rejected, she revels instead in her role as a Philistine saint, a martial heroine no less famous than Samson. "Fame," she reminds him, "is double-mouth'd, / And with contrary blast proclaims most deeds" (971–72); with this reminder she provides room for a Philistine reading of her story. Rather than as treacherous as Babylon she will be thought as brave as Jael who "Smote *Sisera* sleeping through the Temples nail'd" (990). In citing this example of female strength Dalila recalls the initial account in Judges iv, 21 together with Deborah's recapitulation in her song of triumph (Judges v, 26–27), thus anticipating the inclusion of her own story in such songs: "I shall be nam'd among the famousest / Of Women, sung at solemn festivals / Living and dead recorded" (982–84).

Reminding Samson of Jael's physical strength ripostes his threat to tear Dalila "limb from limb" and surely reminds him also of the damage she has brought upon his own head. She anticipates fame for her actions during her lifetime, the "public marks of honor and reward" (992); and that she will become part of Philistine (as Samson of Hebrew) national legend and literature; and she will moreover have a public tomb "with odors visited and annual flowers" (987) which anticipates Manoa's prediction that "Virgins also shall on feastful days / Visit [Samson's] Tomb with flowers" (1741–42). Presumably Dalila's annual flowers will be equally "feastful," commemorating the Dagonalia which, in one of his first scenarios for the play, Milton planned to describe.

Dalila's strong narrative thus counters the play's Hebrew spin controllers, eloquent reminder that while Samson beats the Philistines in this instance the total obliteration of God's enemies which Revelation promises and which the play anticipates lies some way ahead. In the 1660s Milton was keenly aware of the way such ultimate triumphs might be postponed, since he found himself enduring a kind of internal exile in what Nicholas Jose acutely (and Miltonically) describes as a "particular kind of corrupt state: superficial, secular, imperial, greedily mercantile, crypto-Catholic, absolutist . . ."[28]; to which we should add Babylonian, Stuart, Philistine.

The homologies between these last two regimes, and their evident durability, perhaps account for the anxiety felt in the play over the contest between God and Dagon, represented in the counternarratives offered for Samson and Dalila. The Hebrews insist that there can be no such contest since God "Besides whom is no God" (441) must prevail, but their insistence on this point becomes somewhat hysterical, indicating an anxiety that this God may not in fact prevail and that, like Dalila, Dagon will prove to be a redoubtable opponent.

For the Hebrews Dagon is a sea idol merely, the worship of whom is marked by theatrical shows and processions such as those that take place on this particular festival day. These material demonstrations of Dagon's followers make him, they hope, inferior to the Hebrew God. On the one hand they fear that Dagon having entered the "lists with God" (463) may indeed triumph; on the other they fear that Samson will be included as token of victory in Dagonite rituals, and that through this display God will be "Disglorified, blasphem'd, and had in scorn" (442). In the Messenger's account it does indeed seem as if the Philistines view Samson as the chief emblem of Dagon's victory, paraded as part of a neo-Roman triumphal procession, part captive and, as former strongman, part circus freak, thus realizing Samson's fear that he will become indistinguishable from the

Philistine "Gymnic Artists, Wrestlers, Riders, Runners, / Jugglers and Dancers, Antics, Mummers, Mimics" (1324–25). Samson's anxiety operates on a personal as well as on a spiritual/nationalistic level: that he will be transformed into a vulgar piece of Philistine entertainment and that this will testify to Dagon's and Philistia's triumph, since what Samson nightmarishly imagines is exactly the kind of noisy carnival spectacle Dagon apparently delights in.

The Hebrews are adamant that the "interminable" (307) and "uncontrollable" (1754) God of Abraham is a cut above this outré idol. He does not require such treachery as Dalila practices to discover and betray Samson's secrets, for example. For Samson, this proves that Dagon is nothing but an idol, a false, not true, God:

> gods unable
> To acquit themselves and prosecute their foes
> But by ungodly deeds, the contradiction
> Of their own deity, Gods cannot be.   (896–99)

Nor does Samson's God require the Hollywood Babylon style of public festival, complete with mobs of howling revelers "Drunk with Idolatry, drunk with Wine" (1670) worked into Bacchic frenzy. Yet the Hebrew God does have a theatrical sensibility. The danger of Dagon as an opponent is shown by the way his spectacle is countered by another "horrid" spectacle, more lurid and certainly more catastrophic than the first. If Dagon were not such a dangerous adversary he could surely be more easily dismissed. Instead Samson counters with a rival spectacle, the theatre of God's judgments in which, like the final Apocalypse it anticipates, the victory of 'good' is no less spectacular than the temporary triumphs of evil. "In effect", Loewenstein notes, "the contest . . . becomes a contest of dramatic spectacles, namely the drama of Dagon versus the drama of God."[29] Samson is goaded into this demonstration partly by Harapha. He sneers at Samson's godly strength as "black enchantments, some Magician's Art" (1133), asserting of the Hebrews what they do of the Philistines, and peppers his speech with pagan oaths: "O *Baäl-zebub!*" (1231), "By *Astaroth*" (1242), suggesting, however comically, that not just the sea idol but the Lord of the Flies and the Phoenician Moon-Goddess have entered the lists against the God of Abraham. "Harapha's episode is therefore crucial to the advancement of the struggle between two forms of worship."[30] Thus, as the chorus recognizes, "matters . . . are strain'd / Up to the height" (1348–89).

Recognizing this also, and with a theatrical sense as keen as any of the Philistines, Samson waits until Dagon's festival is at its height, in the "blaze of noon" (80) before unleashing his coup de theatre/coup d'état, which the Chorus review in suitably theatrical terms as a "great event" (1756). They even describe their spiritual transformation as an orthodox Aristotelian catharsis, not only assuring themselves that what they have heard was a piece of divine fireworks executed on the wicked, but that, also, they are reacting as they should to a piece of prophetic tragic drama "with calm of mind, all passion spent" (1758). In short they are cheering themselves up. It was a goodly "horrid spectacle" of which they were godly spectators or rather auditors; and so they give themselves permission to leave. They claim to have been dismissed by the "unsearchable . . . highest wisdom" (1746–07, 1757) but they have received no such direct instruction. Rather they read that intention via the Messenger's interpretive account of Samson's final actions. For them this constitutes sufficient proof that Samson has returned finally to being a faithful champion, a prayer warrior. Their certainty has frequently been read as Milton's, but it is simplistic to underread the play's competing spectacles, the intricacies of spin controlling its protoapocalypse as underwriting unequivocally the Chorus' claim that "All is best / . . . And ever best found in the close" (1745; 1748).[31] The play as I have described it might be called not Samson but Samsons Agonistes: a series of Samsons, those spun by Samson, Dalila, Manoa, Harapha, the Messenger, and the Chorus, which compete for our attention and from which it is for each of us to choose our place of rest. Wittreich's hope that we can recover an originary Samson endorsed by Milton as the "true form of the Samson story" seems to me fruitless and naive. But he is surely right to suggest that, in its multiple Samsons, the play anticipates the tangled history of its exegesis.[32]

These competing Samsons, as I have shown, are invested one way or another in the book of Revelation. That investment, by turns ethical, emotional, and aesthetic, is shared by Milton throughout his career. For the last twenty years Barbara K. Lewalski's "Samson Agonistes and the Tragedy of the Apocalypse"[33] has been the canonical statement on this subject. Following Lewalski's lead it is a commonplace of Samson Agonistes criticism to gesture toward David Pareus's famous commentary on Revelation as the main source for Apocalypse in the play. There can be no quarrel with this, since in any case Milton identifies Pareus in his introductory remarks on "that Sort of Dramatic Poem which is call'd Tragedy."[34] The problem is that Lewalski underreads both Milton and Pareus on this point. The Apocalypse's tragedy, she says, is Antichrist's; if Samson Agonistes is an apocalyptic tragedy then Samson's end must also perforce be Antichristian. Wittreich enthusiastically endorses her point: "here is the tragedy of Antichrist and of all those who endorse him in history."[35]

But Pareus does not just prophesy Antichrist's tragic fall "the *Catastrophe* of all evils"; he shows as a consequence "the Churches Victory, and Eternall Glory."[36] If *Samson Agonistes* is, like Revelation, a *"Dramaticall Prophesie"*[37] then perhaps its spectacle anticipates as well the "promised end": the Chorus certainly thinks so. For them the drama shows us in the Philistine defeat the tragic end expected for antichristian peoples, an "image of that horror," while at the same time showing the promised end for God's faithful prayer warriors. We need not think that Milton endorses the Chorus' triumphalism to grasp that through their reactions in particular, Revelation is drawn on as a fictive construct, a site of aesthetic as well as ethical potential. And both that aesthetic and ethic are taken from Pareus. From his preface it would seem that Milton was indeed more interested in using Pareus to justify his artistic rather than his philosophical experiments in the play: "and *Paraeus*, commenting on the *Revelation*, divides the whole Book as a Tragedy, into Acts distinguisht each by a Chorus of Heavenly Harpings and Song Between."[38] Formal considerations seem uppermost also in Milton's earlier reference to Pareus, who in *The Reason of Church Government* is said to confirm that "the Apocalyps of Saint *John* is the majestick image of a high and stately Tragedy."[39]

Milton draws on Pareus in two ways. First he helps justify the form of the drama, allaying Milton's formalist anxiety which makes the preface so overbearing and neurotically defensive; like Pareus's schema for Revelation which "divides the whole book as a Tragedy," so too *Samson Agonistes* breaks into "Acts distinguisht each by a Chorus."[40] Milton's acts are not numbered since the play was never intended for production on royalist, Restoration stages, but what Pareus identifies as the rhythm of apocalypse (action/chorus/action: the rhythm of Greek tragedy also) is evident.

Secondly Pareus calls Revelation "an heavenly *Dramma* or Interlude," "a *Propheticall Drama*, show, or representation," a piece of "Heavenly Theater."[41] He revels, in other words, in Revelation's extravagant theatricality, thus underwriting Milton's claim that Revelation is a "high and stately tragedy"; this underlies, in turn, the highly theatrical exposition and celebration of that tragedy the Hebrew spin controllers offer us in the play. Both the Messenger and the Chorus seem excited as well as awed by Samson's final piece of "Heavenly Theater." The Messenger flees that "horrid spectacle" yet narrates it with great verve. He is appalled at the extent of Samson's destruction yet is no less thrilled by this than the Chorus. It would be as crude a biographical fallacy to suggest that the Messenger was here Milton's spokesperson in the play as to suggest that Samson simply was John Milton, eyeless in London. Nevertheless the play bears witness to Milton's career-long attraction toward Apocalypse as one of those dramatic spectacles Tertullian commends in his *De Spectaculis:*

> What spectacle, indeed, is anything like that of the advent of the Lord, now certain, now glorious, now triumphant? What one is like that of the exultation of the angels? Or the glory of the arisen saints? Or the kingdom of the just? Or the city of New Jerusalem? And there are other spectacles besides, that last and everlasting day of Judgement, that day . . . unlooked-for by the nations, that day derided, when such antiquity of time and so many of those already consumed will be consumed in one fire. (YP I, pp. 489–90)[42]

At the beginning of Milton's polemic career he celebrated the imminence of Judgment Day; through the 1640s and 1650s Apocalypse seemed to recede in time. *Paradise Lost* promises last judgment, but refuses to commit itself as to exactly when it will be. *De Doctrina Christiana* adopts a similar Augustinian position: the Apocalypse will come but its timetable is impossible to predict. Meanwhile both *Paradise Lost* and *Paradise Regained* seem to counsel a retreat into patient domesticity. *Samson Agonistes* is more publicly combative, with its sense that historical change is "turbulent, iconoclastic and dramatic"[43]; such a *Samson Agonistes* accords with recent depictions of post-Restoration dissenting culture either, as Greaves has shown, working to undermine the Stuart regime, or writing assiduously, as Keeble has documented, to inveigh against the monarchy.[44] Milton's readings of Revelation were always complex: he used it in different texts for conflicting purposes. But he never entirely forsook its rhetoric of violence for the pacific consolations of the paradise within. If Samson is partly fashioned in the play as an exemplary text for some future soldier's pocket Bible, then that is at least in part because Milton himself was well aware that there were battles still to be fought.

University of Waikato, New Zealand

NOTES

1. Harold R. Willoughby, *Soldier's Bibles Through Three Centuries* (Chicago, 1944), p. 1.

2. *Cromwell's Soldier's Bible; Being a Reprint, in Facsimile, of "The Souldier's*

Pocket Bible," compiled by Edmund Calamy, and Issued for the Use of the Commonwealth Army in 1643 (London, 1895).

The Soldiers might also have had access to John Field's edition in twenty-fours of the complete Bible, five editions of which were published in 1653 and four again in 1658, as A. S. Herbert notes in his revised edition of T. H. Darlow and H. F. Moule's *Historical Catalogue of Printed Editions of the English Bible 1525–1961* (London, 1968), p. 200.

3. *The Souldiers Pocket Bible*, p. 4.

4. *The Holy Bible with Annotations* (Geneva, 1599), Judges xiii, 5, note b.

5. Ibid., xvi, 28., note A.

6. Jackie Di Salvo, " 'The Lord's battels': *Samson Agonistes* and the Puritan Revolution," in *Milton Studies* IV, ed. James D. Simmonds (Pittsburgh, 1972), p. 40; see also Robert Thomas Fallon, *Captain or Colonel: The Soldier in Milton's Life and Art* (Columbia, Mo., 1984), p. 249.

7. George Whiting, "*Samson Agonistes* and the Geneva Bible," *The Rice Institute Pamphlet* 38 (1951), 23, 33, 34.

8. William Riley Parker, *Milton's Contemporary Reputation* (Columbus, 1940), pp. 263–66.

9. John Milton, *Complete Poems and Major Prose*, ed. Merritt Y. Hughes (New York, 1957). All references to Milton's poems are from this edition.

10. See Stanley Fish, "Spectacle and Evidence in *Samson Agonistes*," *Critical Inquiry* 15 (1989), 584.

11. See Sophie Tomlinson's " 'My Brain the Stage': Margaret Cavendish and the Fantasy of Female Performance," in *Women, Texts and Histories 1575–1760*, ed. Clare Brant and Diane Purkiss (London, 1992), pp. 134–63.

12. Stanley Fish, "Question and Answer in *Samson Agonistes*," in *"Comus" and "Samson Agonistes": A Casebook*, ed. Julian Lovelock (London, 1975), pp. 209–45.

13. Fish, "Spectacle and Evidence," p. 586.

14. David Loewenstein, *Milton and the Drama of History* (Cambridge, 1990), p. 150.

15. Laura Lunger Knoppers, " 'This So Horrid Spectacle': *Samson Agonistes* and the Execution of the Regicides," *English Literary Renaissance* 20 (1990), 487–504.

16. David Masson, *The Life of John Milton*, 6 vols. (London, 1875), vol. II, p. 110.

17. Loewenstein, *Milton*, p. 143 also notes that "Milton's plan to write a work on the subject of Old Testament iconoclasm—namely 'Gideon Idoloclastes' . . . was, to a degree, realized in both polemic and play."

18. Hughes, *Complete Poems*, p. 531.

19. Anthony Low, "The Phoenix and the Sun in *Samson Agonistes*," in *Milton Studies* XIV, ed. James D. Simmonds (Pittsburgh, 1980), p. 230.

20. Fish, "Question and Answer," p. 226.

21. "We blancked them with billes, through all their bright armor," *O.E.D.* s.v. "blank."

22. Ibid., s. v. "catastrophe."

23. Hugh MacCallum, "*Samson Agonistes*: the Deliverer as Judge," in *Milton Studies* XXIII, ed. James D. Simmonds (Pittsburgh, 1987), p. 280.

24. Elizabeth L. Eisenstein, *The Printing Press as an Agent of Change*, (1979; rpt. Cambridge, 1991), pp. 310, 366, 377; "The Reformers offered a different intimacy, the intimacy not of the institution, imaged as the nurturing female body, but of the book, imaged . . . as self, food, and protection: 'As thou readest,' Tyndale writes in the *Prologue to Genesis*, 'think that every syllable pertaineth to thine own self, and suck out the pith of the Scripture, and arm thyself against all assaults.' " Stephen Greenblatt, *Renaissance Self-*

Fashioning: From More to Shakespeare (Chicago, 1980), p. 96. The power of the biblical text to fashion subjectivity in this way is a fundamental assumption in both sixteenth and seventeenth century Protestant texts. Here I disagree vehemently with Fish who sees in the "passage from self to text" nothing but the deliquescence and deconstruction of the self. From his Foucauldian perspective, of course, Greenblatt eventually makes the same claim about his Renaissance selves. See Fish, "Spectacle and Evidence," p. 584, Greenblatt, *Renaissance Self-Fashioning*, pp. 255–57.

25. *O.E.D.* s.v. "phantasy."

26. Nigel Llewellyn, *The Art of Death: Visual Culture in the English Death Ritual c. 1500–c. 1800* (London, 1991), p. 101.

27. Tom Paulin, "Polemics in Paradise: The Republican Epic of John Milton," *TLS* (12 July 1991), 4.

28. Nicholas Jose, *Ideas of the Restoration in English Literature* (Cambridge, Mass., 1984), p. 163.

29. Loewenstein, *Milton*, p. 136.

30. Eid A. Dahiyat, "Harapha and Baal-zeebub/Astaroth in Milton's *Samson Agonistes*," *MQ* 16 (1982), 61.

31. Mary Ann Radzinowicz is an eloquent apologist for this approach to the play, which inextricably links God's, Milton's, the Chorus' and finally the reader's intentions:

The final quatrain of the choral *nunc dimittis* attributes the beneficent action of the tragedy to God, viewing him metaphorically as the tragic poet who can restore to his creatures the delight in his dramatic universe which sends them again into their own creative lives.

"Medicinable Tragedy: the Structure of *Samson Agonistes* and Seventeenth-Century Psychopathology," in *English Drama: Forms and Developments*, ed. Marie Axton and Raymond Williams (Cambridge, 1977), p. 121.

32. Joseph Wittreich, *Interpreting "Samson Agonistes"* (Princeton, 1986), pp. xxviii, 52.

33. Barbara K. Lewalski, "*Samson Agonistes* and the Tragedy of the Apocalypse," *PMLA* 85 (1970), 1050–62.

34. Hughes, *Complete Poems*, p. 549.

35. Wittreich, *Interpreting*, p. 374.

36. David Pareus, *A Commentary Upon the Divine Revelation*, trans. Elias Arnold (Amsterdam, 1644), p. 27.

37. Pareus, *A Commentary*, p. 26.

38. Hughes, *Complete Poems*, p. 549.

39. John Milton, *Complete Prose Works of John Milton*, 8 vols., ed. Don M. Wolfe et al. (New Haven, 1953), vol. I, p. 815. References to Milton's prose are to this edition, and subsequent volume and page references will appear in the text as YP.

40. Hughes, *Complete Poems*, p. 549.

41. Pareus, *A Commentary*, p. 20.

42. Milton commends Tertullian in his commonplace book, the Yale edition of which cites this excerpt from Tertullian.

43. Loewenstein, *Milton*, p. 34.

44. Richard L. Greaves, *Deliver Us from Evil: The Radical Underground in Britain, 1660–1663* (New York, 1986); *Enemies Under His Feet: Radicals and Nonconformists in Britain 1664–1677* (Stanford, 1990); N. H. Keeble, *The Literary Culture of Nonconformity in Later Seventeenth-Century England* (Leicester, 1987).

THE GARDEN WITHIN:
MILTON'S LUDLOW MASQUE
AND THE TRADITION OF CANTICLES

Catherine I. Cox

> Awake, north wind; and come thou south; blow upon my garden, that
> the spices thereof may flow out. Let my beloved come into his
> garden, and eat his pleasant fruit.
>
> —*Song of Songs* xiv, 16

> Eheu quid volui misero mihi! floribus austrum Perditus ————
>
> *Virgil, Eclogue* II, 58–59, as quoted in
> *A Maske Presented at Ludlow Castle* (London 1637)

I N H I S *Commonplace Book* Milton defends public shows against Tertullian's condemnation of all performances by emphasizing in Tertullian's
own prose the spectacle that arises within the mind:

Nevertheless he [Tertullian] does that best in the epilogue of his book as, for
instance, with concise and powerful style he stirs up the mind of the Christian to
better plays, that is, divine and heavenly plays, which, in great number and of
great value, the Christian can anticipate concerning the coming of Christ and the
Last Judgment.[1]

This speculation that "better plays" are apocalyptic dramas staged within
the mind informs Milton's conception of the Ludlow masque, especially as
represented by the 1637 quarto.[2] One tradition, integrally related to the
book of Revelation in Protestant exegesis and the literary and visual arts,
has been overlooked by scholars interested in Milton's reform of the
Caroline masque. This tradition, like Milton's masque, is pastoral, dramatic, apocalyptic, lyrical, and as John Demaray might phrase it, itself a
" 'poetry' of motion."[3] This tradition is the Protestant revisioning of Solomon's Song of Songs.

Because it was designed to be played by the children of Bridgewater,
A Mask Presented at Ludlow Castle contains only minimal echoes of the
"sensually spiritual" Song of Songs.[4] In its deeper structure, however,

23

such as its focus on a woman's lonely search in the wilderness, its study of erroneous choosing, of spiritual invocation and answering, its ceremony of cleansing, anointing, and crowning, and finally in its blending of drama, pastoral, dance, and song, the masque parallels the Song of Songs as it is understood by Protestant translators, commentators, and poets.[5] The bride of Canticles, symbolizing the church or the individual Christian soul, is typically described as a pilgrim or a wandering woman. In *Sion's Sonet Sung by Solomon the King*, Francis Quarles describes the bride's passage in terms reminiscent of the Lady's lonely journey in Milton's masque: "What glorious Angell wanders thus alone, / From earths foule Dungeon to my Fathers Throne!"[6] Lost in the wilderness, the bride is tempted by idolatry and sensual appetite, drawn away from Christ, her true huband, by a false bridegroom (sometimes a tyrannical husband or, like Comus, a false shepherd), pulled down and held immobile by sin, and finally freed by her intense faith and Christ's love of her. The commentaries describe the cleansing, anointing, and adorning of the bride and end in heightened anticipation of the divine nuptial. As in Milton's masque, the contrast between stasis and freedom of movement is emphasized. Joyous movement is expressed in the image of the bounding roe and the bride's response to the groom's invitation to come outdoors and greet the spring.

By examining the relation of *A Mask* first to Revelation and then to the tradition of Canticles, we may better understand the Lady's journey from a position of mazelike wandering to stasis and finally to the freedom she enjoys in the closing dance. For like the pilgrimage of the apocalyptic bride, the Lady's search includes moments of such intense visionary clarity that she with heavenly aid is inspirited to break the chains of paralysis and run quickly to her Christian home. Thus the Lady's experiences and the masque itself direct the spiritual eye to higher and higher vistas—to contemplate "the things which God hath prepared for them that love him."[7]

Blending Reformation symbolism with pastoral lyricism, Milton works within the Protestant tradition that reads Canticles and Revelation intertextually and thus sees in Canticles a pastoral drama of divine love.[8] David Norbrook has effectively demonstrated the affinity of the temptation of Milton's Lady to the trials of the Woman Clothed in the Sun who Wanders in the Wilderness of Revelation xii. Norbrook writes:

The scene in which [Comus] tempts the lady with an enchanted cup had many precedents in sixteenth-century Protestant drama, where representatives of the true faith were shown struggling with the magical temptations of idolatry. The lady's wanderings in the dark link her with the pure woman of *Revelation* who had appeared in the 1613 Aletheia masque, Middleton's civic pageants and in Spenserian poetry but not in most Stuart court masques.[9]

While both Revelation and Canticles emphasize the virgin's wilderness journey and prophesy the divine nuptial of the Bride and the Lamb, the Song of Songs arouses and consoles the soul, for the voice and gifts of the tender lover reassure his espoused that though he may seem to desert her he will always return. The groom may send jewels or ointment, symbolizing the bride's virtues, such as Righteousness, Faith, Hope, Love, and Chastity, or his pledges may be visionary—a glimpse of her allegorized protectors, her heavenly groom (signified by a roe playing upon hills of spices), or her future nuptial. The groom thus leads his bride into the chambers of heavenly contemplation where "he doth giue vnto her an eye of faith, by which she beholdeth the inuisible heauenly riches and treasures of life."[10] These gifts then strengthen the ardent flame of her love, increasing her yearning for her heavenly home and intensifying her faith during persecution.

Milton's Lady undergoes a similar spiritual journey. Alice Egerton, who played the Lady in the masque's first performance, was at fifteen nearing marriageable age, as Comus reminds us when he claims that he will make the Lady his bride. Similar to the bride of Canticles, the Lady indirectly expresses sensually spiritual longing in her song to Echo, a lyric filled with images of forsaken love. The sensual portrayal of Echo who lives unseen in the *"violet-embroider'd vale"* (233) and her attendance by the *"love-lorn Nightingale"* (234) are haunting images of unsatisfied passion, suggesting the Lady's desire for physical and spiritual fulfillment as well as her vulnerability in the forest. Echo, whose harmony replicates the Lady's voice, serves, like Sabrina and Psyche, as a mythical double or echo of the lady. The correspondence crystallizes when the Lady compares her brothers to the object of Echo's desire: *"Canst thou not tell me of a gentle Pair / That likest thy Narcissus are?"* (236–37).[11] The mention of the nightingale calls to mind the tragedy of Philomela, a story of flight, horror, and metamorphosis, a more tragic version of Sabrina's story. The Attendant Spirit significantly refers to the Lady as "poor hapless Nightingale" (566) when he relates to her brothers her pitiful plaint and danger. Although images of sensual longing pervade the Lady's song, those who listen emphasize the purity and sacredness of her passion. Comus calls her lyric "Divine enchanting ravishment"—"raptures" signifying "something holy [lodging] in that breast" (245–47). Similar to Arthur Hildersam's comparison of the bride's desire to the sweetest incense and perfumes rising from the wilderness,[12] the Attendant Spirit describes the Lady's voice as a "stream of rich distill'd Perfumes" (556), producing "strains that might create a soul / Under the ribs of Death" (561–62). This plaintive, "sacred" lyric suggests the love or "rational burning" that Milton speaks of in *The Doctrine and Discipline of Divorce*. Echoing Canticles, Milton states that a "pure and more inbred desire for joyning to it self in conjugall fellowship with a fit conversing soul . . . *is stronger then death*, as the Spouse of Christ thought, *many waters cannot quench it, neither can the floods drown it*" (YP II, p. 251). The Lady's song of "mateless sorrow," her envisioning of her guardian virtues, Faith, Hope, and Chastity, and the "flame of sacred vehemence" (795) that stirs within her when Comus assaults the doctrine of Chastity by wit and rhetoric—these elements of yearning, vision, and zeal underscore the significance of the Canticles tradition in Milton's reformation of the Stuart court masque.

Although we most often think of the Song of Songs as a model for lyrical verse, writers, such as William Baldwin, Francis Quarles, George Gifford, and Antonio Brucioli (as translated by Thomas James), are aware of the interplay of multiple voices and the dramatic structure of the whole. Understanding Canticles as a spectacle that unfolds within the mind, Gifford instructs his reader to,

First look upon it, as vpon a goodly rich peece of work but foulded vp, and then afterward have it vnfoulden and spread before your eyes, to the viewing of euery part thereof. Here be divers persons brought in vttring their parts in it, but especially two which are Louers betrothed each vnto the other. [13]

The drama of Canticles captures the imagination not merely of minor talents; Spenser and Milton also employ its pastoral, lyric, and prophetic style to narrate the spectacle staged within the mind. Both the bride of Spenser's *Epithalamium* and the Lady of Milton's *A Mask* present the female as "a garden inclosed . . . a spring shut up, a fountain sealed" (Canticles iv, 12). In *The Enclosed Garden* Stanley Stewart explains that throughout the Middle Ages, the "garden inclosed" was associated iconographically with Mary, for she is both virgin and nurturing mother. Since Mary is *Mater Ecclesia*, her virginity—the wall enclosing the garden— represents the fortress wall that keeps the church inviolable. According to Stewart, the Catholic and Protestant representations of the church as an enclosed garden are different more in emphasis than in kind. [14] Though the garden is conceived as lovely and powerful in both representations, in Reformation poetry, images of chastity often acquire added militancy for the assaults from the world are virulent and savage. Arthur Hildersam, for example, writes that Christ provides a "wall of fire about her, to keep her from the rage of cruel Enemies . . . which like the wild Boars and Beasts of the field might waste & devour her."[15] Similar to Comus and his bestial followers, these enemies present a sensual threat that must be met with zealous faith and stern, implacable chastity.

In keeping with this tradition, Spenser and Milton counterpose antithetical images and actions to express the feminine beauty as well as the fierce purity of the enclosed garden. Spenser's lyric first echoes Song of Songs in its catalogue of the bride's physical beauty, "Her paps lyke lyllies budded, / Her snowie necke lyke to a marble towre" (176–77), in the praises and celebration of the damsels who are called to dance and carol as they strike their timbrels, and in the adornment of the bride, her golden hair sprinkled with pearls and flowers and "crowned with a girland greene" (155–57).[16] However, as in Milton's masque, the Lady's chastity or inward beauty is paramount. The groom thus turns from outward spectacle, the bride's beauty, to praise her inward, "heavenly guifts" (187). For Spenser the bride is immaculate, and the power of her inward beauty if seen by the eye would astonish the viewer more than "Medusaes mazeful hed" (190). So powerful is her unspotted faith and chastity that her virtues reign as "Queene" (194) ruling the "base affections" (196) so that they dare not "approch to tempt her mind to ill" (199).

Like Spenser's marriage song and the commentaries on Canticles, Milton's masque focuses on the power of the Lady's inward beauty. Since Spenser describes the wedding event itself, rather than the betrothal, the bride is portrayed as immaculate and complete. She is in harmony with her pastoral world. Milton's Lady, however, more in the manner of the veiled bride Una and the warrior bride Britomart of *The Faerie Queene* must confront the temptation of "base affections." The wilderness setting thus contrasts with and impinges on the "enclosed garden," the sanctity and peace of the Lady's mind. As the beast-headed revellers are associated with the "tangl'd Wood" (181), the Lady's beauty is described by the Second Brother in terms of a garden. It is as "the fair Hesperian Tree / Laden with blooming gold" (393–94). The brother then insists that like the precious tree it must be fiercely guarded lest the "hand of bold Incontinence" (397) destroy both blossoms and fruit. The image of the dragon guarding the tree of Hesperus with "unenchanted eye" (395) is rejected by the Elder Brother and replaced by the internalized Medusa. The protector of the garden, the Elder Brother attests, is not external and apart but stands within. Like the groom of *Epithalamium*, he associates the power of chastity with the calcifying power of Medusa. The image is far more violent than in Spenser's marriage song, for the threats to the Garden are active and close. The iconoclastic impulse of Chastity thus freezes and dashes her foe:

> What was that snaky-headed *Gorgon* shield
> That wise *Minerva* wore, unconquer'd Virgin,
> Wherewith she freez'd her foes to congeal'd stone,
> But rigid looks of Chaste austerity
> And noble grace that dash't brute violence
> With sudden adoration and blank awe?   (447–52)

The use of this charged visual metaphor to express the power of an inward state indicates the directional thrust of the masque as a whole—the movement of true spectacle to the inner stage. The words that follow in the brother's discourse describe, like the Lady's earlier envisioning of Chastity, "And thou unblemish't form of Chastity, / I see ye visibly" (215–16), a banishing of antimasque elements:

> So dear to Heav'n is Saintly chastity,
> That when a soul is found sincerely so,
> A thousand liveried Angels lackey her,
> Driving far off each thing of sin and guilt,
> And in clear dream and solemn vision
> Tell her of things that no gross ear can hear.   (453–58)[17]

The brother's verbal masque adds an important element not mentioned in the Lady's earlier speech, the transformation of purity "by degrees" to the "outward shape":

> Till oft converse with heav'nly habitants
> Begin to cast a beam on th'outward shape,
> The unpolluted temple of the mind,
> And turns it by degrees to the soul's essence,
> Till all be made immortal.   (459–63)

For Maryann McGuire, these words point to the Elder Brother's naive belief that outward appearance corresponds to the inward state, a Platonic concept reflected in conventional masques and rejected, says McGuire, by Milton.[18] When viewed as a continuing spiritual and intellectual transformation rather than a completed correspondence, the idea of purification may be read in another way. The progression reverses the kenotic transformation of the Attendant Spirit in the opening; it suggests that the cleansing, perfecting, and glorifying of the saint, ongoing in this life, reach final consummation at the Apocalypse.[19] Explaining a phrase from Canticles, *"Thy countenance (or Aspect) is comly,"* Henoch Clapham describes this transformation that occurs with divine contemplation:

That Son of heauen causeth our face to shine: and this onely, as we become one with him by the apprehension of Faith. Faith purifieth the heart, causeth a change of the soule, inuests vs with Messiahs righteousnesse, as Iaakob was cloathed with his elder brothers garment.[20]

In his epilogue, the Attendant Spirit promises a return to an edenic correspondence between body and soul by referring to the Gardens of Hesperus, an adumbration of the *hortus conclusus,* and the anticipated nuptial of Psyche (soul) and Cupid (body).[21]

The Lady's spiritual growth and glorification paradoxically must come through her contact with and partial contamination by evil. The Attendant Spirit's opening references to "this dim spot, / Which men call Earth" (5–6) and "the rank vapors of this Sin-worn mold" (17) emphasize the effects on all humanity of original sin. The Lady's human predicament makes her exceedingly vulnerable both to evil's deception and to momentary lapses of faith. Unlike the Virgin Mary, who is mystically immaculate, Milton's Lady represents the visible church as well as the individual Christian soldier; she is thus paradoxically spotless and soiled. In Canticles, a voice (identified in Protestant commentaries as the bride) says, "I am black, but comely, O ye daughters of Jerusalem, as the tents of Kedar, as the curtains of Solomon" (i, 5). Acknowledging the presence of original sin, Brucioli emphasizes persecution and the world's limited perspective as keys to understanding the passage. Brucioli's bride explains:

Maruel not to see me blacke with oppressions, for I am faire and beautifull in the desire of heauenly things: true it is, that I am . . . blacke with the remembrance of my sins, but faire in the contemplation & beholding of heavenly matters . . . black in sufferings of momentary and temporary euils, faire in expectation of eternall & euerlasting goods.[22]

While Brucioli stresses persecution, bringing little attention to the bride's sins as an earthly traveler, George Gifford reverses the emphasis:

It is a most cleere case that the holy Church, and all her perfectest children doo want of the beautie while they live here, and are somewhat blacke, partly through sinnes which doo remaine in them, and partlie through afflictions.[23]

Original sin, Gifford explains, forces the church "to commit many sinnes which dimme her beautie, and to omit the doing her duetie in part for her own vine." Thus the bride complains that she is sunburnt: "the sonnes of my mother were angrie with me, they made me the keeper of the vines, but I kept not mine own vine."[24] Mortification of the bride's sins, explains

Gifford, can only come through faith and the process of ingrafting: "We apprehend Christ Iesus, and are ingrafted into him through a true and liuely faith."[25]

Like Brucioli and Gifford, Milton too uses gardening imagery to describe the paradox of the spotless and flawed Church:

INGRAFTING IN CHRIST . . . is the process by which God the Father plants believers in Christ. That is to say, he makes them sharers in Christ, and renders them fit to join, eventually, in one body with Christ. (YP VI, p. 477)

Examining this passage, Stephen R. Honeygosky explains that for Milton "[t]he elect are not flawless, and yet they are perfect because of their incorporation into Christ."[26]

While Milton's Lady remains chaste throughout the masque, her enchantment and capture imply both persecution and spiritual error. The first sign of the Lady's culpability is her conscious movement toward the sounds she perceives as evil; a second, stronger sign is the Lady's ready trust in the shepherd who describes her brothers in idolatrous terms. Before the Lady faces her first test, Milton gives us a means to apprehend the nature of her temptations by allowing Comus to practice his art first on us. Dissonant music, rude bestial dancing, swirling torchlight, glistening costumes, and the figure of Comus amid the dancers, holding his charming rod and the crystal goblet—these images blend, becoming a liquid fire. However, just as the rhythmic power of the dance begins to cast its spell, we recall the Attendant Spirit's opening warning that those who "taste through fond intemperate thirst" (67) degrade their "human count'nance, / Th' express resemblance of the gods" (68–69). With this remembrance, the unholy images of wolves, bears, hogs, and goats lose their kinetic power and convey instead the message of Protestant reform: just as chastity brings spiritual sight and glorification, intemperance muddies the memory and turns human form to bestial. Though these beast-headed revellers are clearly derived from Homer's myth of the enchantress Circe, Protestant revisions of Canticles clarify their Christian implications. Contrasting the bride's ornament—"temperance," Aylett describes the transformation of those who delight in "filth and foul incontinence." For these, "Lust and Wine so far transforme the minde, / Affections beare the sway, and *royall reason* binde." They like "filthy beasts" make "*Swines of Gods faire Images.*"[27] The bestial worshippers of Cotytto have accordingly desecrated the image of the gods—or rather the image of God—in themselves. This scene, which the Lady never sees, reveals to the audience the full flowering of idolatry, the intoxication of "misused Wine" (47).[28] Though suspecting these sounds to be made by midnight revellers "who thank the gods amiss," the Lady curiously moves toward them:

> I should be loath
> To meet the rudenesse, and swill'd insolence
> Of such late Wassailers; yet O where else
> Shall I inform my unacquainted feet
> In the blind mazes of this tangl'd Wood?   (177–81)

Since there are no other people to turn to, the Lady feels she must rely on the guidance of the rude worshippers. Her decision to find them, however, indicates a momentary failure to trust in God's Providence. The Lady soon indicates that she has reached the unholy spot: "This is the place, as well as I may guess, / Whence ev'n now the tumult of loud Mirth / Was rife" (201–03). To heighten her fear and loneliness, the Lady is suddenly cast in total silence and complete darkness.

As though aware of the nearness of evil and of her own spiritual vulnerability, the Lady imagines a shadowy antimasque. Beckoning figures flood her memory, and the mind itself becomes their pageant hall:

> A thousand fantasies
> Begin to throng into my memory,
> Of calling shapes and beck'ning shadows dire,
> And airy tongues that syllable men's names
> On Sands and Shores and desert Wildernesses.   (205–09)

The antimasque has become fully interiorized and more frightening as a power within the mind. In a typical Caroline masque, the antimasque is miraculously routed by the sudden appearance of Virtues or celestial beings who are then revealed to be nobles of the King's court. Just so the Lady welcomes her champions, whose "sacred rays" (425) can assuage her fears and sweep the shadowy images from her mind:

> O welcome pure-ey'd Faith, white-handed Hope,
> Thou hov'ring Angel girt with golden wings,
> And thou unblemish't form of Chastity
> I see ye visibly.   (213–16)

The virtues are here described in the emblematic terms of conventional court masques. Milton, however, reveals no double signification; the virtues are not courtiers and ladies but moral principles, powers not of King Charles but of the Lady herself. The Lady's chastity, the Elder Brother explains, is a "hidden strength / Which if Heav'n gave it, may be term'd her own" (418–19). As in the Song of Songs tradition, the Lady, though confused and near despair, receives visionary comfort and protection. As the phantoms in her mind are banished, the Lady notices that "a sable cloud" has "Turn[ed] forth her silver lining on the night" (221–22)—the outer world thus altering to match her inward state. This internalized masque will serve as a rehearsal for the Lady's resistance to Comus when she looks upon the spectacle of idolatry within his palace.

In bringing before her mind's eye the guardian virtues, Faith, Hope, and Chastity, the Lady clearly distinguishes the shadowy, wilderness antimasque from the masque proper. Less clear, however, is her power of discernment when Comus asserts that he can lead her to her brothers. The flattery that the Lady rejects for herself, she fails to reject when the praise is of her brothers—even though in this case the praise is clearly idolatrous:

> I saw them under a green mantling vine
> That crawls along the side of yon small hill,
> Plucking ripe clusters from the tender shoots;
> Their port was more than human, as they stood;
> I took it for a faëry vision
> Of some gay creatures of the element
> That in the colors of the Rainbow live
> And play i'th' plighted clouds. I was awe-struck,
> And as I past, I worshipt; if those you seek,
> It were a journey like the path to Heav'n
> To help you find them.   (294–304)

This point in the masque, I believe, is critical, for it highlights the weakness that draws the Lady into captivity. The descriptions of the serpentine vine, the overly sensual plucking of fruit, the "more than human" bearing of the boys, and the stranger's response to the "faëry vision"—awe and worship—should serve to warn the Lady. They rather serve to seduce.[29] In Protestant allegories of Canticles, the bride hesitates before opening her door (or heart) to the groom, finding when she opens it that he has departed. Searching for him in dark streets, she asks help of the watchmen, who lead her astray and molest her. Protestant allegorists identify these watchmen as false preachers (shepherds), tricksters, seducers, idolators, and persecutors of the true church. They are the foxes that savagely destroy the tender vines of the holy grape. Like the watchmen's betrayal, Comus presents a false prophecy and a false covenant. He uses the rainbow, a sign to Noah of God's covenant and a symbol of blessing in wedding masques, to veil his dark design. The association of the brothers with sexual metaphors and with idolatry goes beyond the earlier sensual rendering of the brothers in the

Lady's song to Echo. Inexperienced and fearful, the Lady places her trust in the "gentle Shepherd" whose feet she terms "well-practic'd" (310) and whose promise is to give light and direction to her journey. Desperate for her brothers' company, the Lady overlooks the implied terms of her contract. She follows, deceived in part by Comus and deceived in part by herself.

The paradox of the Lady's guilt (her partial culpability in following Comus) and chastity (her firm resistance to unveiled evil) is represented by her captivity. As she explains the significance of the Lady's imprisonment in the enchanted chair, Georgia B. Christopher touches on the paradox of the Lady's innocence and guilt:

This highly verbal Lady caught in the magician's chair is a vivid image of the central tenet of Reformation faith—that the Christian is both sinner and justified saint (*simul iustus et peccator*)—at once bound and free.[30]

Christopher, however, does not develop the implications of the Lady's capture far enough. Her treatment overlooks a crucial, disturbing detail of the scene—the Lady held fast in a chair "[s]mear'd with gums of glutinous heat" (917). In his argument for reading *A Mask* as essentially heuristic, Stanley Fish rightly queries "Whose glutinous heat?"[31] The masque becomes less open-ended, however, when we view it in light of parallel moments described by Protestant commentators of Canticles. Francis Rous, for example, describes the Bride's bondage to the false bridegroom:

Yea this venome hath in it a force and power to draw the wil and affections from that soveraigne good, which is the true and onely beatificall object of the soule, and *to glue and fasten* her to objects of vanity, yea of death and misery.[32] (emphasis mine)

When freed the Bride remembers this life "with her old husband" who is called "concupiscence" as a "painted and glittering misery."[33] She is like a person "awaked from a foolish dreame, or an *inchanted* love, and shee will wonder that shee hath so long beene *bewitched* with vanity, folly, sinne, and misery" (emphasis mine). As in the readings of Canticles, the Lady's cleansing and freedom come through adversity.

Just as the Lady earlier trusted in Faith, Hope, and Chastity when surrounded by darkness and silence, she, now, when tempted by excessive visual and auditory stimulation, asserts a militant confidence in "the sage / And serious doctrine of Virginity" (786–87). The Lady's echoing of Pauline scripture in the forest and her reliance on the doctrine of Virginity when imprisoned strongly suggest the idea of church discipline that Milton describes in *The Reason of Church-Government*. In this pamphlet, published in 1642, Milton contrasts the wolfish greed, extravagance, and impulsiveness of the prelates with the careful planning and instruction of God. Much as God had given "to *David* for *Solomon* . . . a pattern and modell of the Temple," so too he has set forth in scripture the exact discipline for the purification of his church. Milton equates the church's regimen to the careful preparation of a bride who cleanses herself with baths and ointments:

Againe, if Christ be the Churches husband expecting her to be presented before him a pure unspotted virgin; in what could he shew his tender love to her more, then in prescribing his owne wayes which he best knew would be to the improvement of her health and beauty with much greater care doubtlesse then the Persian King could appoint for his Queene *Esther*, those maiden dietings & set prescriptions of baths, & odors, which may render her at last the more amiable to his eye. For of any age or sex, most unfitly may a virgin be left to an uncertaine and arbitrary education. Yea though she be well instructed, yet is she still under a more strait tuition, especially if betroth'd. (YP I, p. 755)

Like the Lady's wilderness education, the purification of Esther requires exacting steps. As prescribed, she would bathe "six months in oil of myrrh, and six months with sweet odours" (Esther ii, 12). In Canticles exegesis, myrrh is often described as a "bitter thing," thus signifying "hard and grievous tribulation," while spices and oils such as cinnamon, spikenard, and aloe indicate the spiritual comforts of God. Milton's correlation of purifying ointments with Scripture finds an analogue in the Songs tradition. Canticles i, 3 reads, "Because of the savour of thy good ointments *thy name is as ointment poured forth*, therefore do the virgins love thee" (emphasis mine). Like James's translation of Brucioli in the following passage, commentators on Canticles often identify ointment with God's Word:

Sweete smeling ointments are to bee vnderstood, the wholsome gifts of the holie Ghost, whence come these *hot and zealous words of faith, hope and charitie*: and these yong damsels, which I told you before were the soules of the elect, renued and regenerated in Christ. (emphasis mine).[34]

Milton's substitution of the term "chastity" for the Pauline "charity" in the Lady's speech emphasizes bridal purity as well as martial vigilance and strict regimen. The "hot and zealous words" of Brucioli thus parallel the "flame of sacred vehemence" (795) that could, if fully kindled in the Lady, move "the brute Earth" with such a force "Till all thy magic structures rear'd so high, / Were shatter'd into heaps o'er thy false head" (798–99). The iconoclastic power of the Lady's speech thus stems not from logic but rather from a fervent conviction in the power of God's Word. In *Of Reformation Touching Church Discipline in England*, Milton defines *discipline* as "the *execution* and applying of *Doctrine* home."[35] The Lady's resistance to the temptation in the wilderness, as she sits immobile though surrounded by bestial shapes, has just this force of "execution." For Milton, the idea of discipline is not merely militant; like the Lady herself and like Sabrina, it is lyrical as well. In words suggesting both the music and grace of a masque and the Lady's earlier envisioning of her guardian virtues, Milton views discipline as both audible and visible experience:

> She [discipline] is that which with her musicall cords preserves and holds all the parts thereof together. . . . And certainly discipline is not only the removall of disorder, but if any visible shape can be given to divine things, the very visible shape and image of vertue, whereby she is not only seene in the regular gestures and motions of her heavenly paces as she walkes, but also makes the harmony of her voice audible to mortal ears. (YP I, pp. 751–52)

Because it narrates the ordering and purifying harmony of Christian discipline, Milton's masque departs from conventional court masques, both in its dramatic structure and in its dance sequence. As McGuire has shown, Milton rejects the iconographic stasis of the conventional court masque. By presenting the children on a journey, acting sometimes mistakenly with partial knowledge, by decentering the crisis and thus blurring the lines between antimasque and main masque, Milton "treats the virtuous life as a process rather than as a fixed state of being." The conventional masque is a "dynamic emblem," the masque proper dissolving the antimasque when the antic performers recognize virtue in the grace and splendor of the royal masquers. Milton's masque, however, does not "develop iconically," as does the typical court masque, but "approaches dramatic narrative" as the children face separation and temptation.[36] Allegorical treatments of Canticles provide this narrative frame of experience and discipline. The Lady's stationary position in Comus's palace, while reflective of her spiritual error, simultaneously indicates her gathering faith, for she ardently refuses the wine that would allow her motion, though without freedom. In the Song of Songs tradition, false doctrines and false preachers arouse the bride to just indignation. Rous writes: "the fire of love upon opposition kindleth another fire of an holy rage; which is full of anger and scorne, that life or death, or any other creature should offer to separate the soule from her loved Christ Jesus."[37] As the Lady's physical movement stops, the inner stage enlivens. Finding "light within [her] own clear breast," the Lady can "sit i'th' center, and enjoy bright day" (381–82). McGuire explains that "the Lady's stasis in the midst of movement is central to the visual composition of the scene. Aristocratic masquers generally demonstrated the virtue in the dance. Milton's Lady initially proves hers by not dancing."[38] The freeing touch of Sabrina thus rewards the Lady's fidelity just as Christ's grace touches and frees his bride. Brucioli writes: "vnlesse [Christ] put to his helping hand we are not able to stand vp vpon our feet, much lesse to run about."[39] The cleansing and refreshing touch of Sabrina thus enables the Lady to answer the Attendant Spirit's word, "Come" (938).

Dancing too helps to narrate the dynamic of spiritual growth and the internalized spectacle of "the garden inclosed." Milton has clearly organized the three set dances, so that we move not as in the Caroline masque to greater and more astonishing spectacles but to dances of an increasingly subdued, refined, and intimate kind. The glittering revel of Comus that links idolatry to the imagery of spiritual wilderness is replaced by the celebrative dance of the rustics interrupted and replaced, in turn, by the triumphant entry and round of the children before their parents. The rustic dance of community thus gives way to the smaller, more intimate dance of family as the children are presented to their parents before the tableau of Ludlow: *"Here behold so goodly grown / Three fair branches of your own"* (968–69). Spiritual triumph is thus imaged in terms of both a healthy garden and a joyous dance or *"crown of deathless Praise"* (973). When dedicating his translation of Antonio Brucioli's commentary upon Canticles to Sir Thomas Egerton in 1598, Thomas James had complimented his patron, Sir John Egerton's father, by paralleling his patron's good governance to the garden (and implicitly to the wisdom) of Solomon:

For seeing God hath made you a Keeper, and that as it is here in the Canticles, of many vines, and that you have kept your vines so, that of the frute thereof hath bene made wine right comfortable vnto many drooping hearts in this land, what remaineth there in me, but to be confident in your Honors kind acceptance of this booke.[40]

Similar to this tribute to the Lord Keeper of the Great Seal of England, the rustic celebration and the presentation of the children as three fair, strong branches assert the flourishing spiritual health of the line of Egerton as well as the prospect of good governance for the garden that is Wales. The main masquers thus enter into a society reflecting biblical values. The image of Ludlow Castle with the children's dance before their parents becomes an earthly shadow of the heavenly city-garden itself.[41] This final outward spectacle, refined and intimate, is indeed a supreme compliment befitting the occasion of Sir Thomas Egerton's installation as Lord President of Wales. The children's triumphant dance will yield in turn to the sublime revel of Hesperus that is narrated by the Attendant Spirit and thus seen only by the mind's eye. The outward journey of the Lady thus stirs the spirit to comprehend greater mysteries. As imaginative participants in the masque, we, like the Lady, are invited to come forth and greet the spring.

J. W. Saunders correctly comments on the triumph at the masque's close:

> The Tempter is finally defeated, not because the Brothers charm him with their "divine Philosophy," nor because the Lady outwits him in dialectic, but because Milton pours into the defence of Chastity all his finest erotic imagery; the real victory in the drama belongs to Sabrina and to the epilogue which . . . persuades with music and not with logic.[42]

It is here in the passages associated with Sabrina and the closing words of the Attendant Spirit that we feel the impress of the Canticles tradition most fully. George Wither anticipates Milton's association of the nymph Sabrina with bridal joy. In his *Epithalamium*, written to honor the union of Princess Elizabeth and Fredrick the Fifth, Count of Palatine, Wither invokes the nymph Sabrina to attend the waking bride:

> Where's *Sabrina*, with her daughters,
> That doe sport about her waters:
> Those that with their lockes of *Amber*,
> Haunt the fruitfull hills of Camber.[43]   (315–18)

Milton too portrays his Severn goddess with amber hair but places her, like the bridal pair of Canticles, amid lilies:

> *Sabrina fair*
> *Listen where thou art sitting*
> *Under the glassy, cool, translucent wave,*
> *In twisted braids of Lilies knitting*
> *The loose train of thy amber-dropping hair.*   (859–63)

As the bride of Canticles is a field of lilies and a garden of spices, two of which are cinnamon and myrrh, she is also like Sabrina, a stream of purified and purifying water, "a well of living waters, and streams of Lebanon." In the commentaries, water seems less the bride's natural essence than the gift of grace. The Geneva Bible reminds us that "the excellent benefits" of the bride are gifts reflecting "[Christ's] pure bountie and grace without any of her deservings." It glosses chapter v: "The Spouse which should be annoynted of Christ, shall not finde him if she thinks to anoynt him with her good workes." Like her other attributes, including her fragrance, the purity of the bride reflects the groom's love.

As water is associated with the gift of purity, it also symbolizes the bride's fertility. Thus the power of Sabrina's touch as she frees the Lady from "glutinous heat" is found both in its coldness and its wetness. Blessing Sabrina, the Attendant Spirit indeed presents her as a garden of fountains. The purity and serenity of water as it "[tumbles] down the snowy hills," the act of crowning with its symbolism of enclosure, "May thy lofty head be crown'd / With many a tower and terrace round," and the groves of spices, "And here and there thy banks upon / With Groves of myrrh and cinnamon" (927–37)—all are elements used to adorn the bride in the Song of Songs tradition.

Garden imagery then culminates in the Spirit's final speech that takes the Hesperian image from its earlier context of fear and violation to that of peace and promise. As the masque moves fully to the interior stage, the mind's eye looks upward. The rainbow now seals a true covenant as it "Waters the odorous banks" (993), making the flowers flourish in colors matching its own. The tree of Hesperus, like the apple tree of the Song of Songs tradition, which is a reminder of the sheltering cross,[44] becomes the center of joyous celebration:

> All amidst the Gardens fair
> Of *Hesperus*, and his daughters three
> That sing about the golden tree:
> Along the crisped shades and bow'rs
> Revels the spruce and jocund Spring,
> The Graces and the rosy-bosom'd Hours,
> Thither all their bounties bring.   (981–87)

The garden dance now flourishes in the imagination. Its elegance and pastoral beauty adumbrate the *hortus conclusus*, the return of Eden and the marriage of the Lamb and the Bride at the Apocalypse. Yet in this idyllic garden we see the contrast of profane and holy love, the terms of the Lady's conflict. Venus sadly watches the sleeping, wounded Adonis while far above "in spangled sheen" (1003), Psyche and Cupid embrace, awaiting their nuptial and the births of their offspring "Youth and Joy" (1011). Psyche's anticipated wedding suitably marks the Lady's victory over loneliness and carnal desire. In *Tetrachordon*, Milton uses the Song of Songs to explain how God's ordination of matrimony at the world's creation testifies to his loving provision against loneliness:

And in the Song of Songs, which is generally beleev'd, even in the jolliest expressions to figure the spousal of the Church with Christ, [Salomon] sings of a thousand raptures between those two lovely ones farre on the hither side of carnall enjoyment. By these instances, and more which might be brought, we may imagine how indulgently God provided against mans lonelines. (YP II, p. 597)

Milton further explains that we are given the capacity to experience marital joy "proportionably to our fal'n estate . . . els were his ordinance at least in vain, and we for all his gift still empty handed" (YP II, p. 597). Thus the celestial betrothal of the epilogue, rather than the earthly riches of Comus's earlier argument, signifies God's manifold bounty. For her constancy and zeal, Milton's Lady is promised solace and joy in human marriage. However, like "unspotted" Psyche who triumphs by her "wand'ring labors long" (1006–09), she, and indeed all of God's faithful disciples, must await the more blissful and ecstatic union—the divine nuptial that exists beyond "the green earth's end" (1014).

Texas A&M University—Corpus Christi

NOTES

I wish to extend my appreciation to Ira Granville Clark, Susan Elaine Marshall, Vanessa Furse Jackson, and Robert S. Jackson for their invaluable suggestions and to the National Endowment for the Humanities for offering me the opportunity to study with John N. King at the Summer Seminar for College Teachers (1990), "The Protestant Imagination: From Tyndale to Milton."

1. *Complete Prose Works of John Milton*, 8 vols., ed. Don M. Wolfe et al. (New Haven, 1953–82), vol. I, p. 490. Subsequent references will appear in the text as YP followed by volume and page number.

2. While all versions of *A Mask Presented at Ludlow Castle* contain apocalyptic references, the 1637 quarto, that includes the Lady's speeches on the "sage / and serious doctrine of Virginity" and on Faith, Hope, and Chastity as well as the Attendant Spirit's description of the betrothal of Cupid and Psyche, is the most developed version of inner drama. *Ode on the Morning of Christ's Nativity* provides an example of an early biblical "drama of the mind," celebrating the mysteries of the incarnation and the final "unmasking"—the Apocalypse.

3. John M. Demaray, "The Temple of the Mind: Cosmic Iconography in Milton's *A Mask*," MQ XXI (1987), 60.

4. Although the Lady yearns for companionship and solace, she does not directly express her longing in the sensual imagery of Canticles, but speaks as is appropriate for a sister and a daughter. The images of desire for the beloved are thus moved into brief mythological narratives, such as the Lady's song to Echo, which alludes to the meandering search of the wood nymph for her beloved Narcissus, and the Attendant Spirit's closing description of "*Psyche* sweet entranc't," who awaits her divine union with Cupid.

5. My examination of the tradition of Canticles includes the following sixteenth and seventeenth century commentaries and poems: Robert Aylett's *The Brides Ornaments, Viz. Five Meditations, Morall and Divine* (1625); William Baldwin's *The Canticles or Balades of*

Salomon (1549); Antonio Brucioli's *A Commentary Vpon the Canticle of Canticles, written first in Italian by Antonio Brucioli, and now translated into English by Th. James* (1598); Henoch Clapham's *Three Partes of Salomon his Song of Songs, Expounded* (1603); Dudley Fenner's *The Song of Songs translated out of the Hebrue into English Meeter* (1587); George Gifford's *Fifteen Sermons Vpon the Song of Salomon* (1598); Arthur Hildersam's *The Song of Songs Paraphrased* (though this text was printed in 1672, Hildersam lived from 1563 to 1632); Francis Rous's *The Mysticall Marriage: Experimentall Discoveries of the Heavenly Marriage between a Soule and her Saviour* (1635); Francis Quarles's *Sions Sonets Sung by Solomon the King, and Periphras'd by Francis Qvarles* (1625).

6. Quarles, *Sion's Sonets Sung by Solomon the King*, C3ᵛ.

7. Protestant interpreters of Canticles typically call upon 1 Corinthians ii, 9, 10 to describe the mysteries of heavenly contemplation.

8. In *The Reason of Church-Government Urged against Prelaty*, Milton recommends that writers use both Revelation and Canticles as dramatic models. While "the Apocalypse of St. John is the majestick image of high and stately Tragedy," (YP I,L p. 815), the "Song of Salomon" provides a model of "divine pastoral Drama." (YP I, p. 815). See Barbara Lewalski, *Protestant Poetics and the Seventeenth-Century Religious Lyric* (Princeton, 1979), p. 61.

9. David Norbrook, "The Reformation of the Masque" in *The Court Masque*, ed. David Lindley (New Hampshire, 1984), p. 105. For the Ludlow masque's relation to Revelation, see also, William B. Hunter, Jr. "The Liturgical Context of *Comus*," *English Language Notes* X (1972), 11–15. In "The Mysteries in Milton's *Masque*," *Milton Studies*, vol. VI, ed. James D. Simmonds (Pittsburgh, 1974), p. 117, Alice-Lyle Scoufos contends that in writing his masque Milton employed the tradition of medieval apocalyptic drama as well as its Protestant adaptations. While in the medieval cycle the heroine represents the inviolable church and her trials in the latter days, Protestant reformers, such as Thomas Kirchmayer and John Foxe, identify her with the persecuted church of their own time. Though Scoufos does not refer to the influence of Canticles on this drama, one can see it clearly in act V of Foxe's *Christus Triumphans*. Bearing the stigmas of suffering, which she calls "gemmae" (13), Ecclesia prays, "Cito, ueni cito, Domine" (43). Suddenly Ecclesia becomes aware of light and the fragrance of perfume. Bridal clothes and thrones with books upon them descend from heaven as a promise of the groom's return. Thus the play, that began with "Christ['s] welcom[ing] of Psyche as his bride" (Scoufos, p. 134), closes with the ceremonial dressing and crowning of Ecclesia, an epithalamion beseeching the bridegroom to hurry, and a final warning to the audience by the Chorus of Virgins to be ready "lest the bridegroom, when he comes, reject you as you sleep" (p. 371), in *Two Latin Comedies by John Foxe the Martyrologist*, ed. John Hazel Smith (Ithaca, N.Y., 1973). Numerous scholars have suggested the significance of the bridal theme in Milton's masque. In "Hail Wedded Love," *ELH* XIII (1946), 79–97, William Haller contends that Milton's Lady is modeled after Edmund Spenser's chaste warrior Britomart, who searches in the forest for her betrothed. In *Milton & the Masque Tradition* (Cambridge, Mass., 1958), John Demaray states, "*Comus* serves as the best evidence that Milton and Lawes believed in wedding poetry and spectacle" (p. 130).

10. Gifford, *Fifteen Sermons*, p. 34.

11. In my text, references to Milton's poetry are to *John Milton: Complete Poems and Major Prose*, ed. Merritt Y. Hughes (New York, 1957).

12. Hildersam, *Song of Songs Paraphrased*, p. 35.

13. Gifford, *Fifteen Sermons*, p. 14.

14. Stanley Stewart, *The Enclosed Garden: The Tradition and the Image in Seventeenth Century Poetry* (Madison, Wis., 1966), p. 50.

15. Hildersam, *Song of Songs Paraphrased*, p. 49. On the iconographic significance of the wall, see Stewart, *The Enclosed Garden*, p. 39.

16. All quotations from Edmund Spenser's *Epithalamium* come from *The Yale Edition of the Shorter Poems of Edmund Spenser*, ed. William A. Oram, et al. (New Haven, 1989). Contrasting or identifying outward and inward ornaments as Spenser does in his *Epithalamium* is conventional in allegorical treatments of Canticles. Protestant writers consistently stress the militancy of the bride's spiritual gifts, finding evidence in Song of Songs i, 5 and vi, 13. The groom's command in Spenser's lyric, "Open the temple gates unto my love, / Open them wide that she may enter in (204–05)," echoing Isaiah xxvi, "Open ye the gates, that the righteous nation which keepeth the truth may enter in," heightens the prophetic significance of the nuptial. This allusion to the mystical marriage parallels the Marriage Ceremony in *The Book of Common Prayer, 1559*, which reminds the congregation that the marriage of the bride and groom signifies "the mystical union, that is betwixt Christ and his Church." In *The Works of Edmund Spenser: A Variorum Edition*, vol. II, ed. Edwin Greeenlaw, et al. (Baltimore, 1947), Van Winkle writes: "the printer of *Complaints*, 1591 attributes to Spenser a translation of *Canticum Canticorum* (now lost)," p. 474. Also see John King's *Spenser's Poetry and the Reformation Tradition* (Princeton, 1990), p. 73.

17. Descriptions of angels who protect and refresh the pure in heart and celebrate their glorification are frequent in treatments of Canticles. Thus Quarles describes the Bride as a garden of "pleasures walled about / With armed Angels, to keepe Ruine out" (*Sions Sonets*, D2), and Aylett exclaims, "Lo! th' Angells-Being doth in zeale consist; / Whose *sacred ardour* doth all flames transcend, / Wherewith they oft enlight our minds darke mist" (*Brides Ornaments*, p. 14).

18. Maryann McGuire, *Milton's Puritan Masque* (Athens, Ga., 1983), pp. 127–28.

19. Michael Lieb, *The Sinews of Ulysses: Form and Convention in Milton's Works* (Pittsburgh, 1989), pp. 45–48. Lieb describes the theological significance of kenosis in Milton's masque: "That the Attendant Spirit deigns to appear in the 'likeness of a swain' . . . gives added impetus to Milton's handling of the Christian perspective, for in the *Nativity* ode, Christ likewise appears as the Good Shepherd (see John x; 1 Pet. ii, 25, v, 4) or the 'mighty *Pan* / . . . kindly come to live with [us] below' " (89–90).

20. Clapham, *Three Partes of Salomon*, p. 171. The parenthetical phrase in the quotation from Canticles is Clapham's. Dudley Fenner writes of spiritual transformation: "we maye beholde with open face, as in a glasse or mirrour, the glorie of the Lorde, and are chaunged into the same image, from glory to glory, as by the Spirit of God" (B8v). See also, Rous, *The Mysticall Marriage*, p. 367.

21. Stewart, *The Enclosed Garden*, p. 44.

22. Brucioli, *A Commentary Vpon the Canticle of Canticles*, B3r–B3v.

23. Gifford, *Fifteen Sermons*, p. 39.

24. Ibid., p. 39.

25. Ibid., p. 62.

26. Stephen R. Honeygosky, *Milton's House of God: The Invisible and Visible Church* (Columbia, Mo., 1993), p. 58. Honeygosky considers the idea of "ingrafting" crucial to Milton's concept of "[i]ncomplete glorification," p. 60. The following statement, stressing the organic relation between God and the elect, goes far to explain the perseverance of Milton's Lady in the wilderness: "While God is responsible for 'regeneration, growth, and preserva-

tion,' man is responsible for the effects, *faith, charity*, and so on.' The divine 'proximate causes' and their human-based 'effects' 'combine to produce the ASSURANCE OF SALVATION and the PERSEVERANCE OF THE SAINTS'," p. 60.

27. Aylett, *Brides Ornaments*, pp. 23–24.

28. In analogues of Milton's masque, the homoerotic rites of Cotytto and Comus are travesties of the celebrations of holy matrimony. See Juvenal's "Satire II" in *The Sixteen Satires*, trans. Peter Green (Middlesex, England, 1967), p. 78, and Erycius Puteanus's neo-Latin *Comus, or the Cimmerian Banquet: A Dream*, in Watson Kirkconnell's *Awake the Courteous Echo* (Toronto, 1973), pp. 52–61.

David Norbrook, *Poetry and Politics in the English Renaissance* (London, 1984), comments on the symbolism of the enchanted cup:

> In a long tradition of apocalyptic literature, the temptations of idolatry had been represented as an enchanted cup; idolatry was defined as spiritual fornication, so that true faith became identified with chastity. (p. 252)

Milton himself interprets fornication very broadly to include any sort of sinful behavior, including idolatry. See *Tetrachordon*, YP II, pp. 672–73 and *De doctrina Christiana*, YP VI, p. 378.

29. See Sears Jayne's "The Subject of Milton's Ludlow Mask," *PMLA* LXXIV (Dec. 1959), 539 and C. L. Barber's "*A Mask Presented at Ludlow Castle:* The Masque as a Masque," in *The Lyrical and Dramatic Milton*, ed. Joseph H. Summers (New York, 1965), p. 50. Both Jayne and Barber regard the moment as spiritual and moral temptation. Barber writes: "Comus' fabrication opens an exquisite vista, exactly in the manner of the masque. It is his supreme moment as a tempter, because a sight of her brothers is just what the Lady, prisoned from them in darkness, most desires."

30. Georgia B. Christopher, *Milton and the Science of the Saints* (Princeton, 1982), p. 52.

31. Stanley E. Fish, "Problem Solving in *Comus*," in *Illustrious Evidence: Approaches to English Literature of the Early Seventeenth Century*, ed. Earl Miner (Berkeley and Los Angeles, 1975), p. 41.

32. Rous, *The Mysticall Marriage*, p. 23.

33. Ibid., p. 41.

34. Brucioli, *A Commentary Vpon the Canticle of Canticles*, A6ʳ.

35. YP I, p. 751, glosses the term *discipline* by referring to *Of Reformation*. "[Milton] uses the word primarily in its Latin meaning, with a military connotation. In addition he is thinking of it as the complement of doctrine: doctrine the attribute of the teacher, and discipline the property of the disciple." Fenner regards Discipline as the hedge or defense of the garden, keeping it pure for Christ (C8ᵛ).

36. McGuire, *Milton's Puritan Masque*, pp. 61–65.

37. Rous, *The Mysticall Marriage*, p. 79.

38. McGuire, *Milton's Puritan Masque*, p. 116.

39. Brucioli, *A Commentary Vpon the Canticle of Canticles*, B1ᵛ.

40. Thomas James's dedication to Brucioli's *A Commentary Vpon the Canticle of Canticles*, 5ᵛ–6ʳ.

41. Kathleen M. Swaim in "Allegorical Poetry in Milton's Ludlow Mask," *Milton Studies*, vol. XVI, ed. James D. Simmonds (Pittsburgh, 1982), p. 172 states, "The woods of *A Mask* point now to Welsh groves and now to Spenserian forests of delusive and entangling moral and spiritual pilgrimage. As the goal of such a journey, the great hall of Ludlow Castle

with its festive assembly points both to parental home and to heavenly mansions, both to the inaugural celebration and to participation in the supernal community of realized virtue."

42. J. W. Saunders, "Milton, Diomede, and Amaryllis," *ELH* XXII (1955), 277.

43. George Wither, *Epithalamion* in *The English Spenserians*, ed. William B. Hunter (Salt Lake City, 1977), p. 300.

44. Stewart explains, "The apple tree in the Song of Songs represented the Grace bestowed by the Passion" (*The Enclosed Garden*, p. 73).

"UNION OF MIND, OR IN BOTH ONE SOUL" ALLEGORIES OF ADAM AND EVE IN *PARADISE LOST*

Kenneth Borris

T HROUGH SATAN'S JOURNEY and the war in heaven, *Paradise Lost* clearly includes and reinterprets motifs of figurative questing and armed conflict from allegorical heroic poetry; but Milton also appropriates its technical and thematic repertoire for heroic expression. Composite characterization was the most allegorically potent resource for epic portrayal of heroism, as in Edmund Spenser's *The Faerie Queene* and Torquato Tasso's *Gerusalemme liberata* according to his "Allegoria del poema" appended to most early editions. *Paradise Lost* likewise explores the nature of heroism partly through configurations of characters, personalized psychic projections, and symbolic settings. Satan's character unfolds through interaction with personified Sin, Death, and other progeny generated by his mental involvements with evil: Milton clearly considered techniques of composite characterization indispensable for his epic. But they have far wider applications in *Paradise Lost*.[1]

Aside from Milton's Satan, Adam and Eve would most readily have such potential, for their biblical story was widely considered an allegory about the created order of the human mind. Although various Miltonists have applied that approach, their arguments have been often ignored, or opposed in ways that assume Milton's couple would be necessarily reduced or oversimplified by any allegorical interpretation. Barbara Pavlock, for instance, recently rejects allegorical assessment of Eve because her character is complex; and this line of argument typifies previous critical banishments of allegory from Milton's Eden.[2] But allegory would thus have to be schematic in some simple sense, or consist of something like one-to-one correspondences, even though very fluid and polysemous capacities of the mode have now been critically acknowledged for decades.

Further impeding consideration of allegory in Milton's Eden is the common assumption that, since the literary authority of the mode had been declining, its presence there is unlikely. For Milton also, then, emergent mechanist and materialist philosophies had jeopardized the

45

prior metaphysical underpinnings of allegory by questioning the status of universals and the broadly Platonic cosmology of correspondences.[3] But, besides oversimplifying the literary history of allegory, this a priori rationale misrepresents Milton's intellectual development. Addressing challenges of the new philosophies by meeting them on their own ground, Milton came to promote free will, afterlife, theism, and Christianity within his own redefined metaphysical context that, in his view, rendered his central beliefs sustainable amidst the pressures of shifting intellectual paradigms. This recuperative enterprise need not involve any attenuation of allegory, for it revises former images of reality in a way that could well enable a renewal of the mode.

For example, Milton's distinctive animist materialism reflects the new prestige of material existence as a main criterion of reality; yet matter itself, in his scheme, derives *ex Deo.* All creation commonly participates in that divine substance, then, which is in turn the basis for the cosmic correspondences that pervade Milton's universe. Fully reflected in *Paradise Lost,* this Miltonic doctrine has the hitherto unnoticed effect of giving allegory some new metaphysical reinforcement, for allegorical correlations would thus become substantiated, so to speak, by metonymic links implicit in the universally shared material substrate created *ex Deo.* Excepting its fallen creatures, Milton's cosmos itself amounts to a diffuse allegory of his God, composed of the rapport of all its constituents as divinely authorized signs expressively participating in divine being. In a universe of monist materialism, moreover, physical and spiritual conditions interpenetrate as manifestations of one substance, so that images more readily concretize ideas and inner states. Better metaphysical conditions could hardly be imagined for theological allegory, which could serve at least, then, as a pragmatic vehicle for the poetic realization of this monist perspective.

Accordingly, the perfect sympathies of Milton's prelapsarian Eden can serve not only as indications of what was impaired or lost in the Fall, but also as an extended figure for the spiritual gains to be realized through recovery of an inner paradise and reintegration into divine harmonies. Likewise, the appearance, behavior, and relationship of Adam and Eve both before and after the Fall can readily body forth spiritual conditions and psychological allegory. Rather than warranting assumptions that *Paradise Lost* excludes, attenuates, or simplifies allegory, Milton's relation to intellectual developments in the period implies that, insofar as the poem involves the mode, its uses and functions would tend to be more self-conscious, critically self-reflexive, heuristic, and provisional, yet dedicated to advancing knowledge of the moral and theological issues that profoundly exercised this poet.

Aside from a priori critical assumptions like those I have rejected, the question of Edenic allegory in *Paradise Lost* largely depends on whether textual features such as diction, imagery, and allusions invite allegorical reading of the couple, and if so, to what extent. Surprisingly, the controversy has not received any such concentrated evaluation to date, and so I focus here on assessment of those potential indicators in relation to relevant generic conventions and the characteristics of some widely influential allegories of Adam and Eve.

Since Eden and the Fall had long been interpreted allegorically, Milton and his more knowledgeable readers had to at least assess that capacity of his subject.[4] Milton could have endeavored to preclude such readings altogether by stating explicitly that his couple are not "allegoric," or by dismissing the traditional allegories with one of his brusque narratorial interjections, such as "thus they relate, / Erring."[5] But the poet provides no such directives; critical assertions that allegory has little or no relevance to *Paradise Lost* are at best supposititious. Instead, the poem clearly aligns Adam and Eve to some extent with qualities attached to their respective psychological meanings in once-familiar allegories of the Fall. Moreover, Spenser and Tasso among others had encouraged allegorically composite characterization in heroic poetry; so many passages of *Paradise Lost* similarly appear to allegorize the couple through wordplay that this effect seems quite deliberate.

Whereas prior allegorical interpretations of Milton's Adam and Eve each argue exclusively for one such reading alone, I find them complementary. They focus on the Fall's occurrence, so that the poet uses allegory to deepen and extend his analysis of that central crux, as with Satan's cosmic journey.[6] And they share a basic structure. Adam and Eve correspond to a binary hierarchy dominated by the Adamic term, which becomes destabilized and degraded in the Fall; Adam's acquiescence confirms the potential for this disruption first manifested through Eve, so that his part incurs final responsibility for sinful action.[7] Just as the Fall involves a transition from one kind of consciousness to another, analysts of Milton's allegory tend to correlate this structure with psychological patterns.[8] His primary human couple thus express a composite model of the human mind as it should be, before the Fall; as it succumbs to and perpetuates the inner processes of sin; and finally as it becomes regenerate.

To date there are two main approaches of this kind, and they corre-

spond to age-old allegories of the Fall which I will call Philonic and Augustinian. These biblical interpretations are likewise distinct yet complementary, though that seems not to have been previously noticed either. Although they do not exhaust the figurative resources of Milton's Edenic
fiction, comparison of these traditional allegorizations with his portrayal of
Adam and Eve can most effectively challenge the apparently dominant
view that his Eden excludes the mode. Not only does this procedure enable
more comprehensive argument, but these particular allegories had an abiding ideological authority that makes their reflection in *Paradise Lost* more
inherently probable than putative alternatives lacking comparable historical precedent.[9] Milton's Edenic narrative accommodates both the Philonic
and Augustinian perspectives, just as seventeenth-century thought still
tended to be loosely syncretic, and complex allegory can readily coordinate
analogous conceptual patterns within one narrative structure.[10]

The allegorical aspects of Milton's representation of Adam and Eve
render it all the more complex. The couple are in one sense a conjoint
whole, to be interpreted according to composite notions of the psyche, yet
also diversely characterized individuals whose depiction somewhat queries
ascendant seventeenth-century notions of gender roles, which were partly
based on the Philonic and Augustinian allegories themselves. The poem
thus challenges the adequacy of the allegorical readings, even as it generates them, and leaves the question of their validity finally open.[11] Moreover, insofar as these allegories are distinct interpretations, their conjoint
expression in a single narrative vehicle promotes further exploration of the
meaning of the Fall by playing each off against the other. I will take the
characters' complexity for granted, and instead attend to neglected or
unnoticed textual aspects of their allegorical dimension. Rather than re-
ducing the scope of the poem's characterizations and significance, the
Edenic allegories augment their plenitude by contributing to a counter-
point of perspectives on the Fall that provocatively sets assumptions of the
traditional allegories over against questions of human diversity, the relative
status of the sexes, and the problem of evil.

PHILONIC AND AUGUSTINIAN ALLEGORIES OF THE FALL

Even when acknowledging these allegories, Miltonists usually under-
estimate their influence in the sixteenth and seventeenth centuries. However, Milton's heuristic inclusion of them in *Paradise Lost* reflects their
common currency. Analogous in structure, they were actively used to
further various ideological interests, and together constitute one of the
most powerful conceptual paradigms of the time. Vestiges likely persist in
current cultural assumptions.

Probably the most common allegory of Adam and Eve originated with Philo Judaeus. It broadly relates Eve to the senses, passions, appetites, will, body, or flesh; Adam to reason or mind; and the serpent or temptation to pleasure. That "slimy serpent, . . . twisted into a hundred coils, never ceases to lie in wait for the heel of the woman, whom he once corrupted," Erasmus declares. "By woman I mean the carnal part of man. This is our Eve, through whom the cunning serpent lures our mind towards deadly pleasures."[12]

Many found this notion alluring. Often explicitly adduced in support of some favored doctrine, it also performed such functions implicitly and unconsciously. Joseph Glanvill's *Vanity of Dogmatizing* uses the Philonic allegory for epistemological explanation: the "*Woman* in us, still prosecutes a deceit, like that begun in the *Garden*," so that "we scarse see any thing now but through our *Passions*." Some use it to advance ideas of human transcendental potential, or explore the implications of sin for humanity, like Sir Henry Vane and Henry More. In Jean Bodin's *République*, or *Six Bookes of a Commonweale*, the Philonic allegory serves to define the extent of a husband's power over his wife; Milton's *Commonplace Book* cites that particular chapter as a reference favoring divorce, and Bodin is a featured authority in *Reason of Church-Government*. The proclamation of male headship in Genesis iii, 16, Bodin claims, morally expresses "the commaund the soule hath over the bodie, and reason over affection. For that reasonable part of understanding, is in man as the Husband; and Affection, as the Woman. . . . Wherefore the woman in holy writ is oftentimes taken for affection" [i.e., figuratively]. For Bodin, that allegory underwrites masculine marital supremacy, thus giving males certain rights to obtain divorce. Although some such texts could have influenced Milton directly, these examples demonstrate the ideological force of the Philonic allegory, and the diversity of its cultural applications.[13]

Though variously applied, this allegory explains the Fall as the turning of mind away from God, toward commitment to the senses, material world, and human desires. Adam's eating of the forbidden fruit at Eve's suggestion thus expresses archetypal inversion of rightful psychic order, reproduced in every sin. Hence the biblical narrative of Adam and Eve becomes a means of understanding and controlling potential for evil according to a correlative bipartite conception of the soul. In Philo's formulations especially, the allegory depreciates women by associating them with the sense perceptions and material world that he presumes inferior. Yet, unless inept, exponents of this allegory observe that the decisive fault belongs to the higher, Adamic element for acceding to inappropriate propositions of the lower, since otherwise no sin could be enacted. The allegory assumes that women as well as men have such bipartite souls, though the higher capacity would usually have been thought weaker in females. Milton himself terms Philo a "gravis author" in *Pro Populo Anglicano Defensio*, mentions his writings in *Doctrine and Discipline of Divorce* and *Tetrachordon*, and propounds a quasi-Philonic marital allegory of Intellect and Will in the Seventh Prolusion.[14]

A further allegory of the Fall expressed in Saint Augustine's *De Trinitate* was also current for such diverse writers as Heinrich Cornelius Agrippa, Hendrik Niclaes, founder of the Familists, and Martin Luther, among others. The serpent correlates with the senses, then, and Adam and Eve respectively with higher and lower modes of reason. While not rejecting the Philonic allegory, Augustine argues that his interpretation more aptly relates Eve to the specifically human rational faculty, and instead assigns the sensory faculty, common to beasts as well as humans, to the snake.

In both sexes, Augustine assumes, the human mind surpasses beasts in having two rational capacities. Dealing with the regulation or cognition of temporal and physical things, *ratio inferior* collects, organizes, and reflects upon sense impressions for practical management of everyday affairs through production of general and comparative principles and judgments. Transcending this *scientia, ratio superior* should adhere contemplatively to the eternal reasons of the intelligible realm, enabling a true intellectual understanding that must ever inform its lower counterpart, as man heads woman, in Augustine's view. Just as in matrimony "there is one flesh of two, so the nature of the mind" properly embraces both capacities, and thus conforms to truth and images God. Sin becomes possible if the lower reason is concupiscently preoccupied with worldly concerns in themselves; such conditions correspond to Eve's eating of the apple. But sin becomes complete only if the "head gives its consent, that is, if . . . the masculine part in the watch-tower of counsel does not check and restrain" the lower reason, and thus also "eats what is forbidden," as it were. Selfishly entangled in its own interests and powers, then, the mind turns against God, excludes itself from participation with other creatures in the divine community of creation, and loses the "vision of eternal things."[15]

The Philonic and Augustinian allegories are sufficiently different to constitute distinct interpretations, yet similar enough in their structure and premises to remain complementary. In the latter, Eve still signifies the element more closely bound to physical existence, the lower or carnal reason. Augustine's scheme transfers the analytic categories of the Philonic allegory to the intellect itself, to scrutinize more closely how it becomes subject to the senses and thus to sin. Using the same hierarchical system of relations, both allegories assume that the more intellectual part of the soul has an especial divine orientation, and properly rules the mind; but that primal order is upset by promotion of the part deemed more physical or worldly, and hence less worthy. In both, moreover, the Adamic term is the executive function, ultimately responsible for the Fall or any sin:

I. Edenic or Godly Soul

$$\frac{\text{Adam}}{\text{Eve}} : \frac{\text{reason}}{\text{senses, passions}} : \frac{\text{mind}}{\text{body, flesh}} : \frac{\text{transcendental reason}}{\text{carnal reason}}$$

II. Fallen Soul

$$\frac{\text{Eve}}{\text{Adam}} : \frac{\text{senses, passions}}{\text{reason}} : \frac{\text{body, flesh}}{\text{mind}} : \frac{\text{carnal reason}}{\text{transcendental reason}}$$

Renaissance thought was shot through with such conceptual structures predicated according to its patriarchal hierarchy of genders. The tendency to align Eve and femininity with anything considered inferior followed not only from the biblical portrayal of gender and sexuality, especially in Genesis and the Pauline epistles, but also from the Aristotelian grounding of the intellectual disciplines. For "the philosopher," the male principle is definitively perfected, formative, and active, but the female deprived, material, and passive. Moreover, the dominant Renaissance notions of opposition and difference, on which male assessment of females greatly depended, were implicated in primitive Pythagorean dualities that pejoratively correlate woman with plurality, darkness, and evil.[16]

Reflections of these patterns of thought, the Philonic and Augustinian allegories are not to be condemned so much as the cultural formulation of femininity that authorized them. Ideas of woman were so fraught with admonitory associations that all the related vocabulary, including terms such as "female," "woman," and "feminine," tended to be strongly figurative, and associated with sensuality and the passions. Sir Philip Sidney elaborately explores the potential of such usage in the *Arcadias* through Pyrocles' disguise as an Amazon, but most obviously when, in the Second Eclogues of the *Old Arcadia,* Dicus correlates feminine subordination of a male with enslavement of "Reason . . . to servile Sence." Since masculinity was so strongly linked with reason, marriage itself often figured rational subjection of passions. The case of Eve tended to crystallize the ostensibly inferior significance of femininity over against privileged masculine criteria, in all respects.[17]

As analogies between external and internal conceptions of order were produced and standardized, so the favored political, sexual, and psychological hierarchies were correlated for seeming corroboration and mutual reinforcement, in keeping with the ascendant cosmology of correspondences. The resultant artificial construction appeared a natural means for understanding and defining both interpersonal and psychic relations, and thus to some extent delimited the very possibilities of thought and social interaction. In this sense, Adam and Eve became a dominant cultural exemplar implicitly warning against inversion of the approved hierarchies of mind, political authority, and gender.[18]

Milton's poetic representation of the supposedly original man and woman could hardly avoid absorbing and reflecting some of these ideological pressures. More positively, the cultural significance of Adam and Eve was so richly fraught with allegorical potential of major importance for conceptions of the human condition that a writer who set out to treat that couple in an epically encyclopedic way would have been unlikely to ignore such a potent means of psychic and social reflection.

Moreover, application of the traditional allegories to Adam and Eve had extensive Protestant endorsement. Though tending to reject allegorical exegesis of the Bible as a basis for theological doctrine, numerous Protestant writers, including Luther, approved it for edification. While commentaries on Genesis did not usually find the Philonic allegory doctrinally binding, they nevertheless allowed it "as a proper moral application of the text." Just as many had long considered the story of Eden jointly historical and figurative, so Milton's Eden accommodates that allegorical perspective. In *Doctrine and Discipline of Divorce*, Milton had already condemned the "strictness of a literall interpreting" of the Bible, and poetic contexts would presumably warrant far greater interpretive freedoms, just as Milton's Eden obviously reworks Genesis a great deal (YP II, p. 242). Though Milton sometimes even allegorizes the Old Testament to support doctrinal arguments in his treatises, the Augustinian and Philonic allegories in *Paradise Lost* serve to further spiritual inquiry, edification, moral armament, and epic comprehensiveness. That is in keeping with current cultural practice, for many writers had already appropriated these allegories to pursue their own aims or lines of inquiry.[19]

MILTON'S EDENIC ALLEGORIES

Contrary to Philonic interpreters of Milton's primal couple, such as Denis Saurat, Arnold Stein, Fredson Bowers, A. B. Chambers, and Joseph E. Duncan, others argue, in Augustinian fashion, for the couple's joint relation to aspects of the rational soul. Intellectual contexts invoked by the latter group differ, but their findings are mutually supportive.

Alastair Fowler finds that Milton's depiction of the couple involves a Neoplatonic bipartite analysis of mental faculties: *ratio*, corresponding to Eve, should "reflect obediently, and . . . translate into practical terms, the truth contemplated" by *intellectus* or *mens*. Sin, then, proceeds from willful disruption of that relationship, so that the Fall can be analyzed accordingly. A. Kent Hieatt stresses Augustine's own exposition relating Adam and Eve to higher and lower modes of reason, like Georgia B. Christopher, but rightly observes that for "imaginative, poetic purposes" Fowler's scheme is "virtually the same." Yet the broadly Augustinian account is not in itself sufficient, for *Paradise Lost* evokes the Philonic allegory as well, by also associating Eve with the senses and physical body.[20]

Milton encourages such explorations of his Eden by relating the couple's actions and inner states to Renaissance faculty psychology. Allegorizing its schemes himself, he presents their terms as active personifications, so that correspondences between them and the couple invite its assessment as a psychological composite. Adam addresses Eve twice in this way, defining Reason's proper role. Much before the passage in the separation scene, which I will consider later, Adam creates his initial *allegoria* of psychic functions after Eve's demonic dream: Reason "as chief" properly superintends "many lesser faculties" within "the soul." By rendering elements of the psyche into notional persons, Adam endeavors to assess how "the mind of god or man" relates to "Evil" (*PL* V, 100–19). In reading the Edenic couple's relations allegorically, then, we merely extend to them the approach that Adam himself uses here, according to textual indications, and modulate from simple to complex allegory.

The Miltonic narrator defines the Fall's psychological impact within another such *allegoria*, so that, in a sense, allegorical commentary on Adam and Eve is inherent in the poem:

> understanding *ruled not*, and the will
> *Heard not her lore*, both in *subjection* now
> To sensual appetite, *who from beneath*
> *Usurping over sovereign reason claimed*
> *Superior sway: from thus distempered breast*,
> Adam, estranged in look and altered style,
> Speech intermitted thus to Eve renewed.
>
> (IX, 1127–33; emphasis mine)

Insubordination of reason by senses and desires is clearly a central dynamic of Milton's Fall, and the narrator encourages us to read the inner condition of fallen Adam and Eve accordingly. Since the context concerns the Fall, and since the terms of analysis here—sensual appetite ousting reason—are those of the Philonic allegory and presented in an *allegoria*, they strongly evoke that allegory. Having just subjected himself to Eve, Adam has inverted their original relationship often taken as a figurative model for the apt internal relation of human psychic faculties.

In another *allegoria*, Michael's interpretation of Milton's Fall provides more allegorical commentary broadly evoking Philonic exegesis: When "Reason in man" is "*not obeyed*," "inordinate desires / And *upstart* passions *catch the government*" and "*unworthy powers . . . reign*" within, abrogating rational human liberty (XII, 83–90; emphasis mine). In encouraging Adam to eat the forbidden fruit, Eve would partly relate, then, to the promptings of "ungoverned appetite" (XI, 515–18).

Milton's Father also promotes allegorical perspectives on the Fall, for his account of human ability to resist sin involves a mixed *allegoria* in which various elements of the mind are interactively personified. Though "sin" enslaves inner powers "to foul exorbitant desires," "conscience" persists as God-given "guide" or "umpire" (III, 175–97), in accord with Spenser's allegory of the Palmer and Ruddymane in *The Faerie Queene*. Likewise, the Son's initial warning to humankind, recounted by Raphael, is allegorically tendentious: "beware, / And govern well thy appetite, lest Sin / Surprise thee" (VII, 545–47). Since vigilant resistance against personified Sin depends on *governing* appetite within, the ensuing narrative of the Fall can readily admit a Philonic kind of analysis. In Milton's view, even God reveals his will to human understanding partly through allegory, just as Revelation "soares to a Prophetick pitch in types, and Allegories," according to *Animadversions* (YP I, p. 74). *Paradise Lost* clearly places even the couple's basic capacity to stand within the purview of psychological allegory, as well as the inner consequences of falling.

Through allegorical wordplay, many briefer passages of the poem point more specifically to the Philonic or Augustinian interpretations of Adam and Eve. Diction in allegorical narratives tends to coordinate multiple areas of reference so that it functions within the story while also reflecting the conceptual contents of allegory. Since the mode is quasiintentional and narratively extensive, it exerts special pressures on language by promoting a broad multivalency organized by the requirements of both the allegorical content and its narrative expression. Moreover, any tenor tends to permeate its vehicle to some extent when such compositional doubleness is allegorically protracted.[21]

The interaction of heroic themes and characterization with the technical repertoire of allegory can be clarified through attention to the role of wordplay in Tasso's and Spenser's allegorical epics. Despite intervening shifts in ideology and poetics, Milton knew the *Gerusalemme liberata* and *The Faerie Queene* well, and endeavored critically to subsume their genres and literary practices within the encyclopedic scope of *Paradise Lost*. In any case, the general relations of allegory with wordplay fundamental to my subsequent argument are diachronic, so that Tasso and Spenser remain technically revealing in this specific application.

When expounding allegory in his *Gerusalemme liberata*, Tasso assumes that such expression largely depends on conceptually oriented wordplay:

> *Godfrey* which holdeth the principall place in this storie, is no other in the Allegorie but the *Understanding*, which is signified in many places of the *Poeme* as in that verse, *By thee the counsell given is, by thee the scepter rul'd.* And more plainly in that other: *Thy soule is of the campe both minde and life.* And *Life* is added, bicause in the powers more noble, the lesse noble are contained. [22]

As commander of the crusading army, Tasso's Godfrey governs its affairs, provides its highest deliberative resource, and ensures its continuing vitality. The role of the rational soul was very similarly conceived, for treatises on psychology and moral philosophy ordinarily described it as the rightful ruler, governor, or prince within, sometimes through an elaborate *allegoria;* and innumerable literary texts and allegories followed suit. Tasso's comment on the inclusiveness of the soul's nobler powers reflects the Aristotelian doctrine of the tripartite soul in which the comprehensive being of the exalted rational soul subsumes powers of the subordinate animal and vegetable souls. Further expounding Rinaldo's relation to the irascible appetite, Tasso adduces yet another passage having both narrative and allegorical applications.

Especially important for the heroic poem, this kind of technique suited the conceitful aspects of epic high style. Moreover, it provided means to negotiate between the narrative and the ambitious encyclopedic content prescribed for epic, without detracting from lively presentation of the action. Spenser advises his reader that, if astutely scrutinized, *The Faerie Queene* covertly signifies much beyond its story:

> Of Faerie lond yet if he more inquire,
> By certaine signes here set in sundry place
> He may it find; ne let him then admire,
> But yield his sence to be too blunt and bace,
> That no'te without an hound fine footing trace. [23]

In Spenserian allegory, many have shown, much depends on allusive subtleties of wordplay. Tasso's casual recourse to wordplay for demonstrating his own allegory, together with his assertion that many parts of his poem are similarly expressive, show he could assume that readers associated this kind of literary technique with allegorical heroic poetry and its interpretation. His *Discorsi del poema eroico* finds "riddle and allegory . . . the same in species, or at least in genus," though the high enigmas of the latter are especially apt to "poems full of mystery like the heroic."[24]

Numerous passages in *Paradise Lost* would thus have provoked allegorical exposition from commentators like Tasso. In presenting the Edenic couple, Milton, noted for his high degree of calculated, intellectually self-conscious artistry, activates interpretive conventions of narrative allegory and allegorical heroic poetry, while providing information that evokes traditional allegories about Adam and Eve. The poem's allegorization of the couple seems intentionally Miltonic, then, but in any case a basic and definitive textual feature.

According to Eve, when Adam first speaks after her emergence into self-awareness, he thus defines her being and role: "*Part of my soul* I seek thee, and thee claim / My other half" (IV, 487–88; emphasis mine). Adam's comment has various meanings apt for the literal situation: as the rational consort Adam requested, Eve partakes of the characteristic rationality of his human soul, and together they form a marital unity, "one flesh, one heart, one soul" (VIII, 499). However, according to the compositional and interpretive practices associated with allegory and Renaissance allegorical heroic poetry, the diction further indicates some composite psychological allegory. This significant ambiguity is embedded in the original context for our knowledge of Eve's relation to Adam, describing the first time they meet and establish their relationship. Similar passages appear later. Eve's behavior evincing "Union of mind, or in . . . both one soul" especially delights Adam (VIII, 600–04). When Adam decides to eat the fruit, he exclaims to Eve, "Our state cannot be severed, we are one, / One flesh; to lose thee were to lose my self"; Eve gladly agrees that they have "One heart, one soul in both" (IX, 958–59, 967). While reflecting the couple's conjugal condition, these passages further suggest some joint psychic meaning.

Epic conventions of composite characterization were readily applicable to *Paradise Lost*, since allegorical accounts of Adam and Eve in relation to one soul or union of mind were well known; the Miltonic narrator makes no effort to foreclose on the allegorical resonances in the text. Instead, Milton characterizes the couple so that they provocatively correlate to some extent with the structure of those allegories: "What the *Masculine* part in man is, *Philo* plainly declares. . . . *In us*, saith he, *the Man is the*

Intellect, the Woman the Sense of the Body. Whence you will easily understand, that the *Masculine Faculties* are those that are more *Spiritual* and
Intellectual."[25] Repeatedly associating Adam with the "higher intellectual,"
contemplation, mind, and wisdom, and Eve more with physical beauty and
power to excite the senses and passions, "Milton seems never to tire of
telling his reader of Adam's superior mind and of his reflection of God's
truth and wisdom," while linking Eve "early . . . with the material world of
passions, the senses, and the body."[26] Of course they are complicated characters, not schematically presented. Eve displays much mental agility, for
example, in debating Adam. Nevertheless, they have these primary and
opposed associations, which unfallen and regenerate Eve, Raphael, Michael, the Son, Adam, and Satan all take for granted.

While allegorical meanings cannot adequately substitute for Milton's
Adam and Eve (and that is also true for most agents in *The Faerie
Queene*), these characters serve to some extent as vehicles for their established figurative significances. Thus they enable some further provisional
expression of the mystery of prelapsarian inner harmony and its degrada-
tion. In that sense, Adam eats "Against his better knowledge, not deceived, / But fondly overcome with female charm," or by apparent goods
pleasurably represented through what many would have called his female
faculties (IX, 997–99). When the Son rebukes Adam specifically for invert-
ing assigned gender roles by making Eve his God or guide, that censure
can likewise extend to correlative psychic inversions, as in the Philonic
and Augustinian allegories (X, 145–56). Whether or not *Paradise Lost*
ultimately promotes acceptance of such conceptions, it uses allegorical
technique to encourage their assessment.

The poem most clearly evokes traditional allegorization of the couple
during their separation debate just before the Fall. Consequently, since the
whole scene is also a Miltonic invention "entirely without precedent,"[27]
Milton seems to have conceived and designed it partly for purposes of
allegorical orientation. Adam explains to Eve the inner dangers of temptation for "man," and their consequent need for mutual reinforcement:

> *within himself*
> *The danger lies*, yet lies within his power:
> Against his will he can receive no harm.
> But God left free the will, for what obeys
> *Reason*, is free, and reason he made right,
> But bid *her* well beware, and still erect,
> *Lest by some fair appearing good surprised*
> *She dictate false, and misinform the will*
> *To do what God expressly hath forbid.*

Not then mistrust, but tender love enjoins,
That *I should mind thou oft and mind thou me*.
Firm we subsist, yet possible to swerve,
Since *reason* not impossibly *may meet*
Some specious object by the foe suborned,
And *fall into deception unaware,*
Not keeping strictest watch, as she was warned.
Seek not temptation then, which to avoid
Were better, and most likely if from me
Thou sever not: trial will come unsought.

                                    (IX, 348–66; emphasis mine)

This is the most important psychological *allegoria* in *Paradise Lost*, since it builds on preceding discussions of inner conditions to provide concentrated analysis of danger "within," or the psychology of sin, immediately before the crucial separation and Eve's fall. Just as Eve is about to encounter and succumb to temptation as we well know, we find reason personified here, feminine, and capable of breaking God's commandment through meeting some deceptive apparent good, or subverted object. The micronarrative of the *allegoria* corresponds broadly with the story of Eve's meeting with and deception by the satanically inspired serpent. Since Eve's and Reason's roles in transgressing divine commandments correlate so closely, the text does not just invite but indirectly offers an allegorical reading of the Fall here, mediated through Adam.

This Miltonic expressive maneuver has many technical precedents. In an especially potent allegorical application of wordplay, inset *allegoria* could generate and focus figurative interpretation of surrounding narrative. Milton would have been well acquainted with Spenser's endlessly resourceful exploitations of this technique in *The Faerie Queene*. They range from virtual interpolations of allegorical commentary, as in the introductory stanzas for the cantos about Alma's castle in book II, to the often ingenious figurative resonances of biographies, epic similes, extended mythic comparisons, and other apparent digressions. *Paradise Lost* similarly indicates figurative possibilities of the Fall here, yet in a way that avoids narrow association of them with the Miltonic narrator's privileged perspective. Expressed by means of Adam's still innocent perception of the psyche, they become inadvert, plangent anticipations of the Fall's significance. As Eve herself meets with Satan's devices, the allegory modulates from the relative simplicity of the mixed *allegoria* within Adam's speech, into the dramatized subtleties of its complex mode.

In this specifically psychological context, Adam's warning reemphasizes the couple's reciprocal relation in which he has priority as guide: "I should *mind* thou oft, and *mind* thou me." Milton's emphasis on "mind" within this highly charged figurative passage seems a pointed allegorical allusion indicating Adam's general association with mind in a superior aspect, or at least the privileged prelapsarian status of intellect. The reciprocal relation of higher and lower intellectual faculties is the fundamental pattern of the Augustinian allegory of the Fall. Not only a compact, simple allegory of how sin can occur, Adam's account evokes a traditional allegory of the Fall, while indicating its categories of analysis that apply to the subsequent action.

The separation of Eve from Adam is an allegorical prototype of the Fall that figures forth a paradigmatic inner state of precarious integration from which sin could potentially develop. In the Augustinian account, when *mens* or *ratio superior* can no longer fully inform the lower reason, corresponding to Eve, then the psyche ceases to reflect as a whole the transcendental apprehensions that guarantee its integrity. It could thus be deceived in encountering an apparent good, so that wrongful choices and actions could result if the error extended to final authorization by the higher reason. Because sin can only result from that assent in the Augustinian allegory, and similarly in the Philonic one, the mere separation of Adam and Eve does not allegorically constitute the Fall, *pace* Farwell.[28] Adam's agreement that Eve can garden alone does not imply his approval of everything else that she could do meanwhile. Rather than simply allegorizing the Fall itself, the separation expresses some of the inner conditions of its possibility.

Milton's attraction to this general allegory is not surprising, for it endeavors to promote moral and spiritual edification by analyzing the psychic conditions of the Fall, and thus of sin in general. For the origins of human wrongdoing, the crux for both Philonic and Augustinian allegorists had long been some notional division, at least, between Adam and Eve; hence that kind of figurative inquiry amounted to a topos optionally associated with discussions of the Fall involving their separation. In Leone Ebreo's Philonic version, for example, the "serpent represents the carnal appetite which, when it finds the feminine part somewhat separated from the intellect, her husband, and defying his rigorous laws, first incites and deludes her into defiling herself."[29] Through Adam's *allegoria* and the ensuing separation, Milton analogously exploits the opportunity to probe psychological circumstances from which the Fall could proceed, and prefigures the far more drastic loss of psychic and social integration after the Fall. The poet also exploratively prefigures the Fall from various other standpoints in *Paradise Lost*, most obviously in the genesis of Sin and Death, but also through Satan's allegorical cosmic journey.[30] The complex allegory of the couple has diverse applications: psychological analysis of the Fall relates at once to its mental workings, impact on the mind, and the subsequent operations of sin in humanity.[31]

While Milton's separation scene is closer to the Augustinian allegory than to Philo's, his treatment of the Fall also evokes the latter. As shown, both use the same fundamental structure of opposition in complementary ways. Over against Adam's affinities with mind in *Paradise Lost*, Eve's very attractiveness symbolically focuses sensory attractions and their power to arouse passions, just as her beauty produces "Commotion strange" in Adam (VIII, 530). The text's many moralizing comments on apt discipline of the senses in relation to Adam, Eve, and the Fall strongly encourage Philonic reading of their relationship. Raphael's parting advice to Adam, "take heed lest *passion sway* / *Thy judgement* to do aught, which else free will / Would not admit," accords with Philonic analysis of the Fall; Eve's role in its occurrence can thus be related to the urgencies of Adam's bodily aspect (VIII, 635–37; emphasis mine). For Philo, "mind corresponds to man, the senses to woman; and pleasure encounters and holds parley with the senses first, and through them cheats with her quackeries the sovereign mind itself."[32] The debate between Raphael and Adam about proper response to Eve, then, admits some Philonic reading. Similarly suggestive is Milton's declaration, after the Fall, that "sensual appetite" had usurped control over "sovereign reason" (IX, 1130). In context, that condition implicitly corresponds with Adam's loss of conjugal authority, so that these psychic and social predicaments are correlative, as in Philonic exegesis. In falling, Adam's senses are inflamed, or he flounders in a troubled sea of passion (IX, 1031; X, 718); Michael too associates the Fall with inversion of a privileged psychic hierarchy of reason over passion (XII, 83–90).

Milton's diction reflects and plays on the traditional allegories in far more ways and contexts than can be enumerated here. However, since both allegories promote intellectual capacities, Milton's usage of words like "appetite" and "mind" would thus presumably evince special pressures of meaning, and they indeed provide some practically economical further demonstration.

Appetite seems much more associated with Eve than Adam. When recounting her satanic dream, she exclaims: "pleasant savoury smell / So quickened appetite, that I, methought, / Could not but taste." In that appetitive state, what she beholds is "The earth," expressing the condition of earthly desire. Before the Fall, it is she who assumes responsibilities of preparing fruits "to please / True appetite," as if she then expresses unfallen conditions of fulfilling bodily needs and desires (V, 84–88, 304–05). Her honorific title conferred by the satanically inspired serpent,

"Empress of this fair world," associates her with worldly attractions, at least potentially, and the snake strongly appeals to sensory indulgence and "sharp desire" in tempting her to eat that fruit so "Grateful to appetite": "such pleasure till that hour / at feed or fountain never had I found," he claims (IX, 568–97). Just before Eve eats, "eager appetite" strongly urges her to do so, along with provocative "smell," "touch," "taste," and "eye" (IX, 739–44). Her other motives of self-promotion may express further appetitive perspectives, or wanting "To reach, and feed" figuratively, by engrossing power and privilege. In turning her attention from God, they amount, from a theological viewpoint, to appetitive self-indulgence (IX, 779). Later, the devils' punishment indicates that such "appetite" leads only to chewing "bitter ashes" (X, 564–66). Milton does not render the process of Adam's fall so much in bodily, physical terms. Since Adam's motives largely reflect his attraction to Eve, they can be allegorically correlated with misdirected commitment of higher faculties to what were considered the lower or properly subordinate aspects and impulses of the self.

"Mind" in its various forms appears sixteen times in Adam's vocabulary and only thrice in Eve's. This disproportion, too extreme and incidental merely to reflect Adam's more intellectualized character, indicates some Miltonic association of Adam with intellect itself as in the traditional allegories. Moreover, in all Milton's prose and poetry, "mindless" never appears, except when it is Eve's epithet as the Satanic serpent approaches to tempt her, rejoicing in Adam's absence: his "higher intellectual more I shun" (IX, 431, 483). "Mindless" likely attracted Milton here as nowhere else because, while meaning "heedless" in relation to the story, it affords means of expressing the allegorical lack of presence of mind bound up with the Fall and involvements with sin, and dramatically focused in the couple's separation.

Many passages likewise hint at Adam's allegorical role, as in these further samples. After the angelic picnic "sudden mind" arises in Adam, "to know / Of things above his world, and of their being / Who dwell in heaven" (V, 451–56). The situation and Milton's wording may well allude to Adam's relation to the transcendentally oriented *ratio superior*, or *mens*. When Adam wrongly pledges to join Eve in eating the fruit, Fowler notes, her definition of their relationship significantly omits "mind" altogether, unlike Adam's earlier one (IX, 965–70).[33] And as Adam eats, he specifically takes "no thought" in doing so, just as his allegorical function is vitiated (IX, 1004–05). The Fall radically disrupts the couple's "inward state of mind" (IX, 1125–26), we are told, as Adam himself recognizes later: "from me what can proceed, / But all corrupt, both mind and will

depraved" (X, 824–25). According to the poem's hierarchical conception
of ideal gender relations, confusion of mind is most striking when "lascivious" Adam praises "wanton" Eve for being "sapient" in purveying the
forbidden fruit. Thus mind itself, as Fowler comments, "can no longer be
distinguished from lower faculties of perception" (IX, 1011–20).[34] Yet
Adam finally consoles despairing Eve with "better hopes" to which his
"more attentive mind" rises, *"calling to mind with heed"* that her "seed
shall bruise / The serpent's head" (X, 1006–32; emphasis mine). In this
passage ushering in the couple's regeneration, Adam's mentality improves, and his mediation of divine prophecy is analogous to the role of
mens or *ratio superior.* Adam is Eve's "guide / And head" whose directions
are "just and right," we find, in the further sense that he allegorically
focuses intellectual attributes (IV, 442–43).

Finally, when stressing at the start of Book X that God omnisciently
allowed Satan's temptation of the couple to occur since they were strong
enough to have repulsed him, Milton characterizes it as an "attempt" on
"the mind / Of man" (X, 8–9; emphasis mine). That specification emphasizes the psychological dimension of the Fall and tends to reify the whole
situation allegorically, for a moment, as an archetypal portrayal of the
human mind as tempted, with the couple as a composite depiction of the
psyche.

Much else in the Edenic scenes is similarly expressive. Adam tells us
that, before the Fall, it was his "highth / Of happiness" to behold God (X,
724–25), and while that is the supreme good of humankind from a Christian
viewpoint, the especial association of that vision with Adam here befits his
allegorical relation to *mens* or *ratio superior.* When Raphael advises Adam
that "wisdom" will never desert him if he does not dismiss "her, . . . / By
attributing overmuch to things / Less excellent," his warning accords with
the fundamental assumption of the traditional allegories, that mind should
be oriented toward higher rather than lower things, especially toward God
(VIII, 561–66). In both, inversion of that hierarchy is precisely what precipitates the Fall. Eve's speeches too have allegorical implications. When she
assures Adam that she is "to no end" without him and obeys what he "bid'st /
Unargued" (IV, 442, 635–36), those conditions befit the psychic order promoted by the traditional allegories. After the couple's separation, Adam
promises "Great joy . . . *to his thoughts*" in anticipation of Eve's return;
beyond its literal aptness, his comment may further reflect their allegorical
roles (IX, 843). Meanwhile, in an allegorical irony prefacing the literal
occurrence of Eve's fall, her erratic progress led by the serpent, who "leading swiftly rolled / In tangles, and made intricate seem straight," symbolizes
the condition of mind potentially misled "into fraud" through indulgence of

cupidinous curiosities associated with the lower faculties. Likewise, fallen Adam, yet more disordered within, finds his reasonings have become "mazes" (IX, 631–45; X, 830). The intellective allegories further heighten a rueful irony central to the poem: Eve's supposed tree of knowledge, from which she seeks "intellectual food" of "virtue to make wise," and Adam seeks some enlightenment too, occasions the disruption of harmonious human mental order (IX, 768, 778).

After the Fall, Adam and Eve's happy nuptial league degenerates into quarreling, "And of their vain contest appeared no end" (IX, 1189). While expressing their degraded inner states as individuals, their bickering allegorizes the disrupted relations of faculties within the "distempered breast," where understanding rules not, and sensual appetite conflicts with reason (IX, 1127–33). That distemper seems endless in one sense, because it is to be characteristic of all human progeny. The debacle of the couple's relationship involves the loss of Adam's headship and the hierarchical reciprocity it entailed; the Philonic and Augustinian allegories figuratively correlate that loss with inversion of psychic order due to the Fall. For Raphael, like the Miltonic narrator, love "hath his seat / In reason," enabling ascension to "heavenly love" (V, 589–92; IV, 754–57). Love and apt psychic awareness are complementary in *Paradise Lost*, and naturally suited for mutual expression, just as the prelapsarian relations of the couple reflect the rightful order of the mind, and their postlapsarian difficulties express its subversion.

When rebuking Adam's prejudice that "man's woe" always begins "from woman," Michael stresses that it springs instead "From man's effeminate slackness," who "should better hold his place / By wisdom" (XI, 632–36). This highly compressed remark epitomizes the force of the Philonic and Augustinian allegories within their accustomed vehicle of the couple's relations. Not only enjoining exercise of male authority, Michael uses the notion of masculine and feminine aspects of the psyche to urge males to maintain a rational headship within themselves that is defined by contrast with a pejoratively feminine inner potential, and subordinates it. Michael associates wisdom itself with masculinity, and only its rule within, in his view, can legitimate external authority. "The weaknesses you seek to objectify outside yourself as blameworthy 'woman,' " he implies, "are really within you, for your inversion of apt inner order has emasculated your mind." Similarly, the traditional allegories finally attach human responsibility for the Fall and any sin to the rational element they deem superior and masculine: it improperly empowers the so-called feminine part through wrongful acquiescence and thus forfeits the executive prerogatives of wisdom. More generally, Milton's poem encourages us to interpret the difficulties of human relationships partly as reflections of inner disorders within ourselves.

These ways of considering Adam and Eve as a figurative composite are finally expressions of the epic's focal interest in adherence to the image of God as the ground of creaturely heroism, for the divine image had been primarily understood and defined according to the operations of mind and reason. In Augustine's once-commonplace formulation, "*ubi est imago Dei, id est in mente*"; the original relationship of Milton's Adam with Eve to some extent epitomizes the privileged role of the "higher intellectual" capacities (IX, 483).[35]

ALLEGORY AND EDENIC REPRESENTATION

Since the Philonic and Augustinian allegories had long been widely influential, their inclusion in *Paradise Lost* befits Milton's epically encyclopedic inquiry into the conditions of humanity. Milton uses allegory partly as a poetic means of epic comprehensiveness, for he can thus assimilate relevant bodies of doctrine without dogmatic affirmations, or massively obtruding dialectic upon his narrative.[36] Moreover, to portray the psychic resources of his human heroes, Milton aptly resorts to techniques of composite characterization associated with epic, and that approach furthers the sweepingly inclusive generic survey and revaluation undertaken within his poem. Through complex allegory, the significance of the characters subsumes additional theories of the Fall and the mental processes of sin, and thereby extends examination of social ties as well.

Of course, this allegorically informed perspective on Adam and Eve's relationship and the Fall in *Paradise Lost* does not imply that they are static personifications. Complex allegory can more or less fuse with dramatic portrayal of fully developed characters, as with Milton's allegorical treatment of Satan's journey. Milton presses this option much further than Spenser and Tasso, partly because dramatization of psychological complexity and personal motives is not germane to romance: a much stronger element in the generic mixtures of *The Faerie Queene* and *Gerusalemme liberata*. Yet even Milton's challenging Satan at last becomes the much simpler, obviously pejorative Great Dragon, for the poet is more concerned to manipulate the potential registers of literary representation, as befits his thematic purposes, than maintain any consistent verisimilitude.

Moreover, except when conforming strictly to clear biblical precedent, Milton's specifics of description for persons and places in *Paradise Lost* are to some extent provisional evocations of what could be considered "true" if veracity were assessed according to utility for edification. The landscapes of his heaven, hell, and Eden are at least partly symbolic, and so are all their inhabitants.[37] When inventive in this poem, Milton seeks to reflect some perceived truth through devices of indirect expression: analogies between situations or events depicted, figurative correspondences, or provocative realignments or recombinations of diverse roles and references traditional in the Bible, literature, or visual arts.

Milton's Adam and Eve themselves seem monumental and hieratic types of humankind, wellsprings of human potential, and yet they also impress us as complicated individuals whose qualities and motivations appear endlessly pursuable. That they further participate in psychological allegories does not reduce but amplifies the scope of their realization and of its assessment of human conditions postulated in intellectual history. Milton's Adam and Eve are thematic representatives, to some extent, because the poem and its treatment of the Fall have such vast significance. To find them also carrying some allegorical freight should not be surprising, then, if we recall that allegory need not be naively simple or univocal, and that Milton's narrative is replete with metaphorical interconnections anyway, and situated in a universe of sympathies and correspondences highly conducive to this mode.

Recent advocates of Milton's "feminism" might still consider the traditional allegories irrelevant on the a priori grounds that they contradict feminist principles. But, though Milton seems "misogynist" to others, his thought tends in both directions and so does *Paradise Lost*, just as variously divided estimates of women typify sixteenth- and seventeenth-century male writings. Milton's *Doctrine and Discipline of Divorce* assumes that marital breakdown usually occurs because the wife is inadequate; in his *History of Britain*, "nothing" is "more awry from the Law of God and Nature, then that a Woman should give Laws to Men" (YP, II, pp. 247, 306, 324–25; YP V, p. 32). Even when Milton's Michael rebukes Adam's misogyny, his correction still assumes that Adam's fault or "slackness" is itself "effeminate" (XI, 634). And Michael introduces the vision of mortality and "Diseases dire" to Adam so that he may "know / *What misery the inabstinence of Eve* / Shall bring on *men*" (XI, 474–77; emphasis mine). Whatever the extent of Milton's "feminism," its expression seems tactlessly vexed by contrary impulses.[38]

Likewise, by including the Philonic and Augustinian allegories in *Paradise Lost*, Milton disseminates perspectives that depreciate women, without placing those views in any unequivocally critical context. These allegories at least allow that the psychological structure expressed by Adam and Eve exists within women as well, who can thus be informed by an inner "Adamic" part. Since the allegories hold the masculine part finally responsible for the Fall and any human sin, they counter the cultural tendency to blame Eve and women. Yet, in keeping with certain Aristotelian and biblical doctrines, those allegories assume that woman is subordinate to man, just as they posit a "feminine" symbolic category that remains properly subject to a "masculine" one. Milton's cultural predicament virtually precluded any feminist assessment of such prejudicial ideologies. During the Renaissance, these allegories were variously endorsed by many prestigious writers, and never explicitly challenged, so far as I have found, on grounds of injustice to women, even though Saint Augustine himself had criticized the Philonic allegory on that basis.[39]

However, as Joan Webber and Marilyn Farwell argue, Milton's portrayal of Adam and Eve's conjugal union endows each not only with an existence related to the other, in which they form a composite in both literal and allegorical ways, but also with a sense of individualized personality. Hence Milton "mitigates androgynous and allegorical interpretation of Eve," and the traditional allegories do not themselves epitomize the poem's whole representation of either males or females.[40] To this we can add two corollaries. Rather than functioning in the poem as privileged glosses, then, the traditional allegories become heuristic devices, played off each other and the couple's diverse traits as individuals; and so the allegories are themselves to be queried even as they are used to explore the meaning of the Fall.

In this sense, Milton's provisional approach is somewhat analogous to More's treatment of Philonic exegesis: "I call the whole Interpretation but a *Conjecture.*"[41] Likewise, by Milton's time these particular allegories were not so much recited as used strategically to advance personal views and investigations. Milton presses this trend much further, so that they virtually become symbols of the difficulties of human endeavors to comprehend, govern, or ameliorate evil. While the Edenic allegories cannot wholly account for the Fall and its dynamics as represented in *Paradise Lost,* the poem attributes to them at least some value for edification. They complement its explicit comments on the proper roles of reason and passion, and its broader concerns with the fit place and bounds of knowledge, and the qualities of human intellect and the divine image. Milton's relatively detached expression of these allegories may reflect the newly questionable status of their metaphysical context. However, even if the Philonic and Augustinian allegories were finally rejected in the poem, that would entail evaluative confrontation with them and their versions of the Fall, human potential, and the relative status of the sexes, so that they would still remain important for our knowledge of *Paradise Lost.*

The poem surveys theories of evil and the Fall, including the traditional allegories, to broaden the scope of active understanding. Milton finds evil a baffling abyss of humanly unfathomable depth, perversity, and confusion: effecting some negation of creatures' divinely appointed characteristics and potential, it possesses mysteriously vast capacities, he finds, for proliferation, metamorphosis, and apparent corrosion of divine order. All possible faults, Milton assumes in *De doctrina Christiana*, were implicit in the first disobedience; in *Tetrachordon*, any attempt to limit or control sin is like trying to bind "a girdle about . . . *Chaos*" (YP II, p. 658; YP VI, p. 383). Confronting this intractable problem, Milton pragmatically presents multiple perspectives on its psychological implications. In *Paradise Lost*, for example, Adam and Eve's decisions to eat the forbidden fruit continue to bait critical inquiry, since the poem yields diverse insights. Likewise, the traditional allegories seem presented not for any hasty denial or assent, but to further prudential contemplation of the problem of evil. As in its elaborate representation of Satan, the poem implicates readers in exploring the appeals and processes of sin, to induce a strengthened virtue through educative trial.[42]

In portraying the biblically first couple, then, Milton appropriates allegorical devices to position them in a more searching context, the better to question and assess the origins and effects of sin: a theme to which he repeatedly recurs in *Paradise Lost*, just as the poem assumes that the very loss of paradise consists in involvement with evil. As Balachandra Rajan observes, "Milton is unique in his readiness to explore what has to be called the psychology of Adam and Eve."[43] In doing so Milton proceeds in diverse ways, including portentous dreams, analytic discourses, concatenations of suggestive images, and dense networks of allusion, but also through allegorical techniques, which were a prime vehicle for inquiry into the psyche. Archetypes of humanity in one sense, Adam and Eve afforded ready means for staging general psychological explorations. Though treating Milton's Adam and Eve simply as Philonic allegory, like Saurat, is reductive, so is ignoring the allegorical aspects of the couple's relationship, which are developed clearly enough in the text. Those interpretive perspectives were so diffused in cultural assumptions of the time that they would have been difficult to avoid or preclude altogether in such an extensive treatment of Eden.

In any case, whereas most studies of Milton's poetry tend to treat allegory cursorily or avoid it altogether, its status has fundamental interpretive importance. Many passages could thus have significance beyond what is conventionally attributed to them, and numerous current readings amount to allegories that are unacknowledged as such.[44] Moreover, on account of the intimate developmental connections of allegory with theism and cosmology, this Christian metaphysical poet's revision of the mode is a primary index of the relation of his theology and metaphysics to his poetics. That relationship would have been central for the composition of his later poems, and especially *Paradise Lost,* his epic of human conditions within a cosmos depicted as a divine creation.

McGill University

NOTES

1. On Satan's journey and the war in heaven in relation to allegorical epic, see Kenneth Borris, "Allegory in *Paradise Lost:* Satan's Cosmic Journey," in *Milton Studies,* vol. XXVI, ed. James D. Simmonds (Pittsburgh, 1991), pp. 101–34; and Joseph Wittreich, " 'All Angelic Natures Joined in One': Epic Convention and Prophetic Interiority in the Council Scenes of *Paradise Lost,*" in *Milton Studies,* vol. XVII, ed. Richard S. Ide and Joseph Wittreich (Pittsburgh, 1983), pp. 43–74. On composite characterization in epic and its relations with allegory, see, e.g., Ernst Robert Curtius, *European Literature and the Latin Middle Ages,* trans. Willard R. Trask (New York, 1953), pp. 167–79; James Nohrnberg, *The Analogy of "The Faerie Queene"* (Princeton, 1976), pp. 22–67; John M. Steadman, "The Arming of an Archetype: Heroic Virtue and the Conventions of Literary Epic," in *Concepts of the Hero in the Middle Ages and Renaissance,* ed. Norman T. Burns and Christopher J. Reagan (Albany, 1975), pp. 147–96; and Wittreich " 'All Angelic Natures Joined in One,' " *passim.* On "allegorical subcharacters," see Angus Fletcher, *Allegory: The Theory of a Symbolic Mode* (Ithaca, 1964), pp. 1–69, 279–303.

2. Barbara Pavlock, *Eros, Imitation, and the Epic Tradition* (Ithaca, 1990), pp. 189–90; similarly Christopher Hill, *Milton and the English Revolution* (London, 1977), p. 342. Likewise, despite observing that Adam may be "related to Eve allegorically as reason is to will," Mary Nyquist claims it is "difficult" to consider them allegorical in the separation scene because, "instead of suggesting an allegorical equation, the dialogue dramatically presents Eve and Adam suddenly failing to act out the roles assigned them" ("Reading the Fall: Discourse and Drama in *Paradise Lost,*" *ELR* XIV [1984], 209). But only allegory at its very simplest would deal in *equations;* besides, failing to perform assigned roles is precisely what makes sin possible in the traditional allegories. For Diane Kelsey McColley, Milton's fall cannot allegorically be "a matter of one part of man . . . perverting the rest" because Milton "was not a dualist who opposed matter and spirit" (*Milton's Eve* [Urbana, 1983], pp. 11–15). But the poem repeatedly subordinates passions and senses to mind, and McColley oversimplifies the traditional allegories and underestimates the mode: e.g., while attributing the fundamental fault to the Adamic part, they hold both parts responsible, and would thus not be incompatible with Milton's kind of morally gradated monism.

3. A recent statement of this view is Stephen M. Fallon's *Milton Among the Philosophers: Poetry and Materialism in Seventeenth-Century England* (Ithaca, 1981). His claim that Sin and Death constitute the only allegory in *Paradise Lost* (pp. 182–83) rests on this dubious series of inferences which assumes that Milton, a highly independent thinker, must have followed current philosophical trends concerning allegory without any markedly divergent initiatives of his own, even though he did not merely accept the philosophies involved, as Fallon concedes.

4. Edenic allegories had popular as well as learnèd currency. See Christopher Hill on Gerrard Winstanley and Richard Coppin, in *The World Turned Upside Down: Radical Ideas During the English Revolution* (Harmondsworth, 1975), pp. 143–45, 221.

5. Citing *Paradise Regained*, IV, 390, and *Paradise Lost*, I, 746–47, from *The Poems of John Milton*, ed. John Carey and Alastair Fowler (London, 1968). For Milton's poetry, I use the Carey-Fowler edition throughout, cited as *Poems*.

6. On Satan's journey as an allegorical analysis of evil, see Borris, "Allegory in *Paradise Lost*," pp. 101–34.

7. Compare, e.g., Saint Augustine's Philonic allegory of sin's three phases: "suggestion" arises with the "serpent" of bodily sensations; then "taking pleasure . . . lies in the carnal appetite, as it were in Eve; and *the consent lies in the reason, as it were in the man: and . . . the man is driven forth, as it were, from paradise, i.e. from the most blessed light of righteousness.*" *The Sermon on the Mount*, trans. Rev. William Findlay, in *Works*, ed. Rev. Marcus Dods, vol. VIII (Edinburgh, 1873), p. 27; emphasis mine.

8. On topical Miltonic allegory, see Hill, *Milton*, pp. 375–80; such interpretations complement psychological ones, since analogies between social and psychic orders were conventional. Cf. Georgia B. Christopher, *Milton and the Science of the Saints* (Princeton, 1982), pp. 146–57.

9. Nearly all previous inquiries into the possibilities of allegory in Milton's Eden relate to either of the two traditional options. However, in Anthony C. Yu's "Life in the Garden: Freedom and the Image of God in *Paradise Lost*," *Journal of Religion* LX (1980), 247–71, e.g., Milton's couple conjointly represent the divine image, though Yu does not acknowledge that this impinges on allegory. Origen applies the scheme *spiritus-anima-corpus* to Adam (*spiritus*) and Eve (*anima*) in *In Genesim Homiliae* (I, xv); its implications are analogous to the Augustinian scheme's, which likewise differs from Philo's in making Eve intermediate. See Robert L. Reid, "Man, Woman, Child or Servant: Family Hierarchy as a Figure of Tripartite Psychology in *The Faerie Queene*," *SP* 78 (1981), 372–74.

10. Renaissance allegorical commentators often approached mythography, for example, in just such a way. Compare Perseus' slaying of Gorgon in Sir John Harington's prefatory account of allegory for his Elizabethan translation of Ariosto's *Orlando furioso*; and Alexander Ross's *Mystagogus Poeticus* (London, 1648). On polysemous Renaissance allegory, see Thomas P. Roche, Jr., *The Kindly Flame: A Study of the Third and Fourth Books of Spenser's "Faerie Queene"* (Princeton, 1964), pp. 4–10, 28–31.

11. On composite and individualized aspects of Milton's Adam and Eve, see Marilyn R. Farwell, "Eve, the Separation Scene, and the Renaissance Idea of Androgyny," *Milton Studies*, vol. XVI, ed. James D. Simmonds (Pittsburgh, 1982), pp. 3–20; and Joan Malory Webber, "The Politics of Poetry: Feminism and *Paradise Lost*," *Milton Studies*, vol. XIV, ed. James D. Simmonds (Pittsburgh, 1980), pp. 3–24.

12. Desiderius Erasmus, *Enchiridion Militis Christiani*, trans. Charles Fantazzi, in *Spiritualia: Enchiridion, De Contemptu Mundi, De Vidua Christiana*, ed. John W. O'Malley, vol. LXVI of *Collected Works* (Toronto, 1988), p. 25; cf. Thomas Milles, trans., comp., *The Treasurie of Auncient and Moderne Times*, I (London, 1613), 28–29. See further Philo Judaeus, *Quaestiones et Solutiones in Genesin*, I, 6–41, *De Opificio Mundi*, lvi–lxi, and *Legum Allegoria*, II, vii–xix. All my citations of ancient texts refer to the Loeb Classical Library Series, unless attributed otherwise. On the history of Philo's interpretation, see, e.g., J. M. Evans, *"Paradise Lost" and the Genesis Tradition* (Oxford, 1968), pp. 69–77.

13. Joseph Glanvill, *Vanity of Dogmatizing* (London, 1661), pp. 118–19; compare Sir Thomas Browne, *Pseudodoxia Epidemica*, ed. Robin Robbins, I (Oxford: Clarendon Press, 1981), 5–9. In quoting Renaissance texts, I silently modernize usage of "u" and "i," except for

archaistic Spenser. Cf. Sir Henry Vane, *The Retired Mans Meditations* (London, 1655), pp. 52–60 (compare Milton's "To Sir Henry Vane the Younger," in *Poems*, pp. 328–29); Henry More, *Conjectura Cabbalistica* (London, 1653), pp. 40–51, 67–77, 221–23 (on its possible Miltonic influence, see Marjorie Hope Nicolson, "Milton and the *Conjectura Cabbalistica*," *PQ* VI [1927], 1–18). For Jean Bodin, see *Six Bookes of a Commonweale*, ed. Kenneth Douglas McRae, trans. Richard Knolles (London, 1606; facsim. rpt. Cambridge, 1962), pp. 14–15; cf. *Complete Prose Works of John Milton*, ed. Don M. Wolfe et al., 8 vols. (New Haven, 1953–82), I, pp. 834, 409; subsequently cited as YP. Milton's divorce tracts similarly tend to subordinate women and blame them most for marital breakdowns.

14. Citing *Pro Populo* from *The Works of John Milton*, ed. Frank Allen Patterson et al. (New York, 1931–38), VII, p. 78; cf. Milton's *Seventh Prolusion*, YP I, p. 293.

15. Saint Augustine, *The Trinity*, trans. Stephen McKenna, vol. XLV of *The Fathers of the Church*, ed. Hermigild Dressler, et al. (Washington, 1963), XII (quoting pp. 345, 355–56, 360, 363). Though rejecting this allegory about "the upper and lower part of reason" in his commentary on Genesis, Martin Luther apparently modifies it to express his characteristic anxieties about human reason as a threat to faith. The divine prohibition was "most simple: 'From the tree in the midst of Paradise you shall not eat.' *But reason did not understand* the purpose of these words . . . *Therefore Eve perishes* while she investigates too inquisitively. . . . Thus their temptation is a *true pattern of all temptations* with which Satan assails the Word and Faith" (emphasis mine). Eve's role correlates with an obtuse or overweening personified reason; her fall results specifically from that source, as a fundamental erring Eve within, as it were; and all temptations repeat this pattern. For Luther here, the story of the Fall thus condenses into a figurative archetype probably inspired, at least in part, by the rationally oriented Augustinian allegory. *Lectures on Genesis*, trans. George V. Schick, in *Luther's Works*, ed. Jaroslav Pelikan, vols. I, III (Saint Louis 1958, 1961), vol. I, pp. 157–59, 184–85; cf. vol. III, p. 282. Cf. Thomas Aquinas, *Summa Theologica*, I, Q. 79, Art. 9; and II, II, Q. 165, Art. 2.

On the history of Augustine's interpretation, see A. B. Chambers, "The Falls of Adam and Eve in *Paradise Lost*," in *New Essays on "Paradise Lost*,*"* ed. Thomas Kranidas (Berkeley and Los Angeles, 1969), pp. 118–30; A. Kent Hieatt, "Eve as Reason in a Tradition of Allegorical Interpretation of the Fall," *JWCI* XLIII (1980), 221–26; and Hieatt, "Hans Baldung Grien's Ottawa *Eve* and Its Context," *Art Bulletin* LXV (1983), 290–304. Chambers assumes that the Augustinian and Philonic allegories are the same, and wholly subsumes Augustine's in Philo's, whereas Hieatt considers Augustine's "counter to that of Philo" ("Eve as Reason" 221). But these allegories are distinct yet complementary interpretations of the Fall, and thus capable of simultaneous presentation, as we find in *Paradise Lost*. Just so, Saint Augustine himself expressly distinguishes between these two interpretations in *De Trinitate*, without rejecting the Philonic one (XII, xiii). Not only are the two allegories distinguishable and mutually compatible, but there is clear Augustinian precedent, readily accessible to Milton and others, for understanding them in that way.

16. See Ian Maclean, *The Renaissance Notion of Woman: A Study in the Fortunes of Scholasticism and Medical Science in European Intellectual Life* (Cambridge, 1980).

17. Quoting Sir Philip Sidney's *Poems*, ed. William Ringler (Oxford, 1962), p. 49 (75–76). Compare the iconographical motif of Phyllis riding Aristotle. On inversion of gender hierarchy as a common pejorative figure for psychic ascendancy of "lower nature," see, e.g., John M. Steadman, "Dalila, the Ulysses Myth, and Renaissance Allegorical Tradition," *MLR* LVII (1962), 560–65; and Natalie Zemon Davis, "Women on Top," in her *Society and Culture in Early Modern France* (Stanford, 1975), pp. 124–51. Cf. Joan M. Ferrante, *Woman as Image in Medieval Literature: From the Twelfth Century to Dante* (New York, 1975), chap. 1, appendix.

18. Cf. Saint Augustine's widely influential *Confessions*, trans. William Watts, XII, xxxii (p. 465).

19. First quoting Arnold Williams, *The Common Expositor: An Account of the Commentaries on Genesis 1527–1633* (Chapel Hill, 1948), p. 128. Heinrich Bullinger, e.g., uses one of Augustine's accounts of the Philonic allegory as a means for deepening insight into sin, in his *Decades*, ed. Rev. Thomas Harding, trans. H. I.,. Parker Society, vol. II (Cambridge, 1850), 405–06 (Sermon X, *The Third Decade*). On Protestant views of biblical allegory, see Williams, *The Common Expositor*, p. 21, and George L. Scheper, "Reformation Attitudes Toward Allegory and the Song of Songs," *PMLA* LXXXIX (1974), 551–62. On Milton's literal-cum-figurative Eden, cf. Patricia Parker, *Inescapable Romance: Studies in the Poetics of a Mode* (Princeton, 1979), chap. 3. Compare Sir Walter Raleigh, *The History of the World* (London, 1614), I, iii, 2–3, citing Augustine and Suidas. Consciously figurative Miltonic biblical interpretation appears, e.g., in *Colasterion, Doctrine and Discipline of Divorce*, and *De doctrina Christiana* (YP II, pp. 288, 751; VI, pp. 169, 365).

20. For Philonic discussions, see Denis Saurat, *Milton: Man and Thinker* (New York, 1925), pp. 149–71; Arnold Stein, *Answerable Style: Essays on "Paradise Lost"* (Minneapolis, 1953), chap. 5; Fredson Bowers, "Adam, Eve, and the Fall in *Paradise Lost*," *PMLA* LXXXIV (1969), 264–73; Chambers, "The Falls of Adam and Eve," pp. 118–30; Joseph E. Duncan, *Milton's Earthly Paradise: A Historical Study of Eden* (Minneapolis, 1972), index, s.v. "Adam and Eve: . . . symbolic meaning of"; Russell E. Smith, Jr., "Adam's Fall," *ELH* XXXV (1968), 538–39; and J. M. Evans, "*Paradise Lost*," pp. 250–54, 266–71. Though claiming that Milton was committed "to a literal treatment of the Fall," Evans inconsistently argues that "Adam's and Eve's physical relationship to the garden" is a Philonic image of "their psychological relationship both to their own passions and to each other" (pp. 268, 250). On the allegory focussing on mind, see Fowler's commentary in *Poems*, pp. 874–77n, 885n, 898n, 923n, 932n, 1014n (quoting 875n); Hieatt, "Eve as Reason," pp. 221–26 (quoting p. 226, 25n); and Christopher, *Milton and the Science of the Saints*, pp. 149–57.

21. Cf. Maureen Quilligan, *The Language of Allegory: Defining the Genre* (Ithaca, 1979), index, s.v. "wordplay."

22. Torquato Tasso, "The Allegorie of the Poem," in *Godfrey of Bulloigne*, ed. Kathleen M. Lea and T. M. Gang, trans. Edward Fairfax (Oxford, 1981), pp. 91–92.

23. Edmund Spenser, *The Faerie Queene*, ed. A. C. Hamilton (London, 1977), II.pr.4.

24. Torquato Tasso, *Discourses on the Heroic Poem*, trans. Mariella Cavalchini and Irene Samuel (Oxford, 1973), pp. 151–53.

25. More, *Conjectura Cabbalistica*, p. 221; cf. Leone Ebreo, *The Philosophy of Love*, trans. F. Friedeberg-Seeley and Jean H. Barnes (London, 1937), pp. 354–62. As Chambers observes, "Milton's regular stress on Adam's wisdom and Eve's beauty almost inevitably must have had allegorical overtones for seventeenth-century readers" (p. 128).

26. Farwell, "Eve, the Separation Scene, and the Renaissance Idea of Androgyny," p. 11. Even Pavlock, who excludes allegory from Milton's Eden, considers "Eve . . . less rational and intellectual than Adam" (*Eros, Imitation, and the Epic Tradition*, p. 191). In *Reviving Liberty: Radical Christian Humanism in Milton's Poems* (Cambridge, 1989), pp. 94–95, 216, Joan S. Bennett finds Eve's reasoning inferior to Adam's even in the separation scene, according to Renaissance logical standards such as Milton's in *Artis Logicae*. Adam's mode of thought is "closer to that of the angels" (p. 111), and thus, we can add, analogous to *ratio superior* or *mens*. For Adam and Eve's contrasting qualities, see especially IV, 288–320, 440–91; VIII, 530–636; IX, 481–93; X, 145–56; XI, 634–36.

27. Barbara K. Lewalski, "*Paradise Lost*" and the Rhetoric of Literary Forms (Princeton, 1985), p. 232.

28. On the configurations of such assent, see Fowler, *Poems*, pp. 875–77n; Chambers, "The Falls of Adam and Eve," p. 130; and Philo, *Legum Allegoria*, II, xiv, and *De Opificio Mundi*, lix.

29. Ebreo, *The Philosophy of Love*, pp. 354–62.

30. See Borris, "Allegory in *Paradise Lost*," pp. 101–33.

31. For some further allegorical applications of Eve's fall, see, e.g, Patrick Cullen, *Infernal Triad: The Flesh, the World, and the Devil in Spenser and Milton* (Princeton, 1974), ch. 3; and Bennett, *Reviving Liberty*, chap. 4, where the couple's debate expresses rival claims of "humanistic antinomianism" and "voluntarist antinomianism." That impinges on theological allegory.

32. Philo, *De Opificio Mundi*, lix, trans. F. H. Colson and Rev. G. H. Whitaker.

33. Fowler, *Poems*, p. 912n.

34. Ibid., p. 915n.

35. Saint Augustine, *De Trinitate*, vol. XLII of *Patrologia Series Latina*, ed. Jacques-Paul Migne (Paris, 1865), XIV, xvi, col. 1054. On intellectual definition of the divine image, see Yu, "Life in the Garden," 254–68. On the image as ground for Miltonic epic heroism, see John M. Steadman, "Heroic Virtue and the Divine Image in *Paradise Lost*," *JWCI*, XXII (1959), 88–90.

36. Borris, "Allegory in *Paradise Lost*," pp. 124–27.

37. On this aspect of Milton's cosmos, see Borris, "Allegory in *Paradise Lost*," pp. 106–19; and Merritt Y. Hughes, "Myself Am Hell," *MP* LIV (1956), 80–94.

38. While most emphasizing Milton's proto-feminism, Barbara K. Lewalski acknowledges his contrary impulses in "Milton on Women—Yet Again," in *Problems for Feminist Criticism*, ed. Sally Minogue (London, 1990), pp. 46–69. Quite uncompromising accounts of Miltonic feminism are Philip J. Gallagher, *Milton, the Bible, and Misogyny*, ed. Eugene R. Cunnar and Gail L. Mortimer (Columbia, 1990); and Joseph Anthony Wittreich, *Feminist Milton* (Ithaca, 1989). But, though some female readers prior to this century took some Miltonic passages to support emancipation of women, that is not definitive for the epic as a whole. And compare, e.g., Milton's *Pro Populo Defensio Anglicano* eagerly ridiculing Salmasius for allowing his wife authority (YP IV, eg.., pp. 471, 518); likewise *Eikonoklastes* on the royal marriage (YP III, pp. 420, 537–38).

39. Cf. Hieatt, "Eve as Reason," 221.

40. Quoting Farwell, "Eve, the Separation Scene, and the Renaissance Idea of Androgyny," pp. 14–16. Cf. Webber, "The Politics of Poetry," pp. 3–24. Hugh MacCallum reduces the situation to an either-or dichotomy in *Milton and the Sons of God: The Divine Image in Milton's Epic Poetry* (Toronto, 1986), p. 152: "Adam and Eve are real individuals, not allegorical abstractions." But, in complex allegory, characters can function as individuals narratively, yet also as projections of each other's capacities or perspectives, as with Spenserian heroes. Milton's furtherance of this option reflects the attenuation of romance in *Paradise Lost*: comprehensive expositions of motivation and character are not germane to that genre.

41. More, *Conjectura Cabbalistica*, sig. A7ᵃ.

42. On multiplication of perspectives on the Fall in *Paradise Lost* and Milton's use of allegory for that purpose, see Borris, "Allegory in *Paradise Lost*," pp. 109–27.

43. Balachandra Rajan, *The Lofty Rhyme: A Study of Milton's Major Poetry* (Coral Gables, 1970), pp. 69–70.

44. Cf. Walter R. Davis, "The Languages of Accommodation and the Styles of *Paradise Lost*," in *Milton Studies*, vol. XVIII, ed. James D. Simmonds (Pittsburgh, 1983), pp. 103–27.

PARADISE LOST: PASSIONATE EPIC

William B. Hunter

R ECOGNITION OF THE commonplaces which underlay Renaissance "scientific" thought is itself commonplace today. These dog-
mas did not attach themselves exclusively to any political or religious
party: Royalists and Levelers, Roman Catholics and Anabaptists equally
accepted them as evident truths. The Ptolemaic ordering of the universe,
the four elements of which our world is made, the four analogous humours
which constitute our bodies, their three "souls"—vegetative, sensitive,
and rational—are among the commonplaces described by E. M. W.
Tillyard in his *Elizabethan World Picture.*[1] Scholars have successfully
employed these concepts to explore the writings of such diverse authors
as Geoffrey Chaucer, William Shakespeare, and John Donne. The thesis
of Kester Svendsen's fine book on Milton's scientific knowledge is its
commonplace nature, a fact reflected in Lawrence Babb's equally distinguished expansion of this thesis.[2] One important piece of commonplace
dogma, however, has not found detailed treatment thus far in studies of
Milton's thought: the passions or perturbations or affections or sensual
appetites or emotions as they are variously called, which everyone possesses, then and now.

Although they appear implicitly or explicitly in many of the works of
Milton (and his biography proves that he was not immune to their force),
the passions figure most prominently in *Paradise Lost.* There every created
character feels them—for good in the case of the good angels, and Adam
and Eve before the Fall and at times afterward; for bad in the evil angels, in
Sin and Death, and in our first parents during and after their sin. So
pervasive and vivid are these passionate experiences in *Paradise Lost* that it
can be denominated "the passionate epic"[3] in contrast with its relatively
bloodless companion, *Paradise Regained.* In such contrasts lie some of the
differing receptions of the two poems, as human and thus passionate readers respond to corresponding experiences in the one which are so absent
from the other. It is important to recognize the background of the commonplace from which Milton drew these powerful elements that give life to his
creations.

Inasmuch as discussion of the passions found formal classical treatment, it is in Aristotle's *Nicomachean Ethics*.[4] There in the classification of the virtues (which he argues are not passions "because we are not called good or bad on the ground of our passions, but are so called on the ground of our virtues and our vices" [1105b30]—a doctrine that the French psychologist J. F. Senault would confirm[5]), he lists as passions "appetite, anger, fear, confidence, envy, joy, friendly feeling, hatred, longing, emulation, pity, and in general the feelings that are accompanied by pleasure or pain" (1105b21). Such a listing Thomas Aquinas expanded and transmitted as eleven basic appetites, consisting of love, desire, and pleasure, which are directed toward the good; and hate, fear, and pain, which correspondingly flee evil. These six he categorizes as "concupiscible," merely desirous of some end to be achieved or, as a later writer on passions would say, regarding good or evil "simply."[6] The second class Thomas denominates "irascible," regarding their end as being accompanied with some difficulty. They include fear and courage, hope and despair, and anger. Such a list, recognized by Robert Burton and accepted by F. N. Coeffeteau and Pierre Charron, was simplified in various ways by various authorities—Stephen Batman, for example recognizing joy, hope, dread, and sorrow; Pierre La Primaudaye desire, joy, fear, and grief; and Benedetto Varchi love, hate, joy, and sorrow[7]. Senault observed that there was no general agreement on the number of the passions,[8] but the various lists are not in disagreement on any fundamental point; and neither the Roman Catholic priest Thomas Wright nor the presiding Bishop of the Westminster Assembly, Edward Reynolds, would have been uncomfortable with the list of the other.[9] The poet Sir John Davies gives a similar one, omitting anger:

> But though the *apprehensive* power do pawse,
> The *Motive* vertue then begins to move,
> Which in the heart below doth *passions* cause
> *Joy, griefe,* and *feare,* and *hope,* and *hate,* and *love*.[10]

The *Christian Doctrine*, which has been accepted until recently as by Milton, defines seven: "love, hate; joy, sadness; hope, fear and anger,"[11] which, as its editor Maurice Kelley observes, are quite unoriginal, being derived directly from John Wollebius's *Compendium Theologiae Christianae*. There is no reason to think that Milton himself would not have believed with everyone else in the tradition that all the passions arise from two basic and opposed states, love and hate; there is, he wrote in *Doctrine and Discipline of Divorce*, "a twofold Seminary or stock in nature, from whence are deriv'd the issues of love and hatred distinctly flowing through the whole masse of created things" (YP II, p. 272). As the author of the *Treatise of Melancholy* observed, love and hate "are the first kinds and primitives of the rest: love being a vehement liking, and hate a vehement affection of disliking: from these springe all the derivatives, which arise either from love, or hate, like, or dislike."[12] Because of the commonplace nature of the subject of the passions, of course, none of the several authorities quoted here should be viewed as Milton's "source." Indeed, all of the information cited here can be duplicated in almost any of the other writers, even as we recognize it in our own experience.

All schools of thought judged that the passions or appetites are instruments of the sensitive soul, directly analogous to the will, which is the equivalent instrument of the rational soul and which is often, in fact, called its appetite and should be under its control. As has been mentioned, all of the appetites are good in themselves. Both God the Father in the Old Testament and God the Son in the New Testament are described as being passionate—the latter, for example, when he angrily cleansed the Temple. Thus Senault makes the point that since Christ was human he was not exempt from passions; his resentments were not purely imaginary, but he did not suffer from their disorders in that "He was their absolute Master," as he demonstrates in his continuing calmness in *Paradise Regained*, whereas "Ours for the most part do surprize us."[13] Proper control of them is for Milton a major ethical element as he argues in his *Apology*: each man's "groundwork of nature which God created in him" should have "each . . . passion wrought upon and corrected as it ought," to become the "foundation of every mans peculiar guifts, and vertues" (YP I, p. 900); and again in *Areopagitica*, where he asks, "Wherefore did [God] creat passions within us . . . but that these rightly temper'd are the very ingredients of vertu?" (YP II, p. 527). Only the Stoics had decried the passions unreservedly. As a result they are the only group opposed by all Renaissance writers on the subject, like Senault, whose opening chapter is "An Apology for Passions against the Stoics" or Reynolds, who also devotes a chapter (7) to it. Milton is thus in good company when he had Jesus, who is dispassionate in *Paradise Regained* because of the situation there, decry Stoic "apathy": their "vertuous man" fears neither "God nor man, contemning all / Wealth, pleasure, pain or torment," which is "but vain boast" (IV, 305–07).[14]

For Christians, ethical issues arose in the control, not the Stoic extinction, of the passions by reason. Unchecked, they could be the source of deadly sins. Anger, for example, was universally so recognized when it operated beyond rational control. As Davies comments,

> These passions have a free Commanding might
> And diverse Actions in our life do breed;
> For all Acts done without true reasons light,
> Do from the passion of the *Sense* proceed. (1113–16)

The author of the *Christian Doctrine* observes that "righteousness towards oneself includes . . . the control of one's own inner affections" (YP VI, p. 720). Coeffeteau details the physiological operation: physical sensations, presented to the common sense,

> become capable to be imbraced by the *understanding;* the which under the appearance of things which are profitable or hurtfull, that is to say, under the *forme* of *Good* and *Evill,* represents them unto the *Will:* the which being blind referres it selfe to that which the *understanding* proposeth unto it: And then as *Queene* of the powers of the soule she ordaines what they shall imbrace, & what they shal fly as it pleaseth her; whereunto the *Sensitive Appetite* . . . quickneth all the powers and *passions* over which shee commands. [15]

Evil results when this process is bypassed, the reason no longer ruling the lower powers. As Milton comments on the passionate outbursts between Adam and Eve after their fall, they were shaken by "high Passions, Anger, Hate, / Mistrust, Suspicion, Discord," because

> Understanding rul'd not, and the Will
> Heard not her lore, both in subjection now
> To sensual Appetite, who from beneath
> Usurping over sovran Reason claimd
> Superior sway.   (IX, 1123–24, 27–31)

Although pride is not a basic passion in any of the lists, it was widely recognized as a perturbation which could have evil effects when carried to extremes. As such it becomes, of course, a deadly sin. Charron believes it to be a type of the passion of love, seeking for itself honor and greatness and distinguished from avarice or the love of riches, and sensuality or carnal desire. As with the other perturbations, it exists in both good and bad degrees, the former directed toward a good reputation, the latter seeking greatness and power (see Charron I, pp. 178, 180). Never in *Paradise Lost* is the good goal even hinted at in Satan's case. His character is rather as Charron describes the evil type, which is directed toward the wrong end:

> [It] makes its way through all Laws, and tramples Conscience it self under Foot . . . eraces all Reverence of God, and treads *Religion* under Foot . . . , changes men's Natures, hardens their Hearts, and makes them brutish. . . . It is in it self a tall and stately Quality, and none but great Souls are capable of giving it a Reception. This was the Temptation which seduc'd the *Angels* themselves; a Temptation of all others best accommodated to Their Circumstances, and perhaps the Only one the Perfection of their Nature could be corrupted by. (Charron I, pp. 184–86)

Milton, of course, describes the fall of Satan in exactly the same terms.

The first division made by Charron—of pride as directed toward a good reputation—is echoed elsewhere in Milton's writings. The source is the Aristotelian conception of magnanimity, of which this type of passion was a recognized and valuable part. Continued by the Scholastics, this idea still held power in Milton's day. Burton shows that it is common to those who are beyond the reaches of any other passion (see Burton, subs. XIV), a belief which finds the same expression in Charron, who adds that, besides affecting only the mightiest men, it is also the last desire which the great relinquish—"even wise men" (Charron I, p. 181)—"That last infirmity of Noble mind," as Milton says of himself in *Lycidas*. Significantly, Satan's offer of the glory of the world that opens Book III of *Paradise Regained* Jesus rejects as not being the "true glory and renoun" of divine approbation (60–62). At a lesser level the unfallen Eve yields to Adam "with coy submission, modest pride" in her womanhood (*PL* IV, 310).

Satan falls immediately from seeking glory "to set himself . . . above his Peers" (I, 39), a godlike passion if a sinful one, to much more petty expressions of his emotions. One evil passion, especially pride, it was believed, would lead to others.[16] Early in *Paradise Lost* the transition is made, from pride to envy and revenge. Satan is described as one

> whose guile
> Stird up with Envy and Revenge, deceiv'd
> The Mother of Mankind, what time his Pride
> Had cast him out from Heav'n.   (I, 34–37)

The same transition was recognized by the psychologists. Thus envy is characterized as "a vice that inflicteth those most extreamely, that use it most, and it (immediately) succeedeth Pride, by nature; for a proud man so loveth himselfe, that he grieves that any should excell him, which when he cannot avoid, then he envies them."[17] This state of affairs existed when the divine Son was elevated to glory: then Satan was "fraught / With envie against the Son of God" because he was not able to "bear / Through pride that sight, and thought himself impaired" (V, 661–65).[18] In envying he is truly sinning, for the Renaissance refused to admit anything good in this passion regardless of its degree or the object toward which it was directed. Chaos also "thought himself impaird" by the loss of his territories to the works of creation, though he took no active steps to avenge himself (*PL* II, 998–1000). Francis Bacon states that "Envy is the worst of all passions, and feedeth upon the spirits, and they again upon the body, and so much the more, because it is perpetual, and, as it is said, keepeth no holidays."[19] Burton quotes Jerome Cardan to the effect that it is the only sin without any pleasure attached to it and without any excuse for existence, adding that it is the only passion which never ceases (see Burton, subs. VIII). Finally, Coeffeteau exactly describes Satan's condition: we envy, he says, only "the glory of our like," as Satan views the newly begotten Son. Coeffeteau goes on to show how evil it is in contrast to hatred, which may be just:

> envy is always unjust; for what shew of reason can be found in a passion which doth afflict us for the prosperities of another man, as if hee did us some injury in being happy? But there may be *Hatred* full of justice. . . . [for] althogh you perswade a man, that hee hath not received any wrong from him that is happy and fortunate, yet it doth not quench his envy;

for he cannot bear to see another's prosperity and benefits (Coeffeteau, pp. 201–02, 204), exactly as Satan responds.

Milton similarly interprets the murder of Abel in *Paradise Lost* (XI, 456): Cain's pride acts against his equal and is bad without mitigation. The *Christian Doctrine* advances this episode as an illustration of the envy occurring when "another should have what he cannot obtain himself" (YP VI, p. 746); Satan's attitude toward the salvation of the human race is yet a further example. Needless to say, such a passion can be felt neither by mankind before the Fall nor by any of the sinless beings in heaven. One of Satan's arguments to Eve is that envy cannot "dwell / In heav'nly brests" (IX, 729–30).

Because of the fact that the passions were seated in the sensitive soul—that is, in the part pertaining to bodily and perceptive processes—it was widely believed during the Renaissance that the passions actually altered the body, working various physiological changes which often could be observed by the onlooker. William James supports an analogous insight that part of the experience of emotions is the bodily changes accompanying them. For the Renaissance, if the heart experienced stress, it might react in either of two ways, drawing blood to itself or sending it to the members of the body. In the former case the face would become pale; in the latter, flushed. Thus in a time of fear the heart would rush blood inward to succor itself. All writers are agreed that such was its action and that such was the cause of pallor. In times of external danger which aroused anger or some other passioon in the irascible nature, however, either one of two things might happen: if the danger was moderate and the resulting anger temperate, the blood would flow to the external organs to fortify them. Thus Milton's good angels, prompted by the defiant Satan, "Turnd fierie red" (IV, 978), as might be expected since their passions are temperate, controlled by reason. But when the poet portrays

the emotions of Satan himself it is with the excess as his heart draws blood
to itself in order to fortify itself. Such a pale man, it was recognized, was
more dangerous than the flushed one[20] because, as Phineas Fletcher
states in describing Wrath, his actions are not temperate:

> Fierce was his look, when clad in sparkling tire;
>   But when dead palenesse in his cheek took seisure,
>   And all the bloud in's boyling heart did treasure,
> Then in his wilde revenge kept he nor mean, nor measure.[21]

Thus Satan is "Thrice chang'd with pale" after arriving upon earth because
of three powerful passions which have drawn blood to his heart: anger,
envy, and despair (IV, 115. The argument to Book IV substitutes fear for
anger, which has the same effect).

Yet as Milton clearly knows, the passions, especially anger, may have
yet further exhibition when they are not held under the control of reason.
Paradise Lost records these without giving any particular details, again in
connection with Satan's arrival upon earth. Uriel sees from the sun his
"gestures fierce" and "mad demeanour" with "passions foul obscurd" and
realizes that these are "more then could befall / Spirit of happie sort" (IV,
125–29, 570–71). Such intemperance of anger, Bacon remarks, is revealed
by "swelling, foaming at the mouth, stamping, bending of the fist."[22]
Coeffeteau adds that in the external effects of choler "there are none worse
nor more dangerous then those which disfigure the face of man, and which
make it deformed and unlike unto himselfe"; and thus "of all the Passions of
man, there is not any one more pernitious, nor more dreadfull then *choler.*"
Such a man's "feete and hands are in perpetuall motion" and he "seemes
hideous and fearefull even to his dearest friends."[23] In just this way passion
in Satan "marrd . . . his borrow'd vision" (*PL* IV, 116), and Adam after the
Fall was "estrang'd in look and altered stile" (IX, 1132).

Not surprisingly, the result of being hurt or outraged is that we
desire revenge upon the perpetrator of such a deed.[24] Thus from the
moment of his fall from heaven Satan and his crew directed their anger
against the victorious Son. The purport of most of Book II is the means
of accomplishing this purpose, and there is no question that such is the
main motivating force behind Satan. Again, however, the passion was
generally judged to be bad. Revenge is "a *cowardly* and *effeminate
Passion;* an Argument of a weak and sordid, a narrow and abject
Soul. . . . *Brave* and *Generous Minds* feel little of these Resentments:
They despise and scorn it" (Charron I, p. 217). Moreover, it is likely to
be unjust (as Satan's was), directed to harm an innocent person like
Adam. It is especially bad in that it "extinguishes all Natural Justice,

breaks through all the Restraints of Honour and Duty, and sticks at no
Practice, tho' never so foul and detestable, to accomplish its Bloody
Intentions" (p. 219), a view that Satan reflects just before the temptation:

> But what will not Ambition and Revenge
> Descend to? who aspires must down as low
> As high he soard, obnoxious first or last
> To basest things. Revenge, at first though sweet,
> Bitter ere long back on it self recoils.   (IX, 168–72)

The impossibility of successfully achieving expression of the passion
was recognized by psychologists, even as by Satan: "Experience shews us
daily, that he who endeavours to revenge himself does not effect his whole
Wish, nor is in every point successful" (Charron I, p. 219). In transferring
his revenge to mankind Satan was misdirecting his energies; to achieve
satisfaction from seeing others suffer, the person who inflicts it should see
that the other "should feel the Smart, not be humbled by the Sorrow, and
pay so dear for the Injury he hath done, that he may be made to repent it"
(p. 220). One can thus recognize immediately the difference between
Satan's mode of revenge, whose success against man could hardly make
God repent, and that of Samson, who executed directly upon the Philistines "dearly-bought revenge, yet glorious" (SA, 1660).

The last of the passions which especially pertain to Satan and his
followers in *Paradise Lost* are a pair of basic affections, hope and fear. As
the *Christian Doctrine* says, in their regulation "the cause, the object and
the degree of hope and fear are the chief considerations" (YP VI, p. 721).
Since such regulation determines whether or not fear is bad, it is not evil
in itself; that is, "Even the bravest of men may feel fear" (YP VI, p. 722).
Similarly, La Primaudaye asserts that fear may be good when it is based on
reason, a position upheld by Varchi: "Feare is two-fold, Good and Evill;
Good Feare is that which is grounded upon a good discourse of Reason,
and Argument; standing in awe of blame, reproach and dishonour, more
than of Griefe or Death: Evill Feare is destitute of Reason."[25] In such a
case reason leads us to fear those who may work us harm, those who have
hurt men more powerful than we are, and similar people (see Coeffeteau,
pp. 439–40). This passion was first felt by the apostate angels, Milton tells
us, during the fight upon the plains of heaven: they were

> with pale fear surpris'd,
> Then first with fear surpris'd and sense of pain
> Fled ignominious, to such evil brought
> By sin of disobedience, till that hour
> Not liable to fear or flight or pain.   (VI, 393–97)

Throughout the remainder of time, apparently, they continue to suffer from this affection; certainly it appears prominently in the discourses in hell and in Satan's monologue upon earth. In this description of fear which the evil angels first felt are two items which are characteristic of the passion. In the first place, like anger it is evinced by pallor, and for the same reason noted above. Secondly, it was recognized to be intensified when accompanied by surprise (see Coeffeteau, pp. 448–49).

In general, fear was looked upon as a perturbation which anticipated what was to come. In this respect it was similar to hope. The latter considered a future good, the former a future evil. Thus they were usually paired, the presence of hope implying fear that it might not be attained, and vice versa. Concomitant with hope was courage, the opposite of fear, in order to meet hardship (see Coeffedeau, p. 414); fear was accompanied by despair, also the opposite of hope. Such distinctions must be made in order to recognize the significant expression which Milton gives these passions. For hope even to exist at all, four conditions must be met: first, it must promise a good; second, it must be in the future; third, it must have some difficulty before it which must be overcome (thus it happens always to be mixed with fear); last, it must be possible of achievement (see Coeffeteau, pp. 515–17). Milton, and apparently Satan, was aware that hell certainly could not comply with the first condition though it might with some of the others; hence he comments upon hell as a place where "hope never comes / That comes to all" (I, 66–67). Satan himself is not sure of his position, trusting to hope but prepared to turn to despair (I, 190–91). Finally, his angelic followers themselves look upon him as their main hope amidst fear (I, 274–75), and Satan goes about the business of seducing man as though he were possessed of true hope.

In agreement with the psychology of his day, however, Milton is careful to modify this characterization of Satan. When the latter surveys the beautiful prospect of Eden, he is overcome by the various passions which Uriel from the sun observes in him, concluding "So farwell Hope, and with Hope farwell Fear, / Farwell Remorse: all Good to me is lost" (IV, 108–09). The two passions imply each other and both deal with future events. The man who is most to be feared is he who is afraid of no law and hence sets himself utterly apart from good: "We apprehend our enemies more, when they are not stayed by some honest *Feare* of Justice, or some other respect, but are ready to tread all divine and humaine laws under foote to satisfie their revenge" (Coeffeteau, p. 440). The persons most dangerous in this respect are those "which thinke they have suffered the cruellist afflictions that can be endured in this life," the reason being not far to seek: "these men seeing no relief in their affairs, as they have no more hope, so they cannot *Feare*" (p. 458). Milton thus has characterized the hopeless Satan as being as evil as possible in just such terms: a being entirely lost to good, utterly turned from the control of right reason.

The other passionate primary characters in *Paradise Lost* are, of course, Adam and Eve. Inasmuch as it is quite impossible to imagine sexuality without passion, and God had directed the couple before the Fall to "increase and multiply," they must have experienced such "affections" if as Milton insists they did they had prelapsarian sexual relations. Senault devotes a chapter to the question "Whether there were any Passions in the state of Innocency," which he decides affirmatively. The unfallen Adam's difference from us is that his passions were firmly under the control of his reason and "never shewed themselves till they had received Commandment" from his reason. On the other hand, he did not experience those like sadness or despair before the Fall.[26] The classic authority for this interpretation was Saint Augustine, who devotes many pages of book XIV of *The City of God* to the question.[27] Because the father, however, did not believe that intercourse actually occurred before the Fall the issue for him is only theoretical. In his view "without feeling the allurement of passion goading him on, the husband would have relaxed on his wife's bosom in tranquility of mind." But, he continues, "The possibility that I am speaking of was not in fact experienced by those for whom it was available, because their sin happened first."[28] Milton, in his monistic insistence upon the unity of man's soul and body and the inherent goodness of each,[29] has no problem with asserting the paradisiacal nature of intercourse and of its accompanying passions. In recounting to Raphael this experience of sight and touch he asserts that it exceeds all of the other pleasures of Paradise: "transported I behold, / Transported touch; here passion first I felt, / Commotion strange" (VIII, 529–31). He goes on to add that he found himself in rational command of all enjoyments save this one and wonders whether God made some mistake in Eve's creation. This is a bold admission that in fact his reason was not then in control:

> All higher knowledge in her presence falls
> Degraded, Wisdom in discourse with her
> Looses discount'nanc't, and like folly shews;
> Authority and Reason on her wait.   (VIII, 551–54)

In response the angel warns Adam that man has the sense of touch in common with animals (like the passions it is lodged in the sensitive soul and so must properly be subject to the reason), concluding that "In loving thou dost well, in passion not" (588), though his meaning must be not that the passion is by nature evil but that its lack of rational control to which Adam has confessed is.

The next time that passion enters the life of Eve and Adam is during the temptations themselves. Satan starts his seduction of her somewhat beside his primary purpose, which was to "excite thir minds / With more desire to know, and to reject / Envious commands" (IV, 522–24), where "Envious" in an unusual construction seems to mean the passion of envy in Eve herself. In first praising her beauty at some length (IX, 532–47 and again at 606–12), he is appealing to her pride in herself which in itself is not evil. Good pride, as an earlier quotation from Charron observed, is directed toward a good reputation. Yet of all the passions pride was especially felt by women, who are most likely to misvalue it. Wright (no feminist he) asserts that they possess "pride, for beautie, or some small sparke of wit, indeed for lack of witte, they prize more then right reason requireth, but selfe-love maketh a little to bee much esteemed, where no better can bee had" (Wright, p. 40). Milton, however, makes it clear that in listening to this praise Eve has not yet sinned: she refuses as yet to be drawn to the evil aspects of this passion, playfully suggesting that the overpraise casts doubt on "The vertue of that Fruit" (IX, 615–16). A few lines later the poet emphasizes that she is "yet sinless" (IX, 659).

In his final speech, which alone seems to have been the cause for the Fall, Satan boldly suggests, having won Eve's attention by his previous blandishments, that she turn from God's commands to disbelief of his word and to the goal that she become equal to the highest by eating the fruit. This is again an appeal to pride but an entirely different order from that of his earlier argument; for here it is directed toward the evil desire for greatness or power that Charron described, not toward furthering a good reputation.

In the development of an overwhelming passion such as this, Wright stresses its tendency to resist introduction of ideas or facts which might weigh to discount it: pride ignores "consideration of those things, which may extinguish the passion." Instead, it responds to

an inforcement or constraint, onely to consider those motives or reasons which tend in favour of that passion: for although the maine part of the soules activitie be haled away with the passion, yet there remaineth some sparks of light in the understanding, to perceive what is represented with it (Wright, pp. 50–51).

Even so, Eve in her inner debate before tasting the apple does not introduce the main argument against doing so (that it would transgress God's express command) but develops instead a side issue, the enhancement of her own knowledge and status. She then rationalizes to justify the passion

rather than rule it by reason. Wright describes such a psychological process as being an act of will (the "appetite" of reason): "the wil perceiving
that the soule rejoyceth, she also contenteth her selfe, that the inferiour
appetite should enjoy her pleasure or eschew her grief, with reason, or
against reason, she cares not, so she may be made partaker." Thus the will
coerces the "wit" "to finde out reasons and perswations that all the appetite demandeth, standeth with reason and is lawfull." He concludes that
such "collusion" of reason with will is "one of the roots of all mischiefes,
that now cover the face of the world, that is, a wicked wil commanding the
wit, to finde out reasons to plead for Passions: for this corrupteth, yea
wholly destroyeth the remorse of conscience," with the result that "when
the witte is once perswaded, and no further appellation can be admitted,
then the soule is confirmed almost in malice" (Wright, pp. 53–54). Such is
Eve's inward rationalizing when she sins (IX, 745–79). As her soliloquy
concludes, "What fear I then, rather what know to fear / Under this
ignorance of Good and Evil, / Of God or Death, of Law or Penaltie?" (IX,
773–75), and Milton's ironic comment underlines her proud desire for
exaltation, her "expectation high" (IX, 789–90).

The poem treats the fall of Adam in a very different fashion. There is
no appeal to his pride, either its good or bad aspects; and Satan, of course,
is not involved. Upon hearing what his wife has done, Adam's reaction is
immediate and natural: he is overcome by horror, which latter is the same
as grief or heaviness and a basic passion in the lists of Milton and the
psychologists dealing with a present evil. Its physical manifestation is
pallor like that of fear and for the same reason: the heart draws blood from
the rest of the body to succour itself during the trouble. Thus Adam stood
"speechless . . . and pale" (IX, 894). Charron gives several external symp-
toms: "our Head hanging down, our Eyes fixed upon the Ground, our
Tongue Speechless, our Limbs stiff and Motionless, our Looks Wild and
Confused, our Ears Deaf and Insensible, our Minds void of all Attention
and composed Thought" (Charron I, p. 227). Like the other passions
horror or grief is dangerous in excess. "It is a very dangerous Enemy," he
observes, "destructive to our Quiet and Comfort; and, if good Care be not
taken of it in time, wastes and weakens the Soul, . . . [so that it] adulter-
ates and deposes the whole Man, binds up his Senses, and lays his Virtues
to sleep" (p. 223). As in Eve's case Adam is poorly prepared to meet the
subsequent passion which proves to be his undoing.

His reason being laid to sleep, he resolves to die with Eve. Charron
recognized and deprecated such a degree of grief in man, since it "palls,
and flats his Relish of Goodness, extinguishes the Desire of Reputation,
and takes away the Disposition of doing Worthily, either for himself, or for

anybody else" (p. 231). The cause of Adam's excessive grief is, however, a simultaneous excessive passion, "vehemence of love." It was dogmatically believed that the soul could not successfully rule two passions at the same time; attending to one, it would lose control over the other.[30] Adam, suffering from the two excessive perturbations of love and grief, loses rational control of them, so that his will can lead his reason to rationalize his sin, thus completing his fall. His passions in themselves are not sinful; their direction of the reason to the forbidden end is. "I feel," he says, "the Link of Nature draw me" (IX, 913–14), and goes on to hope like Eve "to be Gods, or Angels Demi-gods" (IX, 937) and to rationalize away the divine judgment of death for sin (IX, 938–49).

After Adam has eaten the fruit Milton reiterates the idea presented in Eve's earlier case that one passion may lead to another. Thus both become intoxicated and then are overcome by carnal desire, followed by the passion of shame, "the last of evils" (IX, 1079), whose force the experienced Augustine had emphasized[31] as basic to sexual intercourse in his discussion of "Th'expense of spirit in a waste of shame." The Renaissance generally looked upon shame, unhappily though one experiences it, as tending to good. A type of grief, shame also embodies "a kinde of feare, which ariseth, for that man doubts some blame and some censure of his actions" (Coeffeteau, p. 496). but the passion itself need not be held blameworthy: "no man can but allow, that it is good to be ashamed of a fault" (Wright, p. 30).

The remainder of Adam and Eve's part in the poem is taken up primarily with one passion, entirely natural to the circumstances: grief. It is true that Milton delineates them as overwhelmed by anger, hate, mistrust, suspicion, and discord against one another (IX, 1123–24); and again when the Son appears to them they evince shame, perturbation, despair, anger, obstinacy, hate, and guile but no love (X, 111–14). In both of these instances Milton is listing a series of passions which have achieved sway over reason and hence show man as a creature confirmed in sin; these are the fallen human condition, though he does not portray his characters in detail with such specific emotions. The poem does, however, create in considerable detail the grief which the guilty couple felt.

Some of the characteristics of this passion have already been given. As reference to Bright's list shows, it deals with evils present to a person. Adam realizes it most poignantly after he has observed the alterations made in the world as a consequence of his sin (X, 720–25). In such a condition, it was recognized, a man might very well long for death, as Adam does (X, 771–82). Eve herself more specifically suggests suicide: "Let us seek Death, or he not found, supply / With our own hands his

Office on our selves" (X, 1001–02). Burton devotes a great part of his
discussion of grief to this question: often the grief-stricken "are weary of
their lives, and feral thoughts to offer violence to their own persons come
into their minds." But, he adds, "by and by, when they come in company
again which they like, or be pleased, *suam sententiam rursus damnant et
vitae solatio delectantur*" (Burton, sec. III, mem. I, subs. II). Adam refuses Eve's suggestion (X, 1013), putting forward in its place that they
seek "Solace of life" as Burton calls it, by taking revenge upon the serpent
(1028–40). This new passion would meet with general approval since it
was directed against the person who had wronged the pair and at the same
time was intended against something vicious.

People knew then as now that there were a great many remedies for
grief, depending upon the circumstances. In a physiological sense, relief
might be obtained by sleep, baths, and tears (see Coeffeteau, p. 348), the
latter expressing superfluous moisture from the brain.[32] It is not then
surprising (as everyone today will understand) that Eve weeps while plead-
ing with Adam (X, 910, 937), or that Michael composed her spirits with
sleep (XII, 595–97). Meanwhile Adam himself has been experiencing
what was diagnosed as a sovereign cure for such a condition as he wit-
nesses the future troubles of the world, for as

a greater evill makes the lesse to be forgotten, so wee may disperse a present
heavinesse, either by shewing that it is not the present misery which we must
lament, but others that are more cruell, which threaten us: As . . . in fortifying
our resolutions with a better hope. (Coeffeteau, p. 344)

He receives final comfort from the doctrine that "the misery wherewith
wee have been crost, is as it were recompensed by some other felicities
which befall us" (p. 342). Through the vision of the world Adam is thus able
to see how God will in the end draw from it "goodness infinite," even
wondering whether he should not rejoice over what has been named the
"fortunate fall." Here he finally achieves what Coeffeteau recognizes as the
last and best remedy for grief: the contemplation of the ultimate goodness
of God, adding that for people to comfort one another as Adam and Eve do
is another remedy (See Coeffeteau, pp. 352, 350–51).

So they prepare to leave the Garden. Adam has learned the great
lesson regarding passions, in "True patience" that they be restrained in
moderation under the governance of reason:

> to temper joy with fear
> And pious sorrow, equally enur'd
> By moderation either state to bear,
> Prosperous or adverse.   (XI, 361–64)

In this he can achieve true patience, a virtue extolled at length in *Samson Agonistes*. With their departure God has changed their outlook from the dangerous passion of grief to the saving one of hope. They drop "natural" tears, not excessive ones. In one another they have a consolation by which they may overcome future grief; they still possess a sufficient portion of right reason and free will by which they can govern their passions, though, as we are sadly aware, their descendents often do not. Neither God nor Milton could do any more for them.

APPENDIX: PROBLEMS OF THE THEOPATHETIC TRADITION

The question of whether God experiences passions has been ably explored by Michael Lieb.[33] The Old Testament is, of course, replete with statements about how Jahweh has various all-too-human feelings. Lieb has traced two interpretations of such passages from early church fathers to Milton's day. One, initiated by Tertullian, accepts such statements literally. The other, beginning with Philo and continued by Augustine, denies that God can suffer these perturbations at all; biblical passages describing them are intended for the reader's response, not as literal statements of fact. This second line of thought, Lieb shows, was normative for Protestant belief in the seventeenth century.

The other reading, the literalist, however, is that adopted by the author of the *Christian Doctrine*. There God hates. God is jealous. Lieb concludes that in this work, which he then assumed with everyone else to be Milton's, "Milton endorses a hermeneutics of passibility . . . that aligns him with such exegetes as Tertullian and Lactantius (as well as the later Origen), through whom the passible was divinized and Scriptures taken at their word. Recalling these figures—and, in fact, going beyond them in extending the range of emotions attributable to God—Milton [or rather, I should emend, the author of the *Christian Doctrine*] broke not only with the orthodox traditions of the early church but with the reformed dogmatics of his own time."[34] Lieb then proceeds to analyze the passibility of God in *Paradise Lost*, refusing to accept the passionless being that other critics have found there.

I have omitted any reference to the emotions of divinity in the foregoing essay because I do not believe that Milton had anything to do with the composition of the *Christian Doctrine*[35] and that it accordingly should not be used to support an interpretation of his ideas as derived from the theopathetic tradition which the treatise supports. In response to Lieb's argument supporting divine passibility in *Paradise Lost*, I think that every example occurs in reports from others, not in direct narrative of the divinity. Examples are, from the Son, "whom thou hat'st, I hate, and can put on / Thy terrors, as I put thy mildness on, / Image of thee in all things" (VI, 734–36); from the angels, "to appease thy wrauth, and end the strife / Of Mercy and Justice in thy face discern'd," for which the Son has offered himself (III, 406–07); or from Adam, in Christ's resurrection "over [God's] wrauth grace shall abound" (XII, 478). This is the way Protestant interpreters of the Bible generally read such passages: as testimony of the observers' perceptions, not as literal reports of the divine experience of passions.

When I turn to God's own statements and the narrator's descriptions of his actions in *Paradise Lost*, like many other readers I do not perceive any emotions in the Divine Being.

Lieb names as examples of critics supporting such an interpretation Irene Samuel, Roland
Frye, and Stanley Fish. They observe only an impassible being in Milton's depiction of the
Father, the standard Protestant view. As Lieb concurs, "Such an outlook is the rule [in the
seventeenth century] rather than the exception. What makes this outlook so interesting is
the extent to which it reflects the antipassible point of view that became the theological norm
from the period of the early church up until Milton's own time."[36] Because I question the
applicability of the views of the *Christian Doctrine* that support a possible understanding of
deity on Milton's part, I must join with these critics who find in *Paradise Lost* an impassible
God and so reinstate Milton on this issue among mainstream Protestant writers, as I must
also accept a decidedly nonhuman—that is, impassible—characterization of the Father in
the poem.

Houston, Texas

NOTES

1. E. M. W. Tillyard, *The Elizabethan World Picture* (New York, 1944).
2. Kester Svendsen, *Milton and Science* (Cambridge, Mass., 1956) and Lawrence
Babb, *The Moral Cosmos of Paradise Lost* (East Lansing, Mich., 1970).
3. Michael Fixler has also found the passions to be prominent in the poem in "Milton's Passionate Epic," *Milton Studies*, vol. I, ed. James D. Simmonds (Pittsburgh, 1969),
pp. 167–92, but his concerns are different from those argued here. I have deliberately
omitted here the complex issues of divine possibility. See the appendix "Problems of the
Theopathetic Tradition."
4. Aristotle, *Nicomachean Ethics*, in *The Basic Works of Aristotle*, ed. Richard
McKeon (New York, 1941).
5. J. F. Senault, *The Use of the Passions*, trans. Henry, Earl of Monmouth (London,
1671), p. 2.
6. Thomas Aquinas, *The Summa Theologica*, trans. the Fathers of the English
Dominican Province, 21 vols. (London, 1912–1925), the first part of part II, q. 23, art. 4;
and F. N. Coeffeteau, *A Table of Humane Passions, with Their Causes and Effects*, trans.
Edward Grimeston (London, 1621), pp. 32–33, hereafter cited as Coeffeteau followed by
page number.
7. In order, Richard Burton, *The Anatomy of Melancholy*, 3 vols. (London, 1926), part
I, sec. II, mem. III, subs. III (all subsequent references are to mem. III and hereafter cited as
Burton followed by subsection number); Coeffeteau, p. 32; Pierre Charron, *Of Wisdom*, trans.
George Stanhope, 2 vols. (London, 1697), vol. I, pp. 174–76, hereafter cited as Charron
followed by volume and page number; Stephen Batman, *Batman Uppon Bartholome, His
Booke De Proprietatibus Rerum* (London, 1582), pp. 13v–14r; Pierre de la Primaudaye, *The
French Academie*, trans. T. Bowers (London, 1614), p. 31; and Benedetto Varchi, *The Blazon
of Jealousie*, trans. Robert Tofte (London, 1615), p. 10, n. C.
8. Senault, The Third Discourse, pp. 21–30, new pagination.
9. Thomas Wright, *The Passions of the Mind in Generall* (London, 1604), facsimile
reprint with an introduction by Thomas O. Sloan (Urbana, Ill., 1971), pp. 22–23, hereafter
cited as Wright followed by page number; and Edward Reynolds, *A Treatise of the Passions*

and Faculties of the Soule of Man (1640), facsimile reprint with an introduction by Margaret Lee Wiley (Gainesville, Fla., 1971), pp. 39–40.

10. Sir John Davies, *Nosce Teipsum*, in *The Poems of Sir John Davies*, ed. Robert Krueger (Oxford, 1975), lines 1105–08.

11. *Complete Prose Works of John Milton*, 8 vols., ed. Don M. Wolfe et al. (New Haven, 1953–82), vol. VI, p. 720. References to Milton's prose are from this edition, and subsequent citations will appear in the text as YP, followed by volume and page number.

12. Timothy Bright, *A Treatise of Melancholy* (1586), facsimile reprint, ed. Hardin Craig (New York, 1940), p. 82.

13. Senault, p. 49.

14. Quotations from Milton's poetry are all from *The Complete Poetry*, ed. John Shawcross (New York, 1971).

15. Coeffeteau, "To the Reader," in *A Table of Human Passions*.

16. La Primaudaye, *French Academie*, p. 235.

17. Varchi, *Blazon of Jealousie*, p. 12, n. G.

18. Coeffeteau states that for the most part envy, the inability to endure the glory of one of our equals, derives from honor (pp. 391, 397–98).

19. Francis Bacon, *The History of Life and Death*, in *The Works of Francis Bacon*, ed. Basil Montague, 3 vols. (Philadephia, 1852), vol. III, p. 495.

20. La Primaudaye, *French Academie*, p. 294.

21. Phineas Fletcher, *The Purple Island*, in *Poetical Works*, ed. Frederick S. Boas (Cambridge, 1909), canto VII, 55.

22. Bacon, *Sylva Sylvarum*, in *Works*, vol. II, p. 96.

23. Coeffeteau, Table of Human Passions, pp. 601–02. Cf. Charron, *Of Wisdom* vol. I, p. 208, and Wright, *Passions of the Mind*, pp. 124–31.

24. Coeffeteau, *Table of Human Passions*, pp. 575–76; La Primaudaye, *French Academie*, p. 497.

25. See La Primaudaye, *French Academie*, p. 262; Varchi, *Blazon of Jealousie*, p. 10, n. C.

26. Senault, *Use of the Passions*, pp. 42, 44.

27. Among the many discussions of sexuality in Milton's writings, see especially C. S. Lewis, *A Preface to "Paradise Lost"* (London, 1949), pp. 68–75, and Wolfgang E. H. Rudat, *The Mutual Commerce: Masters of Classical Allusion in English and American Literature* (Heidelberg, 85), pp. 77–83, for the relationships with Saint Augustine.

28. Saint Augustine, *The City of God*, trans. Henry Bettenson (London, 1972), p. 591.

29. I have discussed this idea at some length in "Milton's Power of Matter," in *The Descent of Urania* (Lewisburg, Pa., 1989), pp. 141–43.

30. As Wright observed, "Our soule being of a determinate power and activitie, cannot attend exactly to too [i.e., two] vehement and intensive operations together." Such an exhausted soul "can not exactly consider the reasons which may disswade her from attending or following such affections," p. 50.

31. Augustine, *City of God*, p. 591.

32. Bacon, *Sylva*, in *Works*, vol. II, p. 96.

33. Michael Lieb, "Reading God: Milton and the Anthropopathetic Tradition," *Milton Studies*, vol. 25, ed. James D. Simmonds (Pittsburgh, 1989), pp. 213–43, as well as his earlier discussion of the wrath of God, " 'Hate in heav'n,': Milton and the *Odium Dei*," *ELH* 53 (1986), 519–39, and his application of its conclusions to bring greater reality to God's

speeches in *Paradise Lost* III, in his *The Sinews of Ulysses* (Pittsburgh, 1989), chapter VI: "The Dialogic Imagination."

34. Lieb, "Reading God," p. 228.

35. William B. Hunter, "The Provenance of the *Christian Doctrine*," *SEL* 32 (1992), 129–42 and 163–66; "The Provenance of the *Christian Doctrine:* Addenda from the Bishop of Salisbury," *SEL* 33 (1993), 191–207; and "Animadversions upon the Remonstrants' Defenses against Burgess and Hunter," *SEL* 34 (1994), 195–203.

36. Lieb, "Reading God," p. 230.

CAREFUL PLOWING:
CULTURE AND AGRICULTURE
IN *PARADISE LOST*

Richard J. DuRocher

"FRUIT" AND "SEED," in that order, frame the opening sentence of *Paradise Lost*. Surprisingly, Milton scholarship has not registered the significance of that emphatic arrangement. The poem begins as follows:

> Of Man's First Disobedience, and the Fruit
> Of that Forbidden Tree, whose mortal taste
> Brought Death into the World, and all our woe,
> With loss of *Eden*, till one greater Man
> Restore us, and regain the blissful Seat,
> Sing Heav'nly Muse, that on the secret top
> Of *Oreb*, or of *Sinai*, didst inspire
> That Shepherd, who first taught the chosen Seed,
> In the Beginning how the Heav'ns and Earth
> Rose out of *Chaos*.[1]

By placing "Fruit" and "Seed" at the line endings which open and close this grand opening utterance, Milton underscores the importance of those natural images to his epic argument. Both words are used initially in a figural sense. The "chosen Seed" describes the descendants of Abraham, God's chosen people. As the Israelites were taught by Moses, Milton's original, the "Seed" is by analogy Milton's audience, a people not so much chosen as freely choosing to learn of divine creation. "Fruit" figures the consequences of the Fall, including human mortality, expulsion from paradise, and "all our woe." Adam reinforces that figural sense by using "consequence" as a gloss on "fruit" in Book VIII. Adam's speech there, recalling the divine command, takes us to the poem's moral center:

> This Paradise I give thee, count it thine
> To Till and keep, and of the Fruit to eat:
> Of every Tree that in the Garden grows
> Eat freely with glad heart; fear here no dearth:

But of the Tree whose operation brings
Knowledge of good and ill, which I have set
The Pledge of thy Obedience and thy Faith,
Amid the Garden by the Tree of Life,
Remember what I warn thee, shun to taste,
And shun the bitter consequence.   (319–28)

By the end of Milton's epic, the figurative meanings of "Fruit" and "Seed" undergo a dazzling reversal summarized by the doctrine of the fortunate fall. Thus, the "Fruit" of the forbidden tree comes to include the incarnate Redeemer, who is specifically identified as both of "Abraham and his seed" and of "the woman's [Eve's] seed."[2] Perhaps this encouraging reversal of the fruit's negative consequences parallels the opening poem's inversion of the apparent biblical order of creation and fall, which Regina Schwartz has noted.[3] Certainly Milton's reversal of the natural generative sequence in his word order, beginning with fruit and ending with seed, points to a continuing process of re-creation. Milton's poetic reversal anticipates George Eliot's metaphoric and philosophic assertion, in the pivotal chapter heading of *Romola,* that "Fruit *is* Seed."[4]

Because the figural senses of "Fruit" and "Seed" in *Paradise Lost* demand recognition, a reader may overlook the words' literal meanings. Yet fruit and seed in the literal sense carry great significance throughout the epic. For Milton as for Adam, the fruit of the forbidden tree actually hung in the Garden of Eden.[5] The seeds of both plants and human beings appear literally many times in the poem. Variants and offshoots of fruit and seed—in leaves, stocks, and flowers—fill the physical landscape of the poem. To put it with childlike simplicity, *Paradise Lost* is a story about picking a fruit. By heralding the imminent significance of fruit and seed in the poem, the opening invocation reveals Milton's attention to the natural process of growth. More important, it implies that the natural process of growth underlies the argument of *Paradise Lost.*

Milton learned about nature as we all do, by experience and observation. Even when he lived in the heart of London, young John Milton grew up surrounded by flourishing natural growth. Despite the increasing urbanization of London during the earlier seventeenth century, England remained a predominantly agricultural society. While at Cambridge, Milton expressed his fascination with agricultural scenes in his Latin and English poetry, as *L'Allegro* most prominently shows:

While the Plowman near at hand,
Whistles o'er the Furrow'd Land,
And the Milkmaid singeth blithe,

And the Mower whets his scythe,
And every Shepherd tells his tale
Under the Hawthorn in the dale.   (63–68)

Milton needed no more inspiration for these verses than what he saw and heard around him. Those tetrameter couplets happily wed images of rustic working life with the poem's spirit of mirth: no small achievement. Still, the plowman who carelessly whistles while he works here represents only a fraction of farming life; the "careful Plowman" whom Milton will include in an epic simile in *Paradise Lost*, the central focus of this essay, involves a more mature, rounded appraisal of agricultural life.

Milton in particular learned a great deal about natural growth through his reading and teaching. For Milton, the Bible held unique and absolute authority among all texts (YP VI, p. 583–585). The primary biblical text concerning natural growth, which Adam's speech, quoted earlier, incorporates, is Genesis ii, 15: "And the Lord God took the man, and put him into / the garden of Eden to dress it and keep it" (Authorized Version). In Adam's speech, Milton has replaced the verb "dress" from the Authorized Version with "till." Tilling appears in the Authorized Version only after the Fall, at Genesis iii, 23, as part of humanity's punishment for sin.[6] Milton's point is unmistakable. By making tilling the garden part of God's original command, the poet asserts that agricultural labor is part of the unfallen way of life.

Milton's treatment of labor in *Paradise Lost* forms part of a far-reaching poetic strategy, scholars have observed. In *The Georgic Revolution,* Anthony Low's sustained meditation on Milton focuses on the remarkably positive treatment of labor in *Paradise Lost*.[7] Milton's Eden revels in what Thomas Rosenmeyer has aptly termed the "Hesiodic" ethic, demanding that a good life furnish evidence of effort and suffering, which is fundamentally opposed to the pastoral pursuit of *otium*.[8] Given the ethical dimension of labor, notably its association with the inward heroism celebrated in the proem to Book IX—"the greater fortitude of patience / And heroic martyrdom unsung"—one can easily see why Milton would endorse the georgic view of labor. In the poet's view, labor cultivates communities as well as individual souls, as Barbara K. Lewalski, Diane McColley, and Mary Ann Radzinowicz have eloquently argued.[9]

Although scarcely considered, Milton's sustained emphasis in *Paradise Lost* on agriculture itself—on tilling and seeding as well as on agricultural theory and practice generally—is also remarkable. The inclusion of agriculture is remarkable if only because Milton could have entirely avoided it. There are three "steps" in human civilization, the Roman linguist and farmer, Marcus Terentius Varro (116–17 B.C.), points out: first, the state of nature, "when men lived on those products which the virgin earth (*inviolata terra*) brought forth"; second, the pastoral stage; and third, the present agricultural age. [10] Milton's story, of course, takes place almost entirely within the original state of nature; the Edenic state is doubly removed from the harsh realities of agriculture. Yet Milton insists on using agricultural allusions throughout *Paradise Lost*. A cursory survey recalls the major agricultural images scattered throughout the poem: the "belated Peasant" in the darkness visible of Book I who refigures Aeneas among the shades; the transplanted "immortal Amaranthus" said to be growing in heaven in Book III; the "careful Plowman" simile concluding Book IV; early in Book IX, Satan's entry into Eden as a city dweller in farming country; Eve's touching yet ironic depiction at the Fall as the "Harvest Queen"; the simile of the mist rising at the "laborer's heel" marking Adam and Eve's departure from Eden at the poem's end. Before the Fall, Adam and Eve are repeatedly shown working their "field," whereas a garden plot would be more strictly accurate. One may even see God as a farmer, particularly in Creation and in response to the war in heaven. [11]

Agriculture is the most fundamental of human sciences. In Milton's view, it is also fundamental to understanding the "organic" art of poetry. This is not to say that poetry requires agricultural metaphors. Rather, the point is that, as Milton explains in *An Apology Against a Pamphlet*, the epic poet must have the *experience* of agriculture—as well as of all essential arts and sciences—before attempting to sing of the subject. One need not harvest a cornfield to acquire agricultural experience any more than one need travel to hell to confront Satan. Led on by what he believed to be God's Spirit, Milton gathered experience about agriculture by reading and teaching. The "four grand authors *De Re Rustica*, Cato, Varro, Columella, and Palladius" Milton taught at the very beginning of his tutorial program, Edward Phillips recalled. [12] With Milton and his students, we need first to retrace those beginning steps if we hope, by the end, to perceive the open goal announced in *Of Education:* "what glorious and magnificent use might be made of poetry, both in divine and humane things" (YP II, pp. 405–06).

My discussion of *Paradise Lost* focuses on the most controversial of Milton's agricultural images, the figure of the "careful Plowman," which has been read allegorically—mistakenly, I believe—as either Satan or God. I choose the plowman image partly because its dependence on Roman literature is so clear, and partly because its workings, once understood, reveal Milton's characteristically luxuriant method of allusion in full flower. Further, I will show how the plowman image becomes the means

by which the poet joins the seventeenth-century controversy over enclosure. My essay aims to retrace Milton's method of "seeding," that is, of
cultivating readers by presenting images of moral choice that can lead to
growth. If beginning with an image of harvesting and ending with seeding
seems backward, it nonetheless conforms to Milton's organic artistry.

I ·

As Edward Phillips's reference to the "four grand authors *De Re
Rustica*" indicates, Milton taught his students the agricultural works of
Marcus Porcius Cato, Marcus Terentius Varro, Lucius Columella, and
Palladius. Phillips's Latin phrase implies that Milton used one—or
more—of the Renaissance editions containing all four writers. Two notable examples are, first, *Libri de re rustica* (Paris: Iehan Petit, 1533),
which contains a fully annotated index by George Alexandrinos as well as
commentary by diverse hands on Columella's versified Book X; and,
second, *Rei Rusticae Auctores Latini Veteres, M. Cato, M. Varro, L.
Columella, Palladius* (Heidelberg, 1595), edited with an analytical index
by Hieronymus Commelinus. Although Phillips emphasizes the unusual
aspect of his uncle's reading program, in fact both texts were frequently
reprinted throughout the mid-seventeenth century.[13] Moreover, Joan
Thirsk has demonstrated that farming enjoyed a newfound favor among
English gentlemen of the late sixteenth and early seventeenth centuries,
thanks largely to the newfound influence of classical agricultural manuals.[14] Thus Milton could have readily acquired both texts, either in
England or during his continental travels of 1638–39, before his teaching
career. A brief survey of those agricultural texts enables us to grasp their
relevance to *Paradise Lost,* their power to cultivate readers no less than
crops.

Commelinus's edition of the Roman authors *De Re Rustica* has one
immediately intriguing feature. On its title page appears a woodcut illustration that visually reinforces a cluster of points that Milton's poem
makes verbally (see figure 1). The central female figure of the woodcut,
recalling similar figures of the Earth, Gaia, or Ceres, is the ruling genius,
the proper tutelary deity, of agriculture. The Greek legend encircling the
various fruits of agriculture specifically identifies the figure as TRUTH
ALL-RULING. The animate sun in her right hand represents the common Renaissance fusion of Apollo, the pagan sun god, and Christ, the Son
of God. In her left hand the woman holds both a book and a stalk, a
composite emblem for the farming manuals contained in the text. Learning and fecundity, wisdom and plenty, are collectively promised by these
ancient authors, the artist suggests. The promise also carries a warning: As

REI RVSTICAE

AVCTORES LATINI
VETERES,

M. CATO   M. VARRO

L. COLVMELLA   PALLADIVS:

Priores tres, e vetuſtiſſ. editionibus; quartus, e veteribus
membranis aliquammultis in locis
emendatiores:

*Cum tribus Indicibus, Capitum, Auctorum, & Rerum
ac Verborum memorabilium.*

Criticorum & Expoſitorum in eosdem atque Geoponicos
Græos Notationes ſeorſum dabuntur.

Ex Hier. Commelini typographio,
ANNO MDXCV.

Figure 1. Photograph courtesy of DePauw University Archives and Special Collections.
Published with permission.

agriculture literally combines soil (*ager*) and tilling (*cultus*), no culture that violates the creative Earth will thrive.

The ethical dimension of agriculture implied by the title page perfectly matches the spirit of Commelinus's text. Turning to the first printed section, the reader encounters Cato's endorsement of farming as a vocation. Other vocations may be more lucrative, Cato admits, but none is more honorable:

> Est interdum praestare mercaturis rem quarerere, nisi tam periculosum sit, et item fenerari, si tam honestum sit. Maoires nostri sic habuerunt et ita in lebigus posiverunt, furem dupli condemnari, feneratorum quadrupli. Quanto peiorem civem existimarint feneratorem quam furem, hinc licet existimare. Et virum bonum quom laudabant, ita laudabant, bonum agricolam bonumque colonum. Amplissime laudari existimabatur qui ita laudabatur. (*De agricultura*, I, 1.)

[It is true that to obtain money by trade is sometimes more profitable, were it not so hazardous; and likewise money-lending, if it were as honourable. Our ancestors held this view and embodied it in their laws, which required that the thief be mulcted double and the usurer fourfold; how much less desirable a citizen they considered the usurer than the thief, one may judge from this. And when they would praise a worthy man their praise took this form: "good husbandman," "good farmer": one so praised was thought to have received the greatest commendation.]

It is this classical view of farming as a praiseworthy way of life, as indeed the best way of life, Thirsk argues, that brought many English gentlemen onto their land as direct overseers in the sixteenth and early seventeenth centuries.[15] Unlike the absentee landlords typical before 1500, good farmers from Tudor days onward dwelt on their land and took a direct hand in its management. No hollow ideal, Cato's view literally caused a revolution in English agricultural practice sixteen centuries later.

The Roman agricultural anthology repeatedly reinforces the notion of farming as a morally honorable pursuit. For example, Columella begins his work by recalling the tale of Cincinnatus, who, summoned from the plough to the dictatorship in order to liberate a beleaguered consul, after victory readily relinquished power and returned to his small ancestral farm. At times, the lessons in the proper farming spirit are rendered in language with the timeless, philosophical tone of Ecclesiastes. Consider the following passage, which concludes Columella's first book. All of the rules and suggestions for farming ultimately reduce to one principle, Columella suggests: doing what is necessary at the proper time.

Unum enim ac solum dominatur in rusticatione, quicquid exigit ratio culturae, semel facere, quippe cum emendatur vel imprudentia vel neglegentia, iam res

ipsa decosit nec in tantum postmodo exuberat, ut et se amissam restituat et
quaestum temporum praeteritorum resarciat. (I, viii, 14)

[For there is only and only one controlling principle in agriculture, namely, to do
once and for all the thing which the method of cultivation requires; since when
ignorance or carelessness has to be rectified, the matter at stake has already
suffered impairment and never recovers thereafter to such an extent as to regain
what it has lost and to restore the profit of time that has passed.]

To everything there is a season; or more emphatically, every season demands that farmers do certain things. Palladius makes this same point by
arranging his manual in calendrical fashion, with the various tasks appear-
ing in their proper months. Linked with the cyclic pattern of a complete
year, quotidian tasks and particular bits of advice accrue the timeless
quality of the seasons.

At other places in the anthology, the language embodying the agricultural ideal has the salty, homespun quality of *Poor Richard's Almanack*.[16]
For example, after discussing in detail the layout and management of a
farm, Cato quips: *frons occipitio prior est* (IV, 7). It is difficult to convey in
English the wit of this pithy maxim. Literally, Cato writes, the forehead is
better than the back of the head. More loosely, we might say, it's better to
look ahead than back. We might come closer yet to Cato's meaning with
an English aphorism: "Foresight is better than hindsight." Cato's remark
may also contain an extra layer of meaning. The Latin word *frons* has the
sense not only of the English word front but also of frond, that is, the first
uncurling of a leaf. In an agricultural context, that sense certainly is
appropriate. A frond from the farmer's seed appears first (*prior*) in the
growing cycle. This sense of *frons* may even carry the sense of an Aristotelian final cause. For a farmer, a growing frond or plant takes priority over
everything else. It is the underlying reason for all of the farmer's ingenuity, labor, and concern.

II

The "careful Plowman" appears toward the end of Book IV of *Paradise Lost*. The image marks the confrontation between Gabriel and his
band of faithful angels, the guardians of Eden, on the one hand, and Satan
alone, whom they have discovered "[s]quat like a Toad, close at the ear of
Eve" (800) on the other. Gabriel's interrogation of Satan has broken down
into threats to drag him to the "infernal pit" and seal him there, which
provokes Satan to his own insulting, violent counterthreats. At that moment, that is, on the border between speech and violent action, the
plowman image appears:

> While thus he [Satan] spake, th'Angelic Squadron bright
> Turn'd fiery red, sharp'ning in mooned horns
> Thir Phalanx, and began to hem him round
> With ported Spears, as thick as when a field
> Of *Ceres* ripe for harvest waving bends
> Her bearded Grove of ears, which way the wind
> Sways them; the careful Plowman doubting stands
> Lest on the threshing floor his hopeful sheaves
> Prove chaff.   (977–85)

As Joseph Summers has said of the epic's opening poem, everything in this magnificent poetic passage happens at once.[17] While Satan speaks, the angelic band changes color, posture, and military formation. The simile of the field of grain specifically adumbrates the density ("as thick as") with which the faithful angels' spears surround Satan. Readers may find that emphasis on density hard to bear in mind, as Milton's verse rapidly unfolds a variety of animated images: the geometric shifting of the angels—from phalanx to crescent to circle; the dangerously swaying grain, in the guise of the goddess Ceres; the worried farmer, nonetheless standing in the scene, transported there by Milton's rapidly associative imagination.

In the midst of threatened violence, then, the figure of the "careful Plowman" appears. He effects a kind of countermovement to the participants' explosive rage, in much the same way as Christ, the "one greater Man" of Milton's opening invocation, opposes the downward slide inherent in "Man's First Disobedience." Although "doubting," the Plowman "stands": a verb associated throughout the Miltonic canon with wise, moral action. "They also serve who only stand and wait," the conclusion of *Sonnet XIX* goes; at the crisis in *Paradise Regained*, the Son will, miraculously, stand. Within the more immediate context of *Paradise Lost*, Adam and Eve have been introduced as "Two of far nobler shape [than the prone beasts] erect and tall, / Godlike erect" (288–89). In that context, we are prepared to see the Plowman as a morally upright figure, in short as a good man. The Plowman does not, however, arrest the threat of angelic violence, which suggests that he lacks the Son's divine, restorative power. The opposing angels remain locked in their adversarial postures until the heavenly scales appear above them, and Satan flees, ending Book IV.

Most of the controversy over the passage has focused on two questions: the Plowman's identity and the cause of his anxiety.[18] Most critics have attempted to see the Plowman as either Satan or God. For example, Alastair Fowler, in his recent edition of *Paradise Lost*, argues against the satanic reading of the passage advanced by William Empson. Satan already is described in a simile nearby, Fowler points out. He advocates the position that the Plowman represents not Satan but God. The form of Fowler's conclusion is revealing: "The ploughman must in some sense be 'like' God" (251). Certainly Fowler's dismissal of the misleading identification of the Plowman as Satan is useful. Unfortunately, Fowler's black-or-white way of reading oversimplifies Milton's poetry and can result only in truncating its coherence and significance. If the Plowman isn't God, however, who is he? And what is a plowman doing at this point in the poem? These questions can be effectively addressed only if we meet the Plowman in the context from which Milton drew him. As my discussion indicates, that context is agricultural.

The exact phrase "careful Plowman" has a clear precedent in book V of Lucius Columella's *De Re Rustica*. Columella uses the phrase *sedulus arator*, or careful plowman, while explaining the precautions to be taken when cultivating vines:

> Nam in bracchiatis plerumque fit, ut aut cruere aut cornibus buom vitium defringantur, saepe etiam stiva, dum sedulus arator vomere perstringere ordinem, et quam proximam partem vitium excolere studet. (V, v, 12)

> [For in vines which grow out into arms it generally happens that the small branches are broken off by the legs or horns of the oxen, and often too by the handle of the plough while the careful ploughman is striving to graze the edge of the row with the ploughshare and to cultivate the ground as near as possible to the vines.]

Given the strong possibility of injuring the plants, the Latin *sedulus* conveys the same combination of anxiety and diligence embodied in the English word "careful." The first definition for the word "careful" in the *O.E.D.*—"Full of grief; mournful, sorrowful"—is appropriate to the losses contemplated by Columella's and Milton's plowmen. The fifth of the *O.E.D.*'s headings—"Applying care to avoid; on one's guard against, cautious, wary"—said to be obsolete after 1728, perhaps best describes Milton's figure. Specifically, the Plowman in *Paradise Lost* is applying care to avoid the loss of his harvest.

In a passage that further clarifies the identity of Milton's figure, Columella describes the harvesting of grain in book II of his *De Re Rustica*. Columella warns against a variety of dangers attending a harvest, and he gives a unique tip on precisely when to gather the crop:

> Sed cum matura fuerit seges, ante quam torreatur vaporibus aestivi sideris, qui sunt vastissimi per exortum Caniculae, celeriter demetatur; nam dispendiosa est cunctatio, primum quod avibus praedam ceterisque animalibus praebet, deinde quod grana et ipsae spicae culmis arentibus et aristis celeriter decidunt. Si

vero procellae ventorum aut turbines incesserunt, maior pars ad terram defluit; propter quae recrastinari non debet, sed aequaliter flaventibus iam satis, ante quam ex toto grana indurescant, cum rubicundum colorem traxerunt, messis facienda est, ut potius in area et in acervo quam in agro grandescant frumenta. Constat enim, si tempestive decisa sint, postea capere incrementum. (II, xx, 1–2)

[But when the grain is ripe it should be quickly harvested before it can be parched by the heat of the summer sun, which is most severe at the rising of the Dog-star; for delay is costly—in the first place because it affords plunder for birds and other creatures, and, secondly, because the kernels and even the heads themselves quickly fall as the stalks and beards wither. And if wind-storms or cyclones strike it, the greater part of it is lost on the ground; for which reason there should be no delay, but when the crop is even golden yellow, before the grains have entirely hardened and after they have taken on a reddish colour, the harvest should be gathered, so that the grain may grow larger on the floor and in the stack rather than in the field. For it is an established fact that, if cut at the proper time, it makes some growth afterwards.]

Modern farmers carefully monitor percentages of moisture in determining when to harvest crops. Lacking such technology, early farmers could nonetheless rely on Columella's idea about color, harvesting the golden yellow grain at the first sign of reddening. In that context, Milton's depiction of the "Angelic Squadron" turning "fiery red" becomes significant rather than decorative. Presumably the red color of the angels extends to their spears, which become the spears of grain waving in the wind. The waving grain has reached the precise moment when it should be harvested. A corroborating sign from Milton's passage that the time is right is the description of the grain as "hopeful sheaves." The crop has ripened, but only the threshing floor will tell whether the ears will prove grain or chaff.

Anxiety runs through this sequence, one should observe. But it is no more God's anxiety than it is Satan's. The doubts of the careful Plowman are entirely human. The anxiety is precisely that of a careful farmer, properly concerned, understandably if overly fretful. For farmers are constantly reading the skies for signs of weather that threatens to devastate their crops. Such doubts and fears, quite familiar in the agricultural economy of Milton's day, place in human perspective the cosmic events of the passage. The confrontation between Gabriel and Satan thus acquires the high anxiety of harvesttime. Despite the fear and concern everyone involved in the harvest experiences, the resolution of the crisis is generally positive and abundant. A rich harvest is also predicted in the eschatological sense to which Milton's epic gestures. The resolution of the harvest, as well as the plot of *Paradise Lost*, will eventually prove comic in Northrop Frye's sense of humanity assumed into divinity.[19]

As a brief check on this interpretation, one might recall the role rustic figures play in Homeric similes. Richmond Lattimore maintains that Homeric similes carry readers from the scene in the poem to the outside, everyday world. Thus they provide a momentary "escape from the heroic."[20] As an example, Lattimore cites *Iliad* IV, 452–456. In this passage, a simile of clashing mountain streams illustrates the clash of heroic armies. The simile contains a precursor of Milton's Plowman:

As when rivers in winter spate running down from the mountains throw together at the meeting of streams the weight of their water out of the great springs behind in the hollow stream-bed, and far away in the mountains the shepherd hears their thunder; such, from the coming together of men, was the shock and the shouting.

"Such similes," Lattimore concludes, "are landscapes, direct from the experience of life, and this one is humanized by the tiny figure of the shepherd set against enormous nature." In Milton's poetry, the tiny figure of the Plowman does precisely that: he humanizes the remote, heroic world of clashing angelic forces. As with Homer, simile for Milton is neither decoration nor allegory. It is, in Lattimore's phrase, "dynamic invention" (44–45), which opens the epic argument into the strangely familiar world that the poet and reader share. As such, it renovates the epic argument by fusing it with the poet's own culture. Careful plowmen need to watch the swirling angels above, but, no less certainly, the angels need the Plowman if their spiritual struggle is to touch Milton's "fit audience."

III

While enjoying an epic precursor in Homer and reflecting the Roman agricultural writers whom Milton taught in school, the image of the "careful Plowman," then, refers to an agrarian world immediately recognizable to Milton's seventeenth-century audience. If we place the Plowman precisely in that cultural milieu, we might gain even sharper resolution on Milton's poem. What cultural associations would the "careful Plowman" carry for Milton's contemporaries?

On the one hand, for those resisting agrarian change in England, the Plowman would conjure up an image of established order. Thus Robert Cecil draws on the Plowman in a speech to the House of Commons in 1601, in supporting a bill intended to halt depopulation by the practice of enclosure. He proclaims, "I do not dwell in the Country, I am not acquainted with the Plough: But I think that whosoever doth not maintain the Plough, destroys this Kingdom."[21] Cecil's oratory prepares a charge of treason against anyone who would in any way fail to "maintain the Plough." Agrarian reformers would disagree that enclosure necessarily weakened or reduced agricultural production. Nonetheless, Cecil's rhetorical use of the "the Plough" drives at something more intangible yet enduring: a vision of a thriving monarchical England upheld by its loyal farmer-citizens. Such a vision is the positive implicit in Cecil's threat: Those who maintain the plough strengthen the kingdom.

Thus one need not be surprised to find that, throughout the 1630's, King Charles and Archbishop Laud vigorously prosecuted landowners who violated antienclosure commissions, thus driving agricultural laborers off the land. One may speculate, as does W. E. Tate, whether Charles operated more out of concern for the poor uprooted rustics or out of desire to extort fines from offenders for his lavish expenses.[22] Certainly the landowners were able to pay the fines, though a sign of their chafing appears in the charge against Laud in 1644 that "he did a little too much countenance the commission for depopulations."[23] As Charles's political situation became more precarious during the 1640's, the monarchy increasingly needed the support of traditional, loyal citizens. Charles took pains to appeal to yeoman and small farmers up to the end—even after his death, as his commissioning of the *Eikon Basilike* indicates.

Yet images of the plough and metaphors of plowing were used during the 1640s and 1650s to support a completely different political agenda, that of the radical left. The image of the plow appears in the Diggers' song, the refrain of which calls singers and listeners to recall that they are "Diggers all." One stanza goes:

> With spades and hoes and ploughs, stand up now!
> With spades and hoes and plowes stand up now!
> Your freedom to uphold, seeing Cavaliers are bold
> To kill you if they could, and rights from you withold,
> Stand up now, Diggers all![24]

The plows incorporated in the Diggers' song have a literal quality, while the more abstract rights the Diggers claim derive from their farming implements.

Early readers of *Paradise Lost* would recall that the Diggers had physically enacted the program of their anthem beginning in 1649. According to the Council of State records for April 16 of that year, William Everard, a cashiered army officer who styled himself a prophet, had begun to dig up the common land on St. George's Hill in Weybridge, Surrey, and to sow it with carrots, parsnips, and beans. Everard was joined by between one and two hundred followers; the names of seventy-three colonists are preserved.[25] Before being summoned, Everard and Gerrard Winstanley, the

Diggers' leaders, appeared in person before the Council and unfolded a detailed Christian-communal-agrarian program. As outlined in the pamphlet, *The True Levellers' Standard Advanced* (London, 1649), the "first reason" for the digging is "that we may work in righteousness and lay the foundation of making the earth a common treasury for all, both rich and poor, that everyone that is born in the land may be fed by the earth his mother that brought him forth, according to the reason that rules in the creation."[26] The Council tolerated the Surrey Diggers until the autumn of 1649, when they were forcibly dispossessed. Nonetheless, during the 1650s, groups of Diggers operated in similar fashion in Middlesex, Bedfordshire, Berkshire, Buckinghamshire, Herefordshire, Huntingdonshire, Northamptonshire, Staffordshire, and Northumberland.[27]

The Diggers may have been motivated partly by a sheer instinct for survival. "The abysmal harvest of 1648 had led to widespread hunger and unemployment, especially among disbanded soldiers," Christopher Hill points out; moreover, the winter of 1648–49 was particularly harsh.[28] Visible from London, St. George's Hill apparently served as a beacon for the poor seeking sustenance. In terms of Milton's image of careful plowing, the Diggers may have contributed both a sense of urgency and potential failure to the scene. The Diggers succeeded in first plowing then seeding, but they failed both literally and metaphorically to bring in a harvest.

In a work that resonates with the "careful Plowman" and the Digger song, Milton's *Sonnet XVI* features the image of plowing as a measure of Oliver Cromwell's success as of May 1652. In the sonnet's opening quatrain, careful plowing is equated with wise generalship:

> Cromwell, our chief of men, who through a cloud
>   Not of war only, but detractions rude,
>   Guided by faith and matchless Fortitude,
>   To peace and truth thy glorious way hast plough'd.

Cromwell has plowed his glorious way to peace and truth, not only through military battles but through the uncertain political process (the "cloud"), by which he has endured harsh criticism ("detractions rude") for his actions. Cromwell's dual achievement, the sonnet insists, has been glorious. At its turn, however, the sonnet insists that Cromwell has more to do, "yet much remains / To conquer still; peace hath her victories / No less renown'd than war" (9–11). What remains for Cromwell and English citizens to achieve is an inner victory, a revolution that would "save free Conscience" from external, secular authorities—including Cromwell himself. The burden of the sonnet is to suggest that such a victory is at least as difficult and as glorious as Cromwell's military ones. Retrospectively, in light of the plowman image from *Paradise Lost,* Cromwell needs to apply in this new field Gabriel's wisdom: "what folly then / To boast what Arms can do, since thine no more / Than Heav'n permits, nor mine" (IV, 1007–09). In working toward that inner revolution, violence will do no good. There is, however, a way. It is the Plowman's way. The wisdom, faith, and "matchless Fortitude" of a careful Plowman, standing through all the dangers farmers know, represent all the resources that human beings can summon to bring in the harvest.

St. Olaf College

NOTES

1. All quotations from Milton's poetry are reproduced from *John Milton: Complete Poems and Major Prose,* ed. Merritt Y. Hughes (Indianapolis, 1957). All references to Milton's prose are to *Complete Prose Works of John Milton,* 8 vols., ed. Don M. Wolfe et al. (New Haven, 1953–82), hereafter cited as YP, followed by volume and page numbers.
2. See the majestic discussion of fruit in Alastair Fowler's introduction to his edition of *Paradise Lost* (London, 1971), pp. 18–19:

> When Milton's exploitation of the semantic field of *fruit* is reviewed, it is found to account for no small proportion of the poem's content. It extends not only to immediate concrete and abstract uses of *fruit* itself (as well as of *fruitless* and *fruition*) but also to almost every other reference to vegetable nature. Thus Eve is herself a 'fairest unsupported flower' (ix 432) and Christ's promise is to her seed; the fallen angels lie like leaves in Vallombrosa (i 302); the serpent is a shoot of fraud (ix 89); and under the Covenant mankind proceeds 'as from a second stock [trunk]' (xii 7). But none of these images would have half so much force were it not for the actual presence of the trees that dominate the physical landscape of the poem. The sacred Biblical Trees of Life and of Knowledge, the emblematic trees and plants of virtue, the ordinary wild natural trees that complete the grotesque surrounding frame—everywhere in Paradise vegetation burgeons luxuriantly. It is natural and inevitable that the universe itself should be thought of as a plant whose 'bright consummate flower' is breathed in heaven (v 481). Mankind is as naturally both part and guardian of a plant; and a plant's desecration must inevitably have cosmic repercussions.

For a rare discussion of Milton's poetic use of both fruit and seed imagery, see Kathleen M. Swaim, *Before and After the Fall: Contrasting Modes in "Paradise Lost"* (Amherst, 1986), pp. 62–66. Swaim traces a shift in these images away from natural and toward spiritual signification. Swaim's primary concern in that discussion, however, is to locate the image patterns within Raphael's and Michael's contrasting modes. Thus Swaim views the "recollection" of seed passages as characteristic of the post-lapsarian mode in the epic.
3. Regina M. Schwartz, *Remembering and Repeating: Biblical Creation in "Paradise Lost"* (Cambridge, 1988), pp. 2–3.

4. For the literary kinship of Milton and George Eliot, see Diana Postlethwaite, "When Eliot Reads Milton: The Muse in a Different Voice," *ELH* 57:1 (1990), 197–222.

5. For the alternate reading that Milton's fruit is merely an apple and a "completely arbitrary sign," see R. A. Shoaf, *Milton: Poet of Duality* (New Haven, 1985), p. 31, and Satan, in *Paradise Lost* x, 485–89. In *Naming in Paradise: Milton and the Language of Adam and Eve* (Oxford, 1990), pp. 7–9, John Leonard relates those readings of "fruit"—along with others by C. S. Lewis, Cleanth Brooks, and Christopher Ricks—to the continuing debate over natural language in Eden.

6. For further discussion of the various biblical translations of this verse available to Milton, see Fowler's note to *Paradise Lost* VIII, 320–22, p. 413.

7. Anthony Low, *The Georgic Revolution* (Princeton, 1985), pp. 296–352. Hereafter cited as Low.

8. Thomas G. Rosenmeyer, *The Green Cabinet* (Berkeley and Los Angeles, 1969), pp. 20–23. For pastoralism in *Paradise Lost*, see especially John R. Knott, *Milton's Pastoral Vision* (Chicago, 1971). In *Pastoral and Ideology, Virgil to Valery* (Berkeley and Los Angeles, 1987), p. 160, Annabel Patterson suggests that Milton knowingly said good-bye to pastoral in his 1645 volume of poems.

9. Barbara K. Lewalski, *"Paradise Lost" and the Rhetoric of Literary Forms* (Princeton, 1985), pp. 173–219; and "Milton on Women—Yet Again," in *Problems for Feminist Criticism*, ed. Sally Minogue (London, 1990), especially p. 55: Adam and Eve "are expected to grow, change, and develop in virtue by properly pruning and directing their own impulses as well as their garden." Mary Ann Radzinowicz, "Man as a Probationer of Immortality," in *Approaches to "Paradise Lost"*, ed. C. A. Patrides (London, 1968), pp. 31–51; and *Toward "Samson Agonistes"* (Princeton, 1979), especially pp. 244–45. Diane McColley, in *Milton's Eve* (Urbana, Ill., 1983), focuses on the relation of floral and psychosocial growth in *Paradise Lost*.

10. Marcus Terentius Varro, *Rerum Rusticarum*, or *On Agriculture*, with Marcus Porcius Cato, *On Agriculture*, trans. William Davis Hooper, rev. ed. by Harrison Boyd Ash (1934; rpt. Cambridge, Mass., 1979); Lucius Junius Moderatus Columella, *On Agriculture*, 3 vols., ed. with English translation by Harrison Boyd Ash, E. S. Forster, and Edward H. Heffner (Cambridge, Mass., 1941–79). These editions are from the Loeb Classical Library. Unless otherwise indicated, the English translations of Cato, Varro, and Columella in my text are those of the Loeb editions.

11. Low, *Georgic Revolution*, pp. 316–17.

12. Edward Phillips, "The Life of Milton," in *John Milton*, ed. Hughes, p. 1029.

13. On the publication history of the Roman agricultural manuals, see William D. Hooper and Harrison Boyd Ash, eds., Cato, Marcus Porcius and Marcus Terentius Varro, *De Re Rustica* (Cambridge, Mass., 1979), pp. xx–xxiii; Joan Thirsk, "Making a Fresh Start: Sixteenth-Century Agriculture and the Classical Inspiration," pp. 18–19, in Michael Leslie and Timothy Raylor, eds., *Culture and Agriculture in Early Modern England* (Leicester, 1992).

14. Thirsk, *Culture*, pp. 15–34.

15. Ibid., pp. 15–20, 23–26.

16. The resemblance of Cato's remark to Franklin's style is note by Ash in his edition, p. 12.

17. Joseph H. Summers, *The Muse's Method: An Introduction to "Paradise Lost"* (1962; rpt. Binghamton, 1981), p. 12.

18. Richard Bentley emphasizes in his *Paradise Lost, A New Edition* (London, 1732), that the Plowman is afraid of losing his crop in a storm, which Fowler (p. 251) considers an

erroneous reading. Bentley's "error," however, may have already existed in Milton's imagination and that of his readers, because of Vergil's emphasis on the danger of devastating storms during harvesting in *Georgics* I, 311–34. Given England's northern latitude, that danger would be even more acute than in Rome. In *Milton's God* (London, 1961), p. 172, William Empson reads the simile as a sign that either God is lacking omnipotence (if the anxiety is his) or that Satan has assumed his rightful rule over the angels.

Eschewing the search for exact point-by-point correspondences between the epic's plot and every detail of the similes, Christopher Ricks, in *Milton's Grand Style* (Oxford, 1963), p. 129, finds this simile "beautiful but digressive." As in all great poetry, he maintains, "we cannot do without a sense of disparity as well as of similarity in Milton's similes" (p. 130). Ricks's assumption, which I gratefully acknowledge, underlies my interpretation. My understanding of how metaphors work generally has been shaped by the late Max Black. Particularly I acknowledge Black's notion of interaction in metaphor as set forth in *Models and Metaphors* (Ithaca, N.Y., 1967).

19. Northrop Frye, *Anatomy of Criticism: Four Essays* (Princeton, 1957), p. 43.

20. Richmond Lattimore, trans., *The Iliad of Homer* (Chicago, 1951), p. 42.

21. Robert Cecil, in Sir Simonds D'Ewes, *The Journals of All the Parliaments During the Reign of Queen Elizabeth* (London, 1682), p. 674, cited by Andrew McRae, "Husbandry Manuals and the Language of Agrarian Improvement," in *Culture*, Leslie and Raylor, eds., p. 35.

22. W. E. Tate, *The Enclosure Movement* (New York, 1967), p. 126.

23. Joan Thirsk, "Enclosing and Engrossing," in Thirsk, ed., *The Agrarian History of England and Wales, 1500–1640* (Cambridge, 1967), vol. IV, p. 237; cited in Robert C. Allen, *Enclosure and the Yeoman: The Agricultural Development of the South Midlands, 1450–1850* (Oxford, 1992), p. 77.

24. In Tate, *Enclosure Movement*, p. 149. On the Diggers generally, see also H. N. Brailsford, *The Levellers and the English Revolution*, ed. Christopher Hill (Stanford, 1961), especially pp. 56–67.

25. Christopher Hill, *The World Turned Upside Down: Radical Ideas during the English Revolution* (New York, 1972), p. 91.

26. Gerrard Winstanley, *The Law of Freedom and Other Writings*, ed. Christopher Hill (Cambridge, 1983), p. 84.

27. Tate, *Enclosure Movement*, pp. 148–49.

28. Hill, *World*, p. 87; and "The Religion of Gerrard Winstanley," in *The Collected Essays of Christopher Hill*, vol. 2, (Amherst, 1986), p. 203.

THE STATE OF INNOCENCE: EPIC TO OPERA

Hugh MacCallum

A REVALUATION OF the opera that John Dryden based on *Paradise Lost* appears to be taking place. As long ago as 1966 Bruce King urged that Dryden's whole intelligence was employed in writing *The State of Innocence and the Fall of Man*, and that its imagery and themes dominate his most important work. Recently James Anderson Winn judged the unstaged opera "far more interesting, in literary and biographical terms, than many of Dryden's staged plays." For Jean Gagen it is, while not an unrecognized masterpiece, nonetheless worthy of sustained comparison with *Paradise Lost*.[1] Study of the opera in relation both to Dryden's other writing and to its source has led to a keener appreciation of its merits and interest. My aim is twofold: (1) to show how the genre, argument, and style of Dryden's opera illuminate his response to *Paradise Lost;* 2) to argue that Dryden reacted directly and forcefully to Milton's treatment of innocence and the Fall, but that in other important areas of the story—the depiction of deity, the operation of grace, the representation of man's repentance and reeducation—he largely ignored his source and introduced themes and attitudes which are common to his other writing, especially his drama. Dryden's opera thus offers a distinctive treatment of the story, one which reveals both a strong response to selected features of its source and a revisionary impulse fed by a perception of Milton's epic as a flawed if great achievement.

I

The visit made by Dryden to Milton, first described by John Aubrey and then by others,[2] likely occurred in 1673 or early in 1674, about a year before the older poet's death and perhaps only months before the second edition of *Paradise Lost* in July of 1674. Apparently the purpose of the visit was to obtain Milton's permission to make a rhymed version of *Paradise Lost* for the stage. But undoubtedly Dryden had other motives, both personal and literary, for wishing to talk with the poet whose genius he was to recognize throughout his life, and it seems probable that the conversation touched on various literary matters and that, as Winn suggests, it included Milton's acknowledgment that "*Spencer* was his Original."[3]

109

Dryden had been poet laureate for about five years at the time of the meeting, and although his most important work was still to come, he had already achieved a number of striking successes in poetry and drama. While at the time faced with both practical and literary problems,[4] Dryden nonetheless came to the meeting as a mature and successful poet and dramatist who was close to the height of his career, while Milton, his great work over, was living quietly but not in complete silence, and although officially ignored, was enjoying the attentions of friends and well-wishers.

The curiosity of the younger poet who had probably once been his employee must have been of some interest to Milton, but one wonders what he thought of Dryden's proposal to turn his great epic into rhyme. Winn, who believes that Dryden was by his project claiming status for the epic as a classic, nonetheless detects more than a hint of disapproval in the words by which Milton is said to have granted Dryden's request, giving him leave to "tag" his verses or "points."[5] The reference is to the fashion of ornamenting the ends of laces with metal tips. Rhyme, it seems, is like a new fashion in dress. Some critics have linked the wit of the remark to the note on "The Verse" which Milton prefixed to the second edition of *Paradise Lost*, finding evidence here that he was siding with Sir Robert Howard and against Dryden in the literary controversy about rhyme.[6] But the irony of the response is touched by urbanity, and in any case the language could just as well be Dryden's as Milton's.

Andrew Marvell's fine poem "On Paradise Lost," probably written about the same time as the encounter between Milton and Dryden (it was added to the 1674 edition of Milton's epic), has usually been taken to allude to Dryden's plans for an opera, and while this interpretation has recently been challenged, there is no question that Marvell closes his panegyric with a graceful and provocative comment on the status of rhyme.[7] Marvell finds sublimity to be the mark of Milton's heroic verse, and his image for the poem's success is the soaring flight of the bird of paradise which always keeps on wing with unflagging ease. *Paradise Lost* is a unique achievement, inimitable. Rather than serving as a model to be observed and emulated, it is a prophetic poem which requires the kind of interpretation and admiration given to scripture. Marvell's speaker cannot follow the bard, but remains below in the quotidian world of satire and fashionable verse, where poets "tag" their fancies like "Bushy-points." He thus offers a humorous apology for the fact that his panegyric, unlike his subject, is in rhyme and therefore in bondage to the tinkling sound of like endings. Milton stands apart from the literary fashions of the day, and the elegant frivolity of the age acts as a foil to the soaring creativity of the epic bard whose use of "number, weight, and measure" recalls the acts of divine creativity depicted in Wisdom xi, 20.

Dryden also considered sublimity to be a trait of *Paradise Lost*, but his response to the epic is often ambiguous, and he is alert to its lapses and imperfections. Milton matured before those advances in criticism and language which, according to Dryden, give the contemporary poet an advantage over his predecessors.[8] While a belief in the progress of literary refinement is especially prominent in Dryden's earlier work, in less aggressive forms it reappears in connection with some of his later translations.[9] No doubt in 1674 he wanted to learn from his reworking of a major poem, but it is likely that he also hoped to improve some of its poetry, introducing rhyme and realizing more fully the potential in the work of a poet who had learned his craft under difficult conditions and before the new age of enlightenment.

Throughout his life Dryden's responses to *Paradise Lost* were to be marked by strong reservations as well as generous praise. Milton appears in his criticism as a potent yet somewhat enigmatic force. Much suggests that he considered *Paradise Lost* a generic failure. In the later criticism he argues that it misses the point of the epic, since the story concerns an event which is not prosperous but ends in the loss of happiness rather than its recovery. While he grasped the revision of heroism undertaken in Milton's poem, he did not consider it appropriate to the genre (W IV, pp. 14–17). However, he used Milton's poem as a source of magnificent scenes, images, and speeches which could be adapted in his own work to other genres such as satire, heroic drama, and opera.[10]

We cannot be sure when Dryden reached the conclusions about Milton presented in his later essays. He told John Dennis that at the time of the composition of *The State of Innocence* he did not know half the extent of Milton's excellence.[11] No doubt the act of writing the opera taught him much about this and Winn argues strongly that the work of condensing Milton had a profound effect on Dryden's art.[12] Yet I believe that *The State of Innocence* also contains evidence of a desire to revise and reorganize Milton's materials in such a way that they conform to the literary rules and practices which Milton, whether by error or intent, had broken. Implicit in the revision is most of the criticism which Dryden will later direct at the epic. The task provided an opportunity for Dryden to assert some of his own literary convictions in opposition to the character of his source, and this he does in various ways, including the shift to a new genre, the diminishing of the antagonist, and the interruption of the long Miltonic paragraphs in order to create a more naturalistic form of dialogue.

Present throughout the opera, then, is a sense of countermovement, a pressure to restore the generic and literary norms altered by the Miltonic revolution. The concern is evident even in the preliminary matter added to the version published in 1677, which encourages the reader to approach the opera with certain expectations. For example, the revisionist impulse is recognized and celebrated by the panegyric which Dryden's young friend Nathaniel Lee wrote in praise of *The State of Innocence*. Lee's piece labors under the absurd difficulty of favoring Dryden's opera over Milton's epic, but it remains nonetheless a lively and graceful poem, and Dryden's affectionate mockery of Lee's youthful Muse in his preface should not blind us to the fact that he chose to publish it. The main point made by Lee's poem, as Bernard Harris has well observed, concerns Dryden's talent for transformation and refinement.[13] Milton, Lee argues, left behind him a rude chaos which Dryden's genius has illuminated. This idea is repeated and varied in a series of images. Lee's observations appear to be based on the program of literary reform which Dryden articulated in his earlier writing: Milton's "mystic" and melancholy reason must be cleared and illuminated by the sunlike "sense" of Dryden before it will appeal to a courtly Restoration audience.[14] Lee, unlike Marvell, sees Milton as a rough originator, one who is surpassed by the artful perfecter, Dryden; only the latter achieves harmony and sublimity by combining the "mighty" with the "mild" (DW, pp. 415–16).

The dedication of the opera to Mary of Este, daughter to the Duke of Modena and the bride of the Duke of York, provides a further sign of the difference between Dryden and his predecessor. As Dryden recalled the patronage received by such poets as Ludovico Ariosto and Torquato Tasso from the Estensi ancestors of Mary, he must surely have remembered how Milton turned away from courtly patronage to his "celestial" patroness, the Muse. Dryden was throughout his life suspicious of enthusiasm and claims to prophetic insight, and he never imitates the appeal for inspiration found in the invocations to *Paradise Lost* or adopts a vatic tone similar to that of the Miltonic bard. Dryden's commitment to the ideal of a literature whose mode of production depends on patronage is evident throughout his career, and is expressed some years later in his proposal to write an epic in which he would include representations of "living Friends and Patrons of the Noblest Families" (W IV, pp. 23). Moreover the hyperbolic panegyric on Mary, both playful and earnest, is full of literary overtones.[15] Clearly a strategic political statement which supports James's much-criticized marriage to a Catholic, the dedication also suggests that the poet who is about to rewrite the story of *Paradise Lost* has his own literary agenda which includes romance and mysticism, and that he is restoring the subject which Milton had used as a vehicle for his Protestant individualism to the traditional poetic service of the state and its leaders. Such an introduction raises expectations.

Even in the preface which he wrote for the publication of his operatic version in 1677, calling it "The Author's Apology for Heroic Poetry and Poetic Licence," there are some indications of Dryden's revisionist impulse, although these are more a matter of omission and emphasis than of direct statement. The preface is of course unreserved in its acknowledgment of his dependence on Milton. *Paradise Lost* is "*undoubtedly one of the greatest, most noble, and most sublime poems, which either this Age or Nation has produc'd*" (DW, p. 417). Unlike Marvell, however, Dryden understands this sublimity not in terms of high subject matter but rather of rhetorical strategies and powerful technique. Thus the epic contains bold strokes handled with artful coolness and discretion, and succeeds in imagining things "*quite out of Nature*" or "*whereof we can have no notion*" (DW, p. 422).

Yet while Dryden praises "*the sublime Genius that sometimes errs,*" he also observes that poetic liberties vary according to the age in which the author writes (DW, pp. 417, 424). England is more like strict Rome than free Greece, and the bold liberties of the Homeric Milton are perhaps a bit out of style in a more polished and Virgilian age. Although the "Apology" defends the liberty of heroic poetry, it also through implication supports the adaptation by which Dryden makes *Paradise Lost* accessible to an age of refinement, transposing it into another genre and tagging its verses. While Marvell's panegyric relegates the fashionable elegance of rhyme to the quotidian world of satire, Dryden seeks by rhyme to accommodate the force of *Paradise Lost* to an age which he and Nathaniel Lee sometimes thought of as more "Gallant" than the last, where "our native Language" has become "more refin'd and free" (W XI, pp. 201–02). The preface calls at once for greater naturalism and more literary refinement. The choice of opera as the genre for his work of revision gave Dryden the freedom to try to realize these aims in his retelling of the story.

The choice also shows how responsive Dryden was to contemporary fashions in the theatre. When in April 1674 he entered his dramatization of *Paradise Lost* in the Stationers' Register under the title *The Fall of Angels and Man in Innocence, An Heroick Opera*, there was increasing evidence of a new vogue for mixing drama and music.[16] Dryden was no doubt working out his own theory of opera at this time, but the formal statement of his views did not appear until 1685, when he introduced the libretto of *Albion and Albianus* with a preface. Of the two types of opera there distinguished, the "musical drama" (through sung) and the mixed,

The State of Innocence clearly belongs to the later, being "a *Drama* Written in blank Verse" but "adorn'd with Scenes, Machines, Songs and Dances" (W XV, p. 10). In this kind of semiopera, what Dryden calls "*The Songish Part*" (W XV, p. 4) is separate, and presumably was intended to be managed in large part or entirely by singers rather than actors. Through much of its course it is a heroic and pastoral drama but punctuated by vocal and instrumental interludes. As Montague Summers points out in his edition, there are many signs in the text that Dryden was writing with a lively sense of the requirements of performance, and these include frequent suggestions concerning the use of music.

One episode where music is particularly important, and where the text is clearly designed for singing, is Eve's dream of temptation (V, i). Here the use of three and four stress lines reinforces the stage direction indicating that the passage is to be sung, and at the close there is a refrain for which the two singers join in a "chorus of both" (DW, p. 441). The performers who represent this episode while Eve and Adam sleep are clearly singers, and on their departure the story returns to the actors. Elsewhere his stage directions call for *intermezzi* which are both symphonic and vocal. After the opening spectacle of the fall of the rebel angels, for example, a victory hymn is sung as the faithful angels are "discovered above, brandishing their swords." A song for the defeated angels is also to be provided in which they celebrate their bravery and mourn their fall (DW, p. 430). Later, music and song are to accompany the vision of heaven granted to Adam by Raphael. Dryden's decision to rewrite *Paradise Lost* as dramatic opera shows his appreciation of the importance of music and song in the epic. Milton himself had originally proposed to write a masquelike drama on the Fall, and his early sketches are full of operatic potential; although Dryden could not have known these, he was familiar with Milton's earlier experiments with the masque. The heroic-drama-as-opera must have struck him as an appropriate form because of its ability to combine music with masquelike spectacle and the deployment of "machines" and supernatural persons.

Dryden's task was made more difficult by the fact that his play (unlike the one projected by Milton) has no narrator, and thus he must try to incorporate the commentary and imagery of the epic poet in the speech of the characters. He elaborates upon his source with invention, and there are a significant number of passages which, while prompted by *Paradise Lost*, introduce new viewpoints, imagery, and actions (the rich description of the forbidden tree at DW, p. 452, for example, or the reception of bad news by the "Etherial people" at DW, p. 455). Frequently the elaboration is prompted by the need to adapt the story to stage presentation, and the effect is often to move attention from what is seen to what is spoken. When Milton's Adam first encounters the fallen Eve, he sees that she is carrying a bough with its fruit in her hand, and he listens in silence to her long and hectic speech of apology. The narrator then directs our attention to Adam's slack hand, from which now drops a garland of roses intended as a peace offering, shedding its faded blossoms as if to mark the end of the pastoral world. Dryden tried a different strategy. His Adam celebrates the return of Eve in a songlike passage which dwells on her power over nature. As she begins her apology, however, he interrupts her twice, his broken words showing that "disorder'd connection" which, according to Dryden (DW, p. 421), is fitting in the depiction of a man talking in a passion ("Speak—do not—yet, at last, I must be told," DW, p. 453). When Eve confirms her trespass, Adam does not soliloquize as in the epic but engages her in debate. While Dryden's revision starts from the necessities of providing a text for acting, the result of his alterations involves a wholly new appreciation of the scene, one in which attention moves from the symbolic and gestural statement of feeling to its rhetorical expression through dialogue which produces sudden shifts in point of view.

In dealing with space and setting, Dryden relies on masquelike scenes whose general nature is indicated in the stage directions and, sometimes, by the responses of the characters. The four main settings of Milton's poem are reduced to two—hell and the garden of Eden. While Adam is given a glimpse of heaven to comfort him after the Fall, no scenes are set there. The angels are shown on earth and in hell (and briefly, in spectacle only, falling through chaos). The implications of this change are far-reaching. Milton sets up a basic polarity between heaven and hell which is shaped by parody, the self-centered activities of hell offering a perverted imitation of the God-centered activities of heaven. For Dryden the essential polarity shaping action and language is that of chaos and order. The opera opens with a scene in the abyss and closes with a description of "the war of nature." There are several references to the abyss, which is treated as the original matter out of which are struck the sparks of creative light (DW, p. 456), and also, metaphorically, as the tumult of emotion that is fulfilled in love (DW, p. 438). Since hell has no parodic luster, the conflict of opposites is more simply expressed in terms of darkness versus light. Complicating further the comparison of the two treatments of the cosmos are the differing views of matter held by the two poets. Dryden's characters tend to speak in terms of a dualism of mind and matter, soul and body, while Milton's stress the continuity of matter and spirit, as in Raphael's speech on the scale of being (V, 469). Consequently, the difference between man and angel is more marked in the opera than in the monistic universe of the epic. Thus Dryden's Lucifer acts as Eve's tempter in a "borrow'd shape" (DW, p. 449), while Milton's Satan must "imbrute" himself in the serpent in a parody of the incarnation (IX, 166).

The effort to achieve unity of time produces some striking changes. Of particular significance is the fact that Adam and Eve do not, as in Milton's treatment, possess a past. Their experiences of coming into consciousness, which in the epic are recalled first by Eve (Book IV), then by Adam (Book VIII), are in the opera treated as events in the present. Other episodes and conversations are put back into their chronological sequence, and there are few indications of the lapse of time. We have the impression that Eve's dream is inspired by Lucifer on the first night in Paradise. He threatens that they are not to be allowed "another day" of happiness (III, i; DW, p. 439), and the sequence of events suggests that they do in fact fall the next day, for as soon as the admonitory visit of Raphael is over, Adam and Eve engage in the morning dispute which leads directly to their separation. On his reappearance in the garden (IV, i), however, Lucifer says "Thrice have I beat the wing, and rid with night" (DW, p. 448, as opposed to the seven "continu'd nights" of the flight of Milton's Satan in *PL* IX, 63). The implication that the story has now reached the fifth day is not quite consistent with the action we have witnessed. Dryden includes no suggestion of the thirty-three-day time span which comprehends the action of *Paradise Lost*, nor (except perhaps in the proposed songs and the closing visions) does he draw in time before and time after. The rich sense of layers of time, fold upon fold, which contributes so much to the pleasure of interpreting Milton's epic, has gone.[17]

Nor does Dryden follow Milton in creating a sense of the duration of prelapsarian life. Milton's first couple enjoy a period of time in which they can learn and develop, and this allows for shifting moods and complex feelings. Dryden's characters seem to move without real hesitation or significant ambiguity toward the fall. They do, however, debate. As in his plays, Dryden lets the characters adopt fixed positions and then shows how discussion or argument can lead to sudden changes of attitude. He thus breaks up the long speeches of *Paradise Lost* to create interchange, as in Satan's temptation of Eve. Presenting his characters in time, Milton catches the cumulative movement of thought and feeling, the way their attitudes form and shift as they seek to interpret their lives. Dryden's characters are less introspective and meditative, and tend to develop as a result of rapid and intense exchanges which leave little opportunity for reflection. The reduced time scheme also forces a collapse of character evolution, leaving the impression that the characters are abridged and simplified. Lucifer, for example, in his soliloquy on entering Paradise (DW, p. 437), draws on a number of important speeches by Milton's Satan, including his debate with Abdiel, his speech to the sun, and his ranting speech before he enters the serpent's body. The result of such economy is sometimes flat and unrelentingly epigrammatic. Better is Lucifer's earlier speech marking his approach to earth, where Dryden briefly experiments with blank verse.

Space and time have been given unity, then, and the action has become more obviously sequential. Many of the features of *Paradise Lost* that Dryden was to fault in his criticism are removed. The number of "machining persons" has been greatly reduced. The energy of Satan (now Lucifer) has been muted, so that there is less likelihood the reader will conclude that the knight has been overcome by the giant (W V, p. 276). Stylistically there are also important changes. Gone are those flats where Milton creeps along in a "Track of Scripture" (W III, p. 15; IV, p. 17). The diction includes new and fashionable words as well as common proper names absent in Milton's narrative, and an effort has been made to avoid "antiquated words" and "the perpetual harshness of their sound" (W III, p. 17).[18] Above all there is the introduction of rhyme (for which Dryden thought Milton had a bad ear, W IV, p. 15) and the radical change of pace and tone which this produces. The patterns and rhythms of the couplet increase the sense of self-conscious intellectual control, creating effects quite at odds with Milton's "heroic verse without rhyme."[19] Rather than drawing the sense out "variously from one verse to another," the couplet form as employed by Dryden compresses the sense through repeated small acts of closure or of closure denied, so that his surprises are created within a firm but restricted context of expectation. Milton's blank verse is much less predictable, suspending and varying the meaning through long paragraphs which are shaped by a flexible syntax that seems directed by both thought and feeling. Unlike the insistent forward drive of Dryden's couplets, Milton's syntax makes us look backward as well as forward.

II

Dryden remarks in 1685 that opera as a genre releases the story from the usual limits of human nature and thus admits "that sort of marvellous and surprizing conduct, which is rejected in other Plays" (W XV, p. 3). The story of the state of innocence certainly includes much that is marvelous. Yet since it is derived from scripture, it cannot be considered merely "a poetical tale or fiction," and Dryden had to find a way of dealing with its religious elements. The changes in genre and style which we have noticed are matched by changes in theme, argument, and characterization. Crucial to the shift in perspective is Dryden's decision not to dramatize the deity. In his version it is the angels who provide communication between man and heaven, and who explain Adam's situation to him both before and after the Fall. They replace the Son of God, performing many of the functions exercised either by the Son or the Father in Milton's epic. Thus it is Raphael, not the divine presence, who puts Adam to the test which ends in the creation of Eve and Raphael who pronounces the judgment after the Fall. When Milton's Adam is told that he will be exiled from the garden, he laments that he must leave the place where he talked with God; Dryden's Adam sorrows as he remembers that in the garden he once passed the day with the glorious and winged messengers of heaven. The light that is too bright for human eyes is now a property of the angels rather than of the "skirts" or the mount of God (see *PL*, III, 372–82). Dryden no doubt has in mind the problems of staging the story, but he is also representing it in his own way, making the approach to God less direct and less scriptural.

The change is radical. The lack of scenes set in heaven—and especially of scenes representing the divine council—makes the depiction of God in the opera more impersonal. He is "creator," "maker," "power," and, in a revealing phrase, "th' Eternal mind," but not Father and Son. Like a Stoic or Virgilian deity, he moves through the "Universal Mass" (DW, p. 459). Thus the duties of Adam and Eve to God are not put in terms of filial freedom. In his "Apology," Dryden defends Milton for his choice of "supernatural Argument," saying that even on the principles of Horace he would be blameworthy only if he had mixed Christian deities with heathen ones, as was done by Tasso and Luiz Vaz de Camoëns (DW, p. 424). Yet whenever possible Dryden tones down and demystifies the supernatural elements of Milton's argument. The context in which he presents his story is largely that of natural theology, even though the story itself comes from revelation. Not only is Milton's web of biblical allusions gone, but so too is the sense that through prefiguration, typology, and diction, as well as theological principle, this first dispensation reaches out to the rest of time, making contact of an analogical kind with the gospel era. What Dryden's treatment says to his age, while not specifically deistic, has to do with the kind of ethic possible within a natural theology and shows an interest in beginnings or origins which is characteristic of contemporary social and psychological speculation.

The Miltonic conception of right reason has been replaced in the opera by a less optimistic view of rational discourse. The operation of reason is described first by Lucifer, who observes that in man it is "lodg'd in Sense" (DW, p. 429), and that as a consequence man's soul must issue from the prison of the flesh by discourse. The prolonged effort needed to achieve the "faint light" capable of assisting will and understanding is caught in the image of a "long Chain of thought" (DW, p. 459). This does not sound promising, and although Adam rejoices in his use of mental powers at first, he soon appears daunted by the problem of understanding the implications of free will. His debate about this topic with the angels makes repeated use of the image of the chain, which now becomes a metaphor for necessity.

The preoccupation with a devotional relation to God, an "I-thou" relation, which is characteristic of meditational poetry in the first half of the century and also incorporated into *Paradise Lost* in many ways (and particularly through the invocations), is quite absent from *The State of Innocence*. There are no morning and evening hymns in Dryden's garden. Absent too is the Miltonic emphasis on grace and divine support. Milton's treatment of the reconciliation of Adam and Eve and their subsequent repentance is a good illustration of the way he sought to integrate the human drama with theological and scriptural elements. Dryden's dramatization of this part of the story is quite different: he does not draw attention to the divine hand directing and fostering the process of recovery, nor does the reconciliation of Adam and Eve lead them, as in *Paradise Lost*, to turn to God to seek forgiveness by prayer. Instead, they engage after the judgment in a philosophical debate in which Adam strives to justify God's ways (several of the motifs are taken from the long, turbulent soliloquy uttered by Milton's Adam *before* the reconciliation scene).

Unlike Milton's fallen couple, Dryden's Adam and Eve do not seek to interpret and accept the terms of the judgment. In particular, they seem unaware of the curse upon the serpent. Thus the protoevangelium, the prophecy that the seed of the woman shall bruise the serpent's head, plays no part in Dryden's handling of the story. Revenge upon the enemy is not among the motives of his fallen couple. Instead of the history of the world, they are given visions first of death and then of the "deathless pleasures" of heaven (DW, p. 461). Since the fulfillment of the promise concerning the seed of the woman in the figure of Christ is not part of the consolation offered to fallen man in Dryden's version, there is no identification of "my Redeemer ever blest" (*PL*, XII, 573) as the final embodiment of true heroism. Raphael's emphasis is placed on repentance and the life of temperance, which will enable man to find "*Paradise* within" (DW, p. 462), but in spite of these concluding words, he omits all reference to the importance of grace and to the way in which the raising of Eden in the waste wilderness is only possible through the sacrifice of the Son of God.

Adam is not given an education in things to come, nor in the Miltonic lessons of love and filial obedience. The absence of the divine family, and especially of the Son, is even more striking when we remember the importance of domestic relations in Dryden's heroic drama at this time. In *Aureng-Zebe*, for example, the family debates suggest a secularization of the discussions in Milton's heaven. Years later a passage in *The Hind and the Panther* (II, 499–514) was to reveal what a deep impression the epic's scenes in heaven had made on Dryden.

Unlike his treatment of the deity, Dryden's depiction of man in the state of innocence is often close to its Miltonic source. There are differences, of course, and these are revealing, but it is nonetheless true that Dryden shows himself an astute interpreter of Milton's couple, capable of realizing in dramatic terms many of the significant aspects of their relationship. One feature of the comparison which is particularly difficult to assess precisely concerns Dryden's attitude to the idea of a fall from innocence. Readers have often found his unfallen couple rather worldly and perhaps even marked by a Restoration courtliness. P. S. Havens observes that Dryden is less concerned to portray innocence than "man's familiar failings in their primordial setting."[20] Anne Davidson Ferry finds in Dryden's writing no Fall of man and no ideal of original purity, but only shifts in the terms for human experience which itself remains forever the same. Far from being idealized, she argues, Adam and Eve are allowed to express vanity, suspicion, jealousy, fear, lust, disappointment; these feelings are appropriate to romance, satire, and farce, rather than to the pastoral mode.[21]

Dryden certainly fails to catch the spirit of pastoral eclogue that is so hauntingly present during our introduction to Adam and Eve in Book IV of *Paradise Lost*. His first couple are less decorous and less self-contained and impressive than are Milton's. For Milton, the state of innocence is a special dispensation, while for Dryden it does indeed appear to have much in common with ordinary experience. Yet it was Milton who developed in a striking fashion the view that unfallen and fallen experience are analogous. The originality of Milton's picture of innocence lies partly in the way that his Adam and Eve are not static but learn from experience and grow through trial and error, thus providing both a parallel and a contrast to the life of fallen man. They experience a wide range of feeling, including doubt and the play of contrary impulses. Their reactions display many anticipations of the Fall, but these are often contained in experiences which are educational and prompt further growth. The range of feeling that Dryden permits his unfallen couple would thus seem to derive from an incisive, if one-sided, understanding of Milton's treatment.

It is in representing the state of innocence as it is manifest in the relations of Adam and Eve that Dryden most clearly capitalizes on the dramatic potential of Milton's narrative. After the Fall, the opera moves away from its source, treating the repentance and reeducation of Adam and Eve in a way which ignores Milton's characteristic emphasis on trial and grace. In depicting prelapsarian life, however, Dryden shows a close interest in the issues raised by Milton's unfallen couple and particularly in the question of Adam's authority. This can be seen in his depiction of the experience of Adam and Eve from their first awakening into consciousness to their union in marriage.

In Dryden's work, as in Milton's, Adam is more reflective than Eve, his mind made for contemplation and capable of entertaining abstractions. Adam's opening words, with their famous Cartesian echo ("For that I am / I know, because I think", DW, p. 431) display a philosophical and theological precision which is meant to contrast with the parallel first speech of Eve, with its stress on her uniqueness and on eyesight. "Well hast thou reason'd," says the angel to Adam, and then immediately shocks him with the news that man has been created as a replacement for a race of beings who have fallen from the sky. Confronted at once with this unsettling story (much earlier than in the epic), this Adam, unlike his Miltonic predecessor, shows a characteristic tendency to insecurity and self-doubt. His first reaction to the news is revealing: if angels can fall from bliss, what hope has he, a mere beginner in learning, of keeping heaven's laws? (DW, p. 431) Instead of narrating the story of the rebellion, as in the epic, Raphael simply adjures Adam to follow right reason and praise God.

Adam now takes the initiative in his first conversation by asking for a partner. Here too we feel his insecurity as he opens the subject by lamenting his lack of creativity, his "barren sex" (DW, p. 432). Adam sees that reason and speech without society are impotent, and his distress is alleviated only when he is told that he will be provided with a partner. In the dialogue with Raphael which precedes the creation of Eve (II, i), the angel describes the ideal marriage as a circle of love, reason, and beauty. These are the terms in which he introduces the theme of sovereignty as he advises Adam that he will receive a mate who is

> An equal, yet thy subject, as desig'd,
> For thy soft hours, and to unbend thy mind.
> Thy stronger soul shall her weak reason sway;
> And thou, through love, her beauty shall obey;
> Thou shalt secure her helpless sex from harms
> And she thy cares shall sweeten, with her charms.   (DW, p. 432)

Dryden plays with the paradox arising out of Eve's creation as "equal" yet "subject." In this ideal match, sweetness complements strength. The strong soul which sways the weaker reason of the woman is in this very process showing the response of rational love to ideal beauty. Most elements in the passage come either directly or indirectly from the epic, drawing on such speeches as Raphael's advice to Adam in Book IX: "love refines / The thoughts, and heart enlarges, hath his seat in reason" (*PL* VIII, 589–90). It is true, as Jean Gagen emphasizes,[22] that Dryden strikes a distinctive note when he has Raphael say that Eve is "an equal" (even though the angel immediately qualifies this). Milton's narrator, one remembers, remarks that Adam and Eve are "Not equal, as their sex not equal seem'd" (IV, 296). But in Adam's colloquy with God, as reported in Book VIII of *Paradise Lost*, woman is viewed in terms of fellowship. She is not unequal like the animals, but—in accordance with Adam's wish—fit to participate in all rational delight. Mutual love is possible because Eve, too, expresses the image of God. Far from taking a less patriarchal view of marriage than Milton, the general tenor of Dryden's thought, as expressed in this passage, throws more stress than does its source on the vulnerability of Eve, her "weak reason" and "helpless sex" (DW, p. 432). Milton's Eve, in contrast, is expected to use her reason and is, like Adam, "sufficient to have stood though free to fall" (III, 99). We shall find that Dryden's Eve lacks the strength of mind and character of her original. While he has perceived Milton's criticism of the misogyny expressed by fallen Adam, Dryden incorporates this perception into his work with an unsteady hand.

Dryden's dramatization of the first encounter of Adam and Eve reveals the strong and labile impulses which underlie the condition of mutual dependence praised by Raphael. When, from a distance, Adam first glimpses the newly created Eve, he is ready to yield his "boasted Soveraignty" for "I seek myself, and find not, wanting thee" (DW, p. 435). As he searches for her, Eve is left alone briefly and reveals her initial state of consciousness. She speaks at once of her own uniqueness and deduces that since everything seems to be watching her, she must be of special importance: "I my self am proud of me" (DW, p. 435). Adam's initial response to Eve is to view her as a goddess sent to earth to reign as the "softer Substitute" of the creator. Eve is pleased with his praise and places Adam above the "rest," conceding that "I, next to myself, admire and love thee best" (DW, p. 436). Adam courts her by laying the whole creation at her feet ("freely / I obey"), and their thoughts turn to erotic fulfillment. Eve pauses over the possibility of playing the cruel mistress who requires a long courtship; Adam teeters on the edge of despair and sounds like the

bemused Adam of *Paradise Lost* Book VIII, who confesses a lover's perturbations to Raphael. Despite his protest, Eve hesitates a moment longer,
lingering over the prospect of losing her "much-lov'd Soveraignty" (DW,
p. 436) on granting his suit, and perhaps thereafter of losing Adam's heart
to some new beauty. One half-expects a proviso scene (one remembers,
too, that thoughts of rivals do not occur to Milton's Eve until after the
Fall). By the close of the exchange, however, Adam has persuaded Eve of
his fidelity, and she now performs one of those reversals characteristic of
Dryden's heroes and heroines, surrendering her sovereignty in a new
spirit of humility: "Giving my self, my want of worth I grieve." The circle
of reason, love, and beauty posited by Raphael now seems possible.

The ideal harmony to which Adam and Eve aspire is difficult to
sustain. The issue of sovereignty recurs on several occasions. Eve assumes
an active and energetic role in debate, but I cannot share Jean Gagen's
view that she appears superior to her husband in intelligence. Eve has
only a little in common with such comic heroines as Florimell and Jacinta;
she is not particularly witty, sexy, or irrepressible, but seriously preoccupied with the apparently insoluble problem of combining love and inde-
pendence. She is more like the Cleopatra of *All for Love,* for in both cases
we are aware of the personal and emotional needs which explain and, to a
degree, justify their strategies. Her speeches of passion lack the imaginative and tender lyricism which Milton gives to the words of Eve in Book
IV; it is Dryden's Adam who speaks of the way heaven and nature celebrate their love, while Eve talks in semimystical language (reminiscent of
Dryden's dedication) of erotic trembling, warmth, and ecstatic trance—a
"sweet tumult" of joys in which the self is lost (DW, p. 438). Unlike
Milton's Eve, who is a gracious hostess in her reception of the angelic
visitor and who listens quietly to his stories of war in heaven and creation,
Dryden's Eve finds Raphael's glory too much for her "aking sense" (DW,
p. 443) and departs, leaving her husband to encounter the flood of light
alone.

In representing the events leading to the Fall, Dryden selects episodes from Milton's narrative and handles them in a way which suggests
that Adam and Eve lack a clear sense of direction and are drifting toward
destruction. The line between innocent deliberation and self-serving ratio-
nalization is sometimes blurred. Milton uses Eve's dream as the opportunity for revealing her inner life and her response to evil, but Dryden
simplifies the episode for stage presentation, cutting out many of the
narrative and dialogic elements found in the epic source. His treatment
(III, i) is shaped by his decision to dramatize the dream as a kind of
masque, so that a woman "habited" like Eve and a seeming angel act out

the story while Eve herself sleeps and Lucifer whispers at her ear. The temptation is thus put in the present and externalized, and the music and spectacle which attract Eve are shown directly to the audience rather than being recounted by Eve in a retrospective story of the dream (in the epic she recalls the "love-labour'd song" of the nightingale, and the "pleasing light" of the moon). If, as Winn complains, Dryden's episode is less than serious about the great theological issues of temptation and pride,[23] so too is Milton's, both writers leaving these issues until the waking Eve is directly confronted by the arguments of Satan. The discovery of Lucifer by the angel guards leads next to a debate. The explanation of how dreams occur through the operation of mimic fancy, which in the epic comprises part of the reassurance and advice given to Eve by Adam, is in the opera transferred to Lucifer at the outset of the episode in order to prepare us to witness the masque (DW, p. 440). Adam's comment after the dream consists of only four lines in which he expresses anxiety and prays that heaven avert any "dire presages" to their enemies (DW, p. 443). This is an embattled Adam.

The visit of Raphael and Gabriel (IV, i) is designed to educate Adam in the importance of preventing "ills from within" by the use of reason (DW, p. 444). Adam's attitude during this discussion has repeatedly caused surprise and doubt. He is sober and uncertain, preoccupied with the will but sicklied o'er with the pale cast of thought, and deeply concerned about the fairness of the conditions under which he is to be tried. Against Raphael he argues that foreknowledge and free will are not compatible as attributes of God. Dryden appears to be raising the issues of the Hobbes-Bramhall debate concerning necessitarianism, and critics are not agreed whether he leans to the latter's affirmation of free will within providential design or leaves the matter open for the reader to decide.[24] Certainly the discussion, with its doubts and paradoxes and contradictions, is quite different in effect from the firm account of free will in the corresponding passage from the Heavenly Council of Book III of *Paradise Lost*. Rational biblicism has been replaced by scholastic dialectic.

What is curious is Adam's anxious expression of vulnerability. He argues his case persistently and cleverly. He appears deeply disturbed by the implication that God might foresee man's fall and yet refrain from preventing it. When the angels fly up in their cloud, Adam is left lamenting and dissatisfied: "Why am I not ty'd up from doing ill?" (DW, p. 446). Freedom makes him uneasy, querulous, and his objections to it clearly arise from his wish to reject responsibility. Unlike Milton's Adam, he has a lively sense of the likelihood that man will fall, and he seems rather bitter in his view that it would be better to be "constrain'd to good." An Adam who sees his condition as a "hard state of life" appears to have abandoned completely Milton's justification of God's ways and to speak rather as one who knows only the fallen condition.

Adam's sense of impotence reaches a crisis after he fails to restrain Eve through persuasion and permits her to go out alone to meet trial. During their argument love sentiment is given more direct expression than in the epic source. Eve, embracing Adam at the fatal moment of parting, says "I find / Thou lovs't; because to love is to be kind" (DW, p. 448). Milton's Eve, by contrast, concentrates on the ethics of trial, leaving the question of feeling to implication and to the comments of the narrator ("As one who loves, and some unkindness meets," IX, 273). In a short soliloquy after her departure Adam echoes the argument which the Miltonic Adam of Book VIII addresses to Raphael as he dwells on Eve's power over him: "Reason itself turns folly when she speaks" (DW, p. 448). But the fact that he is talking to himself, not confiding in another, makes all the difference.

Dryden's depiction of the Fall itself stresses Eve's aggressive curiosity and Adam's deliberate resolve. The long, meditative speeches of *Paradise Lost* are replaced by exchanges of argument between two characters, so that the Fall seems less an interior event than the result of a debate. The effect is strengthened by the way his Eve talks with a human figure, "some other Adam," as she thinks (DW, p. 450), and not with a monstrous and magical snake. She turns up at the tree on her own initiative, rather than being led there by the wiles of the serpent. The trial of Eve follows the epic fairly closely (IV, i), although the final oration of Satan is here broken into parts in order to create a dialogue in which the tempter's words are interrupted by Eve's protests. Lucifer stresses sovereignty, and in the first moments after her fall (V, i), Eve thinks that perhaps she will not share her crime with Adam after all, since " 'Tis in my pow'r to be Sovereign now," and "Empire is Sweet" (DW, p. 452). She is flippant and foolishly greedy ("I love the wretch," she remarks airily), but her brief speeches do not catch the winding and corrosive process of corruption expressed in the soliloquies of Milton's Eve.

Adam's fall is presented by Dryden through a dialogic exchange in which Adam proceeds in stages to his decision. This disperses some of the tragic force Milton achieves by making Adam's first speech after Eve's fall a soliloquy revealing that his decision is already made. A lover who can take the time to persuade himself that love comes before all is less moving than one who is wholly absorbed in the fear of loss and chooses without deliberation. Milton's subtle dramatization of the taint of egoism in Adam's love is also absent from Dryden's treatment.

Dryden's couple now commit themselves to a pact of love and death in the high style of romantic suicides. The rhetoric anticipates *All for Love:* "We're both immortal, while so well we love" asserts Eve, and Adam responds, "We'll take up all before, and death shall find / We have drain'd life, and left a void behind" (DW, p. 435). This is an interesting addition to Milton's story, putting into heroic dialogue what is only suggested by the narrator's comments in the epic (IX, 1009–11).

Soon deflated and terrified by divine thunder and descending angels, they discuss their plight. Eve's observations are sharp and witty, yet off-center and wayward. It is Eve who says they cannot shun the piercing sight of God who "from dark chaos stroke the sparks of light" (DW, p. 456), thus displaying her lively sense of God's creative power. But when Adam rebukes her, she takes refuge in self-pity, speaking like a jilted mistress as she reflects on the "curs'd vassalage" of women (DW, p. 456). In the heated exchange which follows, Eve develops a misandry to match Adam's misogyny, and the upshot is a rousing Restoration battle of wits about the "unhappiest of creation," "this helplesse ayd call'd wife" (DW, p. 437). Sovereignty and responsibility are the chief issues again in this scene of quarreling and reconciliation. Eve accuses Adam of failing to act on "Th' Authority you boast . . . Sovereign-like," and Adam retaliates by accusing woman of "boundless will" (DW, p. 456). The double reversal in this scene is carefully managed. As in *Paradise Lost*, Eve is stunned by Adam's misogynistic outburst, and kneels to seek pardon, taking full blame upon herself. But her speech does not immediately effect a change in Adam. Instead, Samson-like, he offers only cold forgiveness ("I pardon you; but see my face no more," DW, p. 457) then warms to a smug conceit, until finally and swiftly he undergoes his own painful moment of recognition: "Forgive me; I am more in fault than you" (DW, p. 458). In *Paradise Lost* the mending of the marriage is the first step toward the healing of man's relations with God, but there is little to suggest this pattern in Dryden's version.

Dryden's treatment of the reeducation of man by an angelic visitor differs from Milton's in a number of important ways. Raphael continues to act as instructor, and both Adam and Eve receive his lessons. However they are not, as in *Paradise Lost*, educated in a discipline of faith that would prepare them for trial. Rather they are led to surrender the illusions of heroic effort and to resign themselves to a life of temperate passivity, waiting in the expectation that at death they will melt into a state of deathless pleasure. During the scene, Adam seems to have lost the intellectual drive that marked his earlier speeches. He is first resigned and dependent, then eager to embrace the mercy of God but stung by his own betrayal of his descendents. Eve, however, begins by asking provocative questions and making challenging evaluations, and she does so in language which recalls speeches uttered by Adam in *Paradise Lost*. She does not, like Milton's Eve, entertain the possibility of self-destruction; rather when Raphael appears she rejects Adam's despondent acceptance of his punishment in words spoken by Milton's Adam in his dark soliloquy of lamentation: "Did we solicit Heav'n to mould our clay?" (DW, p. 458). Adam counters by drawing an answer from the same soliloquy: "Should we a rebel-son's excuse receive / Because he was begat without his leave?" Stunned by Raphael's stern words concerning exile, toil, and domestic thralldom, Eve's spirit begins to fail; she rallies briefly during the visions of death, protesting that life is forced on man, then lapses into grief at the sight of "our dead" (DW, p. 460). Adam then takes the initiative by asking if there is not a more "kindly" manner of returning to clay, and is told that there is and that it lies in the life of temperance. Eve agrees with him that they should seek this natural course and "melt away" (DW, p. 461).

Raphael moves from the picture of death after a temperate life (drawn from the beginning of Michael's history in Book XI of *Paradise Lost*) to a final scene showing the deathless pleasures of heaven, and thus he omits any reference to salvation by Christ, to the love that perfects faith, and to the higher heroism exemplified by the redeemer. He seems oddly lacking in the homiletic impulse, restricting the lessons of repentance to three brief phrases, and leaving an impression of the inevitability of history which might lend support to Adam's earlier doubts concerning free will. At the close Adam does not look back at the lost garden but takes comfort in the vision of heavenly joy that he has been granted. In this version of the *felix culpa*, the blessed are removed from the realm of fate, time, and sorrow, so that their joy becomes self-sufficient and changeless. The expectations once centered on romantic love are fulfilled here. This final vision does not stress the importance of the trial of faith and love in time on earth, but only the surrender of life through the easy way of temperance followed by revival and deathless pleasure. Raphael's prophecy of a paradise within does not seem particularly relevant to this world-surrendering Adam.

Like Milton, Dryden gives the final human words to Eve, but her speech of farewell is quite different from the speech with which her epic namesake greets her husband and prepares for trial. Milton's Eve has a mind and imagination restored by dreams and by faith. Dryden's Eve, by contrast, expresses pathos. Her words draw on those of Milton's Eve in Book XI, during her first rush of despair at the news of banishment. Dryden's version is less precise and less tender than the original, however, and generates a more strident and heroic sense of loss through its repetitions, which recall Satan's farewell to the happy fields of heaven in the epic. "Farthest from what I once enjoy'd, is best" (DW, p. 462), she concludes, with a curious echo of words spoken in quite a different mood by Milton's Satan.

In spite of life-long interest in the epic, Dryden did not succeed in writing one himself. Instead he developed new forms of satire, heroic drama, and panegyric. His innovations involved epic ingredients, and Milton contributed to the development of his style, imagery, and strategy in these modes. While he admired Milton's greatness, he never entirely accepted *Paradise Lost* as a successful expression of the epic genre, probably feeling that much of his own work expressed the same formal and generic dislocations which Milton's poem had introduced. *Paradise Lost* does not embody the epic paradigm employed in Dryden's later criticism, a paradigm Dryden himself realized in his writing only indirectly through the translation of the *Aeneid*.

The State of Innocence shows Dryden coping with some of these issues at a relatively early stage in his career. It is an original work, and it is marked by both dramatic and intellectual vitality, but some of its best effects are not Miltonic: they arise out of Dryden's preoccupations and are expressed in his distinctive voice. He did pick up certain innovations inherent in Milton's telling of the story—the original view of the state of innocence, with its humanizing of Adam and Eve, the subtle treatment of the sovereignty theme—but these he developed in a more naturalistic style which employs debate in order to represent the shifting movements of feeling. The new emphasis in depicting human nature was also accompanied by a change of argument: no longer a justification of the ways of God to man, Dryden's opera omits the Christian doctrine that was crucial to Milton's epic and also the context of biblical allusion and exegesis in which that doctrine was embedded.

The result is a fresh treatment of the story so central to Christian civilization, one that brings the myth into a more direct relation to the contemporary world of the author. While less comprehensive and less satisfying aesthetically, Dryden's retelling expresses the new age, and a comparison of the two versions illuminates the revolution in sensibility that is taking place as Dryden writes. In Dryden's world, grace does not operate intimately, but at arm's length. Sceptical concern about the weakness of reason is no longer balanced by faith in its rectification by the spirit. Human endeavor, troubled by the dichotomy of mind and matter, labors to escape chaos by acts of creativity, but in the end must recognize its own destructive bent and accept the restraints of temperance and patience.

At the heart of the change is a new attitude to the representation of events in time. Dryden abandons the mode of thinking and feeling illustrated by Milton's characters, including his narrator. Their speech represents a process which is meditative, introspective, and interpretative. They engage in an exploration of the self which requires an effort to understand and apply the words of God, and which searches through time past, present and future, seeking the fulfillment of those words. These are habits of representation which connect Milton with the devotional poets of the first half of the century and perhaps with some of the nonconformist writers of the years following the Restoration. Dryden, on the other hand, avoids the long speech of reflection and seeks to create sharply defined debate tied to a line of action which is sequential and which evokes values in an immediate present without much reference to evolving historical consciousness or a providential view of history. His argument centers on the human—man's confusion and weakness, man's repentance and resolve—in a life troubled by the interplay of sense and reason. Dryden must have been aware, at least in part, of how "tagging" the verses of his great predecessor involved wrenching the poetic narrative in a new direction to express new literary and cultural aims. The problem of how to realize these aims in terms of his conception of epic genre was one that he never solved.

University of Toronto

NOTES

1. Bruce King, *Dryden's Major Plays* (Edinburgh, 1966), p. 115; James Anderson Winn, *John Dryden and His World* (New Haven, 1987), p. 265; Jean Gagen, "Anomalies in Eden: Adam and Eve in Dryden's *The State of Innocence*," in *Milton's Legacy in the Arts*, ed. Albert C. Labriola and Edward Sichi, Jr. (University Park, 1988), p. 147. On the other hand, Morris Freedman in "The 'Tagging' of *Paradise Lost:* Rhyme in Dryden's *The State of Innocence*," *MQ* V (1971), 18, remarks that the opera is, "in so many ways unusual for Dryden, a botch" (in support of his negative assessment he refers to the opinions of A. W. Verrall and David Masson); and Earl Miner, in "Dryden's Admired Acquaintance, Mr. Milton," in *Milton Studies*, vol. XI, ed. B. Rajan (Pittsburgh, 1978), p. 10, writes that it was "fundamentally misguided and often seems strained or flat," while conceding that "there are good things also."

2. For accounts of this meeting, see *Early Lives of Milton*, ed. Helen Darbishire (London, 1937), pp. 7, 335, 396. Morris Freedman, in "Dryden's 'Memorable Visit' to

Milton," *HLQ* XVIII (1955), 99–108, argues that the most likely source of the anecdote is Dryden himself (p. 105).

3. Reported by Dryden in the preface to *Fables Ancient and Modern* (1700), in *The Poems and Fables of John Dryden*, ed. James Kinsley (London, 1962), p. 521.

4. Winn notes Dryden's financial and political troubles in the period immediately preceding composition of *The State of Innocence* which also seems to have been a time of literary uncertainty as he reconsidered his career. See *Dryden and His World*, pp. 244–48, 265.

5. "Points" are mentioned in Richardson's account of the meeting which explains that "the Fashion was in those days to wear much Ribbon, which some Adorn'd with Taggs of Metal at the Ends." Darbishire, *Early Lives*, p. 296.

6. Morris Freedman, in "Milton and Dryden on Rhyme," *HLQ* XXIV (1961), 337–44, argues that Milton's note on the verse of *Paradise Lost* comprehends the issues of the Dryden-Howard exchange, often using the same phraseology and formulations, a view questioned by Miner, "Dryden's Admired Acquaintance, Mr. Milton," p. 6.

7. Cited from *John Milton: Complete Poems and Major Prose*, ed. Merritt Y. Hughes (Indianapolis, 1980), pp. 209–10. Milton's poetry is also cited from this edition. Those who think Marvell refers directly to Dryden's project include David Masson in *The Life of Milton*, 7 vols. (1881–94; rpt. Gloucester, Mass., 1965), vol. VI, pp. 715–16; A. W. Verity, ed., *Paradise Lost* (Cambridge, 1910), p. 366; H. M. Margoliouth, ed., *The Poems and Letters of Andrew Marvell*, 2 vols. (1927; rpt. Oxford, 1952), vol. I, pp. 131–32. Freedman, in "Dryden's 'Memorable Visit' to Milton," p. 101, thinks that Marvell is referring to the revision which was in circulation, not to the anecdote of the meeting. Joseph Anthony Wittreich, Jr., questions the relevance of Dryden's project in "Perplexing the explanation: Marvell's 'On Mr. Milton's Paradise lost,' " in *Approaches to Marvell*, ed. C. A. Patrides (London, 1978), pp. 280–305.

8. *The Works of John Dryden*, ed. H. T. Swedenberg, Jr., et al. (Berkeley and Los Angeles, 1956–), vol. XI, ed. John Loftis and David Stuart Rhodes (1978), p. 432. The California Press edition of Dryden's works will be used where possible and referred to as W, subsequent reference being made to the following volumes in addition to volume XI: vol. II, ed. H. T. Swedenberg Jr. (1972); vol. III, ed. Earl Miner (1969); vol. IV, ed. A. B. Chambers and William Frost (1987); vol. XIII, ed. Maximillian E. Novak (1984); vol. XV, ed. Earl Miner (1976). The prefatory poem by S[amuel] B[arrow] also stresses the sublimity of *Paradise Lost* ("*grandia magni / Carmina* Miltoni,") but with particular emphasis on the war in heaven and the triumph of the Son. See Michael Lieb, "S. B.'s in 'Paradisum Amissam': Sublime Commentary," *MQ* XIX (1985), 71–78.

9. See John Dryden, "The Defense of the Epilogue to the Second Part of *The Conquest of Granada*" (1668), in W, vol. XI, pp. 203–18. For later examples of such criticism see Dryden's "Preface to *Troilus and Cressida*," W, vol. XIII, p. 225, and preface to *Fables Ancient and Modern* in *The Poems and Fables of John Dryden*, pp. 528–29.

10. On Dryden's view of Miltonic heroism, see Dustin Griffin, *Regaining Paradise: Milton in the Eighteenth Century* (Cambridge, 1986), p. 153; on his use of Milton's epic as a contemporary classic to be alluded to and otherwise used for norms of value, see Miner, "Dryden's Admired Acquaintance, Mr. Milton," pp. 10–25.

11. John Dennis, *Original Letters*, 2 vols. (1721), vol. I, p. 75, letter dated 25 May 1719 and addressed to Judas Iscariot, Esq., cited in *The Life Records of John Milton*, Joseph Milton French, 5 vols. (New Brunswick, N.J., 1949–58), vol. V, p. 48.

12. Winn, *Dryden and His World*, pp. 267–69.

13. Bernard Harris, " 'That soft seducer, love': Dryden's *The State of Innocence and*

the *Fall of Man*," in *Approaches to "Paradise Lost"*, ed. C. A. Patrides (Toronto, 1968), p. 125. Lee echoes the language with which Dryden speaks of creation as the ordering of chaotic materials, as in the dedication of *The Rival Ladies*.

14. Nathaniel Lee, "To Mr. Dryden, on His Poem of Paradise," in *The Dramatic Works of John Dryden*, ed. Montague Summers, 6 vols. (London, 1931), vol. III, 415–16. Citations from the preliminary matter to *The State of Innocence*, as well as from the opera itself, are from volume III, subsequently referred to as DW.

15. See Winn, *Dryden and His World*, p. 296.

16. In the month when Dryden registered his opera, the Dryden-Davenant version of *The Tempest* was performed with music by Matthew Locke and others and with alterations by Shadwell. Shadwell's *Psyche*, which has been called the archetypal dramatic opera, was performed in 1675, but seems to have been in preparation since 1673. It was itself an adaptation of a French *Tragedie-ballet* staged in Paris in 1671. As Robert D. Hume observes, English opera in the seventeenth century is a miscellany form; it did not achieve a sense of direction in the century, not even when Purcell made his contribution. See Hume, *The Development of English Drama in the Late Seventeenth Century* (1976; rpt. Oxford, 1990), p. 207. For discussion of musical drama in the period, see Curtis Alexander Price, *Henry Purcell and the London Stage* (Cambridge, 1984); Allardyce Nicoll, *A History of Restoration Drama: 1600–1700* (1923; rpt. Cambridge, 1928); E. W. White, *The Rise of English Opera* (London, 1951); W, vol. XV, pp. 336–55.

17. As P. S. Havens observes in "Dryden's 'Tagged' Version of *Paradise Lost*," in *Essays in Dramatic Literature: The Parrott Presentation Volume*, ed. Hardin Craig (Princeton, 1935), p. 386, the five act structure of *The State of Innocence* follows the progression from Protasis to Epitasis, Catastasis and Catastrophe which Dryden records in his *Essay on Dramatic Poetry*.

18. Dryden's distinctive diction includes terms that recall his earlier plays of conquest, such as *slave* and *colonies;* that are more specific than Milton's such as *orange, peach, guava, jessamine* (the last used in *Lycidas*); that carry stronger connotations of our world than Milton normally allows in Eden, such as *partner of my bed, the bending crutch;* that convey new attitudes to sexual relations, such as *softer sex, the wretch, blast*.

19. This phrase and the next are from Milton's note "On the Verse" of *Paradise Lost*. Dryden's criticism of Milton's ear for rhyme is curiously balanced by the opinion of the early Dryden which Milton's widow Elizabeth is said to have attributed to her husband: "no poet, but a good rimist." *Life Records*, vol. V, p. 323.

20. Havens, "Dryden's 'Tagged Version' of *Paradise Lost*," p. 396.

21. Anne Davidson Ferry, *Milton and the Miltonic Dryden* (Cambridge, Mass., 1968), p. 89.

22. Jean Gagen, "Anomalies in Eden," p. 137. Gagen argues that Eve is "assigned a sovereignty over Adam which is considered just and right, not only by her and Adam but by their angelic master as well." This reading of the angel's account ignores the stress he places on the mutual concern which Adam and Eve should show for each other.

23. James Anderson Winn, *"When Beauty Fires the Blood": Love & the Arts in the Age of Dryden* (Ann Arbor, 1992), p. 222.

24. See King, *Dryden's Major Plays*, pp. 95–115.

WHEN GOD PROPOSES:
THEOLOGY AND GENDER IN
TETRACHORDON

Elizabeth Hodgson

IN MILTON'S PENULTIMATE divorce tract *Tetrachordon*, the function of God, men, and women in proposing marriage and then disposing of the marital bond is both immediately obvious and extraordinarily opaque. Since Milton argues from Saint Augustine and from Théodore de Bèze, from civil, legal, and natural precedent, from scripture and from anecdotal evidence, determining the ideological underpinnings of the tract seems a herculean task. To see through and into Milton's deepest strategies only becomes more possible when we focus on the exegetical tactics and theoretical case studies which pervade the text and which help Milton to characterize those marriages which justify divorce. The most important of these themes is Milton's emphasis on a prevalent kind of marriage in which two good but irrevocably unsuited individuals become un"help"ful to each other, only to be saved by a gracious divine law. It is this picture of deserving spouses redeemed by God's just edict which seems analogous to, or part of, Milton's Arminianist insistence on the availability of God's grace to the seeking (and deserving) human. Indeed, this Arminianism of *Tetrachordon* seems one of its defining characteristics. Christopher Hill argues that Milton "needed Arminianism to save God. . . . [he] substitut[ed] for the Calvinist God of arbitrary power an Arminian God of goodness, justice and reasonableness" (p. 275).[1] The tract's model of the sinned-against married couple and God's (Milton's) reasonable response to their undeserved misery seems, in many ways, to support this reading. But, as we will see, the tract's model of gender in marriage fits neither Hill's vision of the Arminianist Milton nor Milton's own claim of charity for husbands *and* wives.

I

Before we can develop this argument we must first clarify what in Milton's tract we can read as Calvinist and what we can read as Arminianist. Needless to say (witness the historians' war on this subject), any

133

such clarification will be reductive and provisional at best.[2] But Milton is not explicitly participating in the complex tangle of arguments over communion tables and altars, sacramentalism, pre- or postlapsarian predestination, Episcopalianism or liturgy, which raged within and between these two ideological schools in the 1640's. So since Calvinism and Arminianism function rather as general analogies in *Tetrachordon,* perhaps a fairly simple set of principles can guide us here.

We should start by reminding ourselves that in the discourse of Milton's culture Arminianism and Calvinism *shared* a belief that their theology depicted a merciful and charitable God.[3] Calvin figures predestination as a "very sweet fruit" (p. 921); God's power to elect the saints, as the Westminster Assembly asserted in the 1640's, was supposed to be a sign of his "free grace and love" (III, v).[4] Arminius likewise stresses that "God presides over the whole world . . . not only in justice, but also in mercy" (III, 286), a mercy allowing sinners to be redeemed by contingent grace.[5] Where these theologies differ is in their sense of how powerful God is in relation to human beings and in how they think God's charity manifests itself. In striving to define more strongly the Reformed antidote for the Roman doctrine of works, Calvin's theology of predestination insists upon God's total control of human destiny. Double predestination, in Calvin's foundational articulation of it, means that God has preordained some people for salvation and others for damnation. In trying to oppose the Roman church's proposal that one work one's way out of purgatory, Calvin in the *Institutes* suggests that "God has ordained some to salvation, others to destruction" (p. 920) in a "plan . . . founded . . . without regard to human worth" (p. 931), "utterly disregarding works" (p. 921). The *Westminster Confession* uses similar language: "by the decree of God, for the manifestation of His glory, some men and angels are predestined unto everlasting life; and others foreordained to everlasting death. . . . without any . . . thing in the creature . . . moving Him thereunto" (III, iii, iv). Calvinism insists upon the utter depravity of the human will, arguing that God alone can determine election or reprobation. Seventeenth-century English Calvinism stressed divine sovereignty, then, reminding its followers of their inability to effect or even affect their own salvation—or damnation. Arminianism in contrast asserts the importance of human free will as well as divine grace. Arminius argues that God's mercy is manifested in grace given to individuals to redeem their own wills, by which argument he emphasizes God's mercy and grace acting locally, not in the predetermined moment of election alone. And Arminius above all argues that we must not characterize God in such a way that we "take away *the free will to that which is evil*" (II, p. 473). As Robert Shelford argues in the 1630's,

"God . . . hath given to man free will, and to maintain this he hath ordained contingencie and added his grace" (Tyacke, p. 53). Arminius declares that God "can not have the right to condemn to eternal punishment a man unless he has become a sinner" (III, p. 320); in this Arminius not only rejects absolute election and reprobation but also stresses that God's divine sovereignty and charity operate according to certain principles of *reason*, obeying certain identifiable laws and subject to the actions of the human will. While Calvin and Calvinist theology assert the absolute absence of any restraints on God's actions, Arminius and Arminianism are prepared to discuss what "the divine right does not permit" (Arminius III, p. 320). So Calvinists would explain that we cannot work our way to heaven because human nature is incapable of the slightest redemptive action; only God, in his great and unsearchable wisdom, has the power to declare us elect or reprobate, and he has done so before or at the beginning of time. The puritan doctrine of "calling" is an extension of this concept; our life's work is also predetermined by God. Arminianists would explain that God chose to give his human creatures free will and that God will not impinge upon his own principled commitment to human liberty of action, though his grace is always available. Arminianism's view of Christ is an extension of this: in *response* to Adam's choice in the Garden of Eden, God offered grace through Jesus.

If we are to apply these principles to *Tetrachordon*, we can find many strategies and arguments that suggest that this tract has a distinctly Arminianist bent. In the tract Milton persistently argues that good civil law, theological exegesis, natural reason and divine will do coincide, as he tries to demonstrate in his long appendix on civil precedents for his proposed divorce law. Milton has an Arminianist confidence that "all sense, and law, and honesty, and therefore surely . . . the meaning of Christ" (p. 621) follow from and define each other in this case.[6] To this end, Milton contrasts images of England's unreasonable, deterministic and judgmental code with his own promise of a scripturally instituted and divinely reasonable divorce plan to which the married couple deserves access. As well as constructing a *reasonable* and gracious God, these images and Milton's scriptural exegeses echo Arminius's own stress on the dignity of human beings and the importance of free will and "contingencie [standing] with the Holy Scripture, against the men which attribute all to fate and necessity" (Tyacke, p. 53).[7]

But Milton's genuinely Arminianist arguments which implicitly oppose Calvinist determinism also take on a certain Calvinist cast of their own in *Tetrachordon*. And this confusion of what seemed opposing ideologies will finally have its most important causes and effects in Milton's central discussions of husbands and wives. It is this intersection between gender and theology which will be the central thrust of my argument; I will increasingly focus on Milton's problematic Calvinisms because their existence in the text becomes such a powerful tool in his depictions of bad wives. We will see that while Milton may attack anti-Arminianist views throughout the tract, his discussions of wives often invoke the powerful and distinctively Calvinist concept of absolute reprobation. In particular we will find striking and disconcerting moments where God's contingent grace actually seems to depend upon an insistence that the wife who doesn't fulfill her calling should be put away to allow the other spouse his destined liberty. Whatever Milton claims about the "good of both sexes," then, a kind of predestinarian language of failed calling and reprobation often creeps into his argument precisely when he deals with the unwifely wife. That coincidence achieves the level of exegetical argument in the tract's concluding discussion of 1 Corinthians vii, a discussion which retrospectively interprets those moments when wives are condemned for the sake of men's freedoms.

In addition to, or rather even as part of, his insistence on contingent divine grace as the sovereign source of liberty from marriage, we will see Milton invoking a gendered and judgmental predestinarianism. So although Milton seems to have reason to emphasize the liberating empowerment of his proposal for no-fault divorce, we must resist the temptation to see this as a vindication of either Milton or Arminianism. For Milton's free will for men at least partly depends upon a divinely inspired reprobation for wives. Milton's emphasis on "the just mans right and privilege, . . . [and] the afflicted mans necessity" (p. 644) excludes wives from such divine justice or mercy. As we will see, the model of arbitrary divine power which had its cultural uses for the committed puritans of Milton's era also has its function here. *Tetrachordon* thus models, but only for husbands, a God who graciously and reasonably proposes divorce.

II

Of course to argue that *Tetrachordon* is ultimately and consistently hostile to "bad" wives is to risk contributing to the increasing use of the divorce tracts as ammunition in the battle over Milton's poetic idea of woman. The debate over *Paradise Lost* and Eve has been extended to the tracts on marriage and divorce which Milton wrote some thirty years earlier; critics attacking and defending Milton's views of women in *Paradise Lost* have by now developed clearly held positions on Milton's divorce tracts which often come as much from their interest in Milton's epic as from their interest in the tracts themselves.[8]

Despite a welcome recent upsurge of interest in Milton's prose in and of itself, to write on gender in the tracts is also to risk being pulled into one of the opposing critical camps which still have a remarkable homogeneity.[9] Most feminist critics accuse Milton defenders of eliding the central question of sexual politics in the divorce tracts; the political allegory invoked by the Yale edition is but one example cited of the historical tendency to metaphorize men and women in these texts.[10] Stephen Fallon's 1990 study describes the generations of "readers [who] have seen the divorce tracts as pivotal works in which Milton redefines his thoughts on Christian liberty, freedom of the will, and Church government" without reference to their central concern with gender and marriage.[11] Most feminist critics would also argue that many scholars absolve Milton by focusing only on his generosity toward wives and his pleas for "the companionate marriage" (Nyquist, p. 99); they complain that Milton's promise on the title page of *Doctrine and Discipline of Divorce* that his text is written "for the good of both sexes" is mistakenly seen as definitive (and as evidence for Eve's equality with Adam in *Paradise Lost*).[12]

Feminist criticism of the tracts has tended to counter this argument by pointing out Milton's "ugly" images of women (Fallon, p. 78), the "rage, petulant accusation, and violent disdain" (Turner, *One Flesh*, p. 229) which are undoubtedly present in the divorce pamphlets and which later appear in Adam's postlapsarian misogyny.[13] Much feminist criticism seeks to explode critical faith in Milton's generous radicalism. Annabel Patterson declares that " 'the good of both sexes' is a claim easily refuted by today's readers of both sexes, who quickly discover the passages of masculinist bias that, no matter what happened later in *Paradise Lost*, cannot be explained away" (p. 85).[14]

Tetrachordon has been the site of much of the feminist/antifeminist debate precisely because it is so rife with temptingly contradictory statements; Fallon perceptively notes how Milton's text is full of dramatic shifts in tone and temper (Fallon, p. 79). But simply to gather up such often-contradicted evidence from the tract to support either view of Milton is to participate in the tendency of this controversy rapidly to degenerate into a "severely restricted . . . debate on Milton and sexual politics" (Nyquist, p. xiv).

I would like to model a theory that it is easiest to understand the roots of Milton's advocacy for human dignity and also his misogyny when we adopt the strengths of both critical schools. Focusing on the relations between the sexes in Milton's work while also considering those genealogies of spiritual culture which intellectual historians emphasize will make it possible to explain Milton's curiously contradictory positions on theology and on women.[15] We can perhaps begin to see that in this tract the virulent judgmentalism so often perceived in Milton's discussions of women is strangely connected to what seems his ideological commitment to human dignity and free will. Whether this connection, this coexistence of seemingly contradictory positions, has implications for the misogynist hostility expressed by Adam or Samson is a question for another study or studies; but we may at least begin to understand this particular effort of Milton's to create a theological frame for such a dynamic.

III

As we begin our discussion of *Tetrachordon* it is important first to understand precisely how Milton constructs the charitable side of his argument for divorce; this is the foundation of his tract and the point from which his gendered attacks will eventually emanate. On the title page of this tract, Milton defines *Tetrachordon*'s topic as "Mariage, or nullities in Mariage," framing divorce itself as an absence of marriage (unlike the *Doctrine and Discipline of Divorce* tract). In doing so, Milton emphasizes the importance of his marriage model and his discussion of the married couple. Indeed, throughout the tract Milton builds his case by creating a model of the marriages which deserve divorce, a model which he will go on to buttress with biblical exegeses. In this scenario of marital woe Milton repeatedly asserts that the couple are blameless and deserving of liberty; this argument is particularly resonant with the Arminianist view of human nature. And to bolster this view Milton criticizes current divorce law, depicting it as an anti-Arminianist institution in which the married couple are constrained by an arbitrary and deterministic legalism.

Whenever Milton argues for divorce through describing this type of marriage, he begs for grace on behalf of the spouses by describing either participant as a "faultles person" (p. 631), a "best spirit" (p. 632), a "blame-lesse" soul (p. 667), "without fault" (p. 613). The "mistake in choosing" is "irreprehensible" (p. 601); in fact, the spouses are not sinning but sinned against, "defrauded of all this originall benignity" (p. 601). These are ones whom "only error, casualty, art or plot hath joynd" (p. 622); they are united "by one mishapp, and no willing trespas of theirs" (p. 632) in "an accidental conjunction of this or that man & woman" (p. 622). Milton's Arminianist work here is to restore the married couple to a position of dignity and worth. Indeed, he says in the opening section of the tract that "nothing now adayes is more degenerately forgott'n, then the true dignity of man, . . . especially in this prime institution of Matrimony" (p. 587).

In order to mitigate our disapprobation of the unhappily married couple, Milton insists upon the pain caused by an unhappy marriage. He repeatedly depicts and emphasizes the horrible results of this kind of union:

Then follows dissimulation, suspicion, fals colours, fals pretences, and wors then these, disturbance, annoyance, vexation, sorrow, temtation eevn . . . then comes disorder, neglect, hatred, and perpetual strife. (P. 631)

We see in the following passage the degree to which marriage law, and not either spouse, becomes the principal agent of misery:

It . . . leaves [the married couple] . . . to unsettl'd imaginations, and degraded hopes, careles of themselvs, their houshold and their freinds, unactive to all public service, dead to the Common-wealth . . . outlaw'd from all the benefits and comforts of married life and posterity. (P. 632)

As a way of heightening his characterization, Milton insinuates that this type of conjugality is harmful not only to individuals but also to the state, for it creates persons who are "dead to the Common-wealth."[16] Though we should not be misled into thinking that the tract is an allegory about peace in the Commonwealth, Milton clearly recognizes the potential for such an analogy and its power for his parliamentary audience.

To evoke further our sympathy for the unhappily bound couple, Milton in good polemical fashion paints the current English legal system as evilly deterministic because it damns his worthy couple to unending misery. Throughout the tract Milton attacks the current law as "opposite both to human and to Christian liberty" (p. 587), declaring that under it a mismatched marriage is "a remediles" (p. 631) situation, "without havn or shoar," "a ransomles captivity" (600–01). Milton declares that "staying can doe no good" (p. 623), for the unhappiness of the marriage is "perpetual" (p. 625) and entails "a whole life lost to all houshold comfort and society" (p. 629). There is "continual . . . hatred" and a "habit of wrath" (p. 631) between the spouses; there "can no more bee peace or comfort to either of them continuing thus joyn'd" (p. 621). Marital disunity is a "naturall unmeetnes" which "ever after cannot be amended" (p. 674); discord is as inevitable as the problems ensuing from putting "a peece of new cloth upon an old garment, . . . [or] new wine into old bottles" (667–68). Milton suggests that if it be not "in the nature of either, and . . . there has bin a remediles mistake, as vain wee goe about to compell them into one flesh, as if wee undertook to weav a garment of drie sand" (p. 605); the key term here is "remediles." "All the Ecclesiastical glue, that Liturgy, or Laymen can compound, is not able to soder up two such incongruous natures into the one flesh of a true beseeming Mariage" (p. 606). Milton here accuses his opponents of a Frankenstein-like attempt to play God and "soder up" bodies into a horrible imitation of the organic Christian "one flesh." Milton's persistent images of "new cloth upon an old garment," "a garment of dry sand," "a habit of wrath," suggest by contrast the tight strong weave of matched fibers in a whole marriage versus the artificial (and toxic) glue of Comus's chair, a "compelled" union. In Milton's suggestive language an unhappy marriage under current English law is as predetermined, inflexible, and void of grace as Calvinism was sometimes claimed to be. The married couple are sentenced to unending misery by the petty tyrant of governmental policy, a tyrant whose arbitrary sentences seem to mimic the God of the Calvinists as their enemies portrayed him.

IV

These dramatic depictions of inescapable misery intentionally privilege Milton's Arminianist assertion that God in fact gives human beings the freedom to choose divorce, a position which reinforces and is reinforced by the structural and argumentative emphases of the whole tract. *Tetrachordon* is a more biblically based argument than either version of the *Doctrine and Discipline of Divorce,* as its title suggests; Milton's goal in this is to make his case even more clearly dependent upon God's divine word than it was previously. He explicitly refers his central arguments back to God's institution of marriage in Genesis i and ii (Nyquist, p. 112), consistently arguing that God's charitable establishment of marriage is the single most important fact in any discussion of conjugality. Christ's word and God's law are both Milton's declared highest standard in interpreting scriptural texts on marriage, and he declares more forcefully than in any earlier tracts that the Mosaic law, because given by God, must be both infallible and authoritative in perpetuity.[17] This emphasis on God's creation of divorce supports Milton's argument that God will grant freedom of choice to human beings whose contingent experience requires an infusion of divine grace.

Milton continues this general insistence upon divine provision by declaring (in opposition to some puritan divines) that marriage is a *"divine institution"* (p. 612). In order to counter the argument that marriage is so holy as to be indissoluble (p. 624), Milton asserts that not only marriage but also divorce itself is a creation of God, "just and pure; for such is God who gave it" (p. 653).[18] At those points when Milton seems to contradict himself by describing marriage as a "civill contract" (p. 621), he does so only to emphasize how easily its commitments should therefore give way to God's divine institution of divorce, the "benignest ordinances of God to man" (p. 623) which not only permit but actively provide for the dissolution of a marriage.

Milton's assertion in his exegesis of Matthew xix that God empowers "real" marriage is but one example of how he sustains this emphasis upon God's intention to authorize free will. Milton bases much of his discussion of Matthew xix on its central phrase, "*What therefore God hath joyned, let no man put asunder*" (p. 650). Milton interprets this as "If God hath joined, let no man put asunder," i.e., marriage is only true marriage where God has facilitated a unity pleasing to the married couple. Milton says:

> shall wee say that God hath joyn'd error, fraud, unfitnesse, wrath, contention, perpetuall lonelinesse, perpetuall discord . . . hate with hate, or hate with love? (P. 650)

Milton then applies this definition of joining to separating:

> if it be, as how oft we see it may be, not of Gods joyning, and his law tells us he joynes not unmachable things but hates to joyne them, as an abominable confusion, then the divine law of *Moses* puts them asunder, his owne divine will in the institution puts them asunder, as oft as the reasons be not extant, for which only God ordain'd their joyning. (P. 651)

God thus authorizes marital success or failure through certain principles: "his law," "the divine law of Moses," "his own divine will in the institution," and finally "the reasons . . . for which only God ordain'd their joyning." Milton asserts that God "intended to found" marriage law "according to naturall reason, not impulsive command" (p. 595), and he suggests that divine divorce law is equally reasonable in protecting the freedom of individuals. Milton also asserts that to provide for human happiness God not only passively gives permission for divorce but will actively intervene and "[put] them asunder," like Moses' miraculous and salvific parting of the Red Sea.

V

Milton thus emphasizes how this reasonable Arminianist God creates and honors access to free will and reasonable choice, the same kind of free will and reason Milton claims for the divorce law which he has been proposing to the English Parliament. In *Tetrachordon*, Milton (perhaps compelled by the indifference and hostility his earlier arguments evoked) stresses *God's* reasonable and gracious provision for divorce even further than he did in previous tracts. And to emphasize by contrast his Arminianist belief in the "just mans right" (p. 644), Milton continues to imply that unhappy spouses under the current regime are victims of a judgmental and deterministic system, a system as guilty as Calvin's God of a perceived lack of grace. As we will now see, he also argues more explicitly that the present law allows couples only two chances at self-determination or choice concerning their own marriages. One is a past and irrevocable moment and the other is a current (though no less irrevocable) moment. Milton thus emphasizes again that the current unhappiness of the married couple is constructed not by themselves but by predetermined laws and narratives which constrain their free will.

Milton describes the first of these determining moments when addressing Christ's declaration in Matthew xix that "*Moses because of the hardnesse of your hearts suffered you to put away your wives, but from the beginning it was not so*" (p. 651). Milton says that "the beginning" was Paradise before the Fall, and that, "In the beginning, had men continu'd perfet, it had bin just that all things should have remain'd, as they began to *Adam & Eve*. . . . While man and woman were both perfet each to other, there needed no divorce" (p. 665). Since Adam and Eve chose to disobey God, though, their decision "alter'd the lore of justice, and put the government of things into a new frame" (p. 665). In other words, after this moment of choice in the garden of Eden (a moment of which Milton has much more to say in *Paradise Lost*), Milton's no-marriage came into being, and divorce became part of the divine provision for humanity. Note how Milton emphasizes that it was Adam and Eve's decision which "alter'd the lore of justice"; many Calvinists might hesitate to attribute so much power to the human will.[19] To Milton, then, this was one moment of human choice, where "our" decision played some part in the nature of "our" marriages. Since, Milton argues, we surrendered our innocence of our own free will, God in his charity has had to intervene on our behalf.

The one other relevant moment of human free will should (one would imagine) lie in the decision to marry. In Milton's definition of marriage he explains that until there is the consent of both parties "the mariage hath no true beeing" (p. 612). Milton then argues against the continuance of unhappy marriages by asserting that "error is not properly consent" (p. 612). Further, he argues that continuing consent to marry is itself at least partly a condition "naturally arising from the very heart of divine institution" (p. 613), the bestowal from God of "a love fitly dispos'd to mutual help and comfort of life" (p. 613). This definition of consent as God-given love means that we are only morally responsible to stay married when our marriage continues to be full of the love which makes (or marks) a divinely

instituted marriage. Milton seeks to remind his readers that God's creation of a successful marriage is contingent upon the circumstances and
experience of the married couple; if they err, if they find themselves
miserable, God collaborates with them in changing their consent to marry
into permission to divorce. Milton argues that nobody is compelled by his
or her own vows to stay married should the marriage not contain "a love
fitly dispos'd to mutual help and comfort."

VI

But now we must address the ways in which this model of God's
merciful protection of man's rightful freedom seems to shift and crack.
Tetrachordon's emphasis on a divine reason which allows and provides for
fallible human choices is plain and plainly analogous to Arminianist theologies. And when the tract describes English divorce law as prescriptive,
judgmental, and condemnatory Milton is labeling that law fundamentally
anti-Arminianist. But even in the above analyses it would be possible to
see Calvinist language in Milton's model of unalterably miserable marriages, in his emphasis on God's provisions for human beings, in his
emphasis on individuals' inability to choose wisely, and in his suggestion
that God alone makes good marriages. It would be quite possible, for
example, to argue that Milton's definition of consent makes God alone
responsible for marital destinies; if free will is so important, we might ask,
how is it that married couples' choices have so little force when it comes to
getting or staying married? Though Milton clearly intends to suggest that
the freedom to divorce is needed for his unhappily married couple, his
depiction of their immovable dislike implies that they become at some
point unable to change their relationship to one another; this invites us to
accept the concept of conjugal determinism. Likewise, when Milton declares that "there is an intimat quality of good or evil, through the whol
progeny of *Adam,* which like a radical heat, or mortal chilnes joyns them,
or disjoyns them irresistibly" (p. 606), Calvinist models of predetermined
destiny seem rather close at hand.

Beyond the sections which describe Milton's particular model of marriage, *Tetrachordon* does not insist on a strict anti-Calvinist stance. When
Milton denounces the tyranny of canon law as the work of the popish
Antichrist and ignorant monks, he makes it clear that Calvinism is not the
only ideology he is opposing; indeed, in some instances Calvin doesn't
seem to be an enemy at all. Milton's explicitly pro-Calvinist argument
against Arminius in the *Doctrine and Discipline of Divorce* (p. 294) propounds a view of the Fall which Milton replicates in *Tetrachordon*, and in

this tract he cites Calvin's exegeses in support of his own (p. 615). All of
these instances make the opposition between Calvinism and Milton's Arminianism increasingly difficult to locate.

But the most important instance of Milton's inconsistent commitment
to Arminianism has to do with wives. In a central reversal which can help us
define the tract's gendered theology, Milton adopts the strongest predestinarian language not against current law but in favour of his own—
along gendered lines. To track this shift we will first focus on what seem like
anomalous moments of vitriolic condemnation of bad wives which adopt
predestinarian categories. Then we will examine the final "string" of the
text, the final biblical passage and Milton's analysis of it, which seems
curiously out of harmony with the Arminianist sound of the argument as a
whole. In its particular emphasis on judgment and exclusion it in fact (again)
recalls one aspect of the Calvinist God important to other puritan divines
and the *Westminster Confession*.[20] In fact, this final breakdown of Milton's
argument for human freedom from necessity has a particularly specific
function, one which can connect together the moments throughout the text
where Milton seems less than gracious toward "unfit" wives. What ties
together the final section of Milton's tract and his scattered damnations is
indeed a similar and singularly un-Arminianist argument which ironically
seems to depend upon God's provisional grace. Now that we understand
how Milton attempts to make divorce a divine and contingent gift, we can
understand more precisely how Milton's God turns against bad wives.

First we should recognize that alongside the Arminianist arguments
in support of "the just mans right" in Milton's exegeses there exists a
whole series of statements which attack bad wives. These arguments reso-
nate with the Arminianist language of deserved liberty, but they also draw
on Calvinist images of failed calling and reprobation to condemn the
woman who fails to be a "meet help" (*Tetrachordon*, p. 595). The tract as a
whole certainly suggests Milton's primary focus on *male* liberties: it repeatedly refers to "our manhood in grace" (p. 636), a force lacking in those who
"*want manliness to expostulate the right of their due ransom*" (p. 585).
This gendering of grace and the "right of . . . ransom" suggests that Milton does really think of human freedom and desert as particularly masculine privileges. He tellingly explains that "although ther bee nothing in
the plain words of this Law, that seems to regard the afflictions of a
wife, . . . yet Expositers determin . . . that God was not uncompassionat
of them also" (p. 626). Such grudging admission that his argument *might*
apply to wives speaks volumes for Milton's position; they are the also-
forgiven, and indeed they are forgiven not by the primary law but by
mere "Expositers."

Beyond these brief comments, the text also begins to develop arguments which support this unequal access to God's grace. In discussing the Genesis texts Milton explains:

seeing woman was purposely made for man, and he her head, it cannot stand before the breath of this divine utterance, that man the portraiture of God, joyning to himself for his intended good and solace an inferiour sexe, should so becom her thrall, whose wilfulnes or inability to be a wife frustrates the occasionall end of her creation, but that he may acquitt himself to freedom by his naturall birthright, and that indeleble character of priority which God crown'd him with. If it be urg'd that sin hath lost him this, the answer is not far to seek, that from her the sin first proceeded. . . . She is not to gain by being first in the transgression, that man should furder loose to her, because already he hath lost by her means. (Pp. 589–90)

As Fredric Jameson has noted (p. 335), Milton strengthens man's position (and his own) by making divorce an issue of political freedom versus "thralldom," "naturall birthright" versus the willfulness of a natural inferior. In doing so Milton adopts and emphasizes the argument that the woman is inherently "less worthy" and more responsible for injuries in marriage because that is what she was made for. This emphasis on divine calling ("that indeleble character of priority which God crown'd him with") and the connected promise of God's charitable intent for Adam combine concepts from seemingly opposite theological ideologies (puritan destiny versus Arminianist grace) so as to defend the liberty of "man" while supporting the rejection of unhelpful wives.[21] Indeed, it seems here that Adam's free will comes from Eve's wifely reprobation.

Again, even while Milton speaks charitably on behalf of "the afflictions of a wife" (p. 626), he engages other theologians concerning their suggestion that divorce was instituted for women, "For certainly if man be liable to injuries in mariage, as well as woman, and man be the worthier person, it were a preposterous law to respect only the less worthy; her whom God made for mariage, and not him at all for whom mariage was made" (p. 627). Here again, Milton emphasizes Eve's calling (to be a wife) over and against Adam's Arminianist liberty. That which justifies him and his actions also predestines her and her fate.

In a more violent moment of antagonism toward the wifely other, he explains:

[Adam] might well know, if God took a rib out of his inside, to form of it a double good to him, he would far sooner dis-joyn it from his outside, to prevent a treble mischief to him: and far sooner cut it quite off . . . then nail it into his body again, to stick for ever there a thorn in his heart. . . . how much . . . is it [nature's]

146   MILTON STUDIES

doctrin to sever by incision, not a true limb so much . . . but an adherent, a sore, the gangrene of a limb, to the recovery of a whole man. (P. 602)

If the woman (Eve) is not the intended "help meet," then, she becomes a gangrenous sore to be excised so that the man can once again be a "whole man." These confused and potent images of rape and castration, phallic nail and thorn, reveal the ways in which God's grace can become, and perhaps requires, Michael's smiting sword.

   The same condemnation of woman on behalf of man's freedom occurs again, "let her bee a wife, let her be a meet help, a solace, not a nothing, not an adversary, . . . can any law or command be so unreasonable as to make men cleav to calamity, to ruin, to perdition?" (p. 605). Milton here makes an unhelpful wife into not just a fallen woman but also the hell into which men will fall (perhaps a precursor of *Paradise Lost*'s Sin) because of her. Milton's plea for a reasonable (not arbitrary) God again twists to strike at the "adversary," who is here not Satan but woman. Milton repeats this notion:

[Proverbs 30]. . . . tells us . . . that a *hated,* or a *hateful* woman, *when shee is married, is a thing for which the earth is disquieted and cannot bear it;* thus giving divine testimony to this divine Law, which bids us nothing more then is the first and most innocent lesson of nature, to turn away peaceably from that which afflicts and hazards our destruction; especially when our staying can doe no good, and is expos'd to all evil.[22] (P. 623)

Note how Milton blurs together "hated" and "hatefull"; a wife has only to be disliked to be sinful because, of course, as Perkins might say, in being disliked she has failed in her calling. Milton invokes punitive terms and applies them to a believing wife in a "fearsomely unilateral form of accusation" (Turner 221) which, ironically, Milton justifies through the same "divine testimony" and "divine law" which he elsewhere claims proposes men's free will and freedom.

VII

   The post-facto exegetical support for these passages which make grace for the husband into punishment for the wife comes in fact at the end of the tract, in Milton's discussion of 1 Corinthians vii, 10–16. The Corinthians passage does not fit the model of wedded believers Milton has been creating, for its subject is marriage between Christians and pagans. For the same reason the Pauline passage does not depend as the earlier texts do upon Milton's interpretation of God's institution of holy marriage. The Pauline text is indeed, from many perspectives, a difficult one for Milton to explain:

If any brother hath a wife that believeth not, and she be pleased to dwell with him, let him not put her away. And the woman which hath an husband that believeth not, and if he be pleased to dwell with her, let her not leave him. . . . But if the unbelieving depart, let him depart. (I Cor. vii, 12–14, Authorized Version)

Milton himself, at the end of his exegesis, says, "Thus much the Apostle on this question between Christian and Pagan, to us now of little use" (690).

Despite—or rather precisely because of—the ostensibly anomalous relationship of this passage to the others in the tract and Milton's dismissal of the text's direct relevance, this lengthy section of *Tetrachordon* is of particular importance in explaining the curious pattern of charity and judgment in the tract. In fact, as we will see, Milton's discussion of the Corinthians text allows him to justify and connect the comments hostile to 'bad' wives which he has been intermittently making through the tract. Specifically, the Apostle's discussion of believers and unbelievers, the saved and the unsaved, will allow Milton to emphasize terms of moral judgment, even in his usually charitable argument. The justification of this moral language allows Milton retroactively to slide it over on top of that model of Christian marriage which he started with and which was based on an absence of moral judgment, a rejection of the very possibility of sin. By juxtaposing Paul's Christian-with-pagan unions with the Christian-Christian marriage which has been his focus, then, Milton can formally categorize the participants in Christian marriage more like "elect" and "nonelect" than the argument to this point would seem explicitly to allow, though we have already seen Milton's facility at creating localized moments of this dynamic. Milton will (in fact) make an analogy between the Pauline text and his original model; he is saying that even in the irreprehensible Christian marriage which has been his focus, one partner is really an infidel and the other a believer. The tendency of the tract's language to lose its equitably generous tone and to begin advocating the divorce of "the Religious from the irreligious, the fit from the unfit" (p. 635)—Milton's abhorrence of mixing "holy with Atheist, hevnly with hellish, fitness with unfitnes, light with darknes" (p. 635)—is here explicitly articulated and justified. Here we find not the Arminianist marriage of true minds but that in which "a Saint is joyn'd with a reprobate" (p. 607).

Ernest Sirluck points out the analogy which Milton creates here between the incompatible spouse and the idolatrous spouse, but he does so without seeing the implications of such a comparison.[23] For in Milton's tract the value of the believer-infidel marriage of the Pauline text is that it

allows him explicitly to criticize bad spouses; he almost completely reverses Paul's charitable advice to the Corinthian church. Milton declares
here that it is almost always contrary to God's command to "dwell with all
the scandals, the houshold persecutions, or alluring temptations" (p. 687)
of an infidel spouse. He details the unpleasantness of the situation: "to
beare indignities against his religion in words or deedes, to be wearied
with seducements, . . . to be tormented with impure and prophane conversation, this must needs be bondage to a christian" (p. 688).

   The similarity of this Christian-pagan marriage to the failed Christian-
Christian marriage we saw earlier is striking; misery, torment, bondage,
unhappiness, and temptation are the common experience of both. Not
surprisingly, the solution for both is also "divorce." Milton suggests that
these infidel spouses should be shunned; he reiterates God's command to
"come out from among them, and be ye separate, . . . and touch not the
unclean thing" (p. 683 n). Milton quotes Chronicles, that "Neither should
we love them that hate the Lord" (p. 682), and he refers to Genesis: "God
hath put enmity between the seed of the woman, and the seed of the
Serpent" (p. 682). He begins this section by referring to Christ's declaration
that "he who hates not father or mother, wife, or children hindring his
christian cours, . . . cannot be a Disciple" (p. 682), and he opens the whole
discussion thus, "the Gospel . . . requires [of us] . . . rather then our christian love should come into danger of backsliding, to forsake all relations how
neer so ever, and the wife expresly, with promise of a high reward" (p. 682).
Repeatedly Milton invokes the language of absolute necessity and of
opposition/separation to describe the utter dissimilarity between believing
and unbelieving spouse and the spiritual compulsion the believer is therefore under to "touch not the unclean thing." Divine law, Milton asserts,
requires that these husbands and wives be divorced so that the one not be
contaminated by the damnable influence of the other.

   As in the "backsliding" passage quoted above, which in fact opens
Milton's exegesis of 1 Corinthians, it is clear that in the discussion of
Paul's text Milton's wrath is directed much more toward the wife in
particular as a liability to the pilgrim's progress. This is why Milton wants
to equate the two members of a Christian marriage with a saint and a
sinner; it enables him to say that the (male) "saint" spouse must, not just
for peace's sake but for salvation's sake, leave the (female) "sinner" spouse.
This argument would seem to run counter to Milton's earlier description
of innocent unhappiness; but Milton can make it because the logic of his
emphasis on divine provision can invert or extend itself: generosity toward "husband" can now equal rejection/damnation of "wife." Or, per-

haps, his own emphasis on God's gracious willingness to divide simply provides Milton with too ready an analogy with the parable of the sheep and the goats, the elect and the reprobate. As Turner says, "the characteristic movement of the divorce tracts is one of oscillation" (p. 204); this twist of divine will from grace to judgment is the logic controlling those oscillations. Milton's exegesis of Paul's letter at the end of the tract thus helps us to understand more clearly the patterns of mercy and attack which so disconcert its readers. For here Milton can argue explicitly that some spouses should be divorced because they are evil and noxious; and since the tract has tended throughout to apply damning labels to wives rather than husbands, this final section of the tract provides exegetical support for *Tetrachordon*'s theological subtext. That Milton particularly emphasizes the importance of fleeing "the wife expresly" (p. 682) only confirms what this section of the text implies: Arminianist free will is not the only motive or justification for *men's* right to divorce.

VIII

To complicate but also clarify this theological contradiction in Milton's tract, it may be helpful to consider that although predestination and its daughter doctrine of vocational calling were supposed, as the Westminster Assembly asserted, to be a sign of God's "free grace and love" (III, v), the Puritans also declared that the "doctrine . . . of predestination is to be handled with special prudence and care" (III, vii) because it contains such potential for anxiety rather than thankfulness. Even in Calvin's *Institutes* the problem of knowing whether or not one is elect manifests itself in lengthy discussions of "the manner of the call itself" (p. 967), "the right and wrong way to attain certainty of election" (p. 968), "general and special calling" (p. 974), and "the cause of hardness of heart" (p. 981). And indeed Calvin's charitable God rapidly disappears into one whose punishment is most noticeable:

We shall never be clearly persuaded . . . that our salvation flows from the wellspring of God's free mercy until we come to know his eternal election, which illumines God's grace by this contrast: that he . . . gives to some what he denies to others. (P. 921)

Only the "contrast" between "us" and "others" (a construction suggested by Calvin's consistent use of the first-person plural pronoun) can provide "us" with the necessary assurance of God's grace and "free mercy." It is only because some are damned that "we" can be confident in the mercy granted to "us." Knowledge of election depends upon the knowledge that some are eternally reprobate. Even the earliest Calvinist doctrines, then, contain this tendency to damn the other.

Historians have long noted that English Puritans and Reformers of the seventeenth century were certainly as preoccupied with this problem of assurance as Calvin was. The *Westminster Confession* reaffirms God's "sovereign power over His creatures" to save *or* damn while simultaneously declaring that predestination's main purpose is to assure men "of their eternal election" (III, viii). Arthur Dent in *The Plaine Man's Pathway to Heaven* acknowledges that the central problem is "know[ing] in your selfe, and for your selfe, that you are one of the Elect" (p. 253).[24] Dent's handbook provides in response three separate series of "infallible" signs of election, each numbering eight or more. Richard Rogers's *Garden of Spirituall Flowers* (London, 1616) has a similar collection of "signs," "tokens," and "actions" of regeneration; headings include "seven signes of true Repentance" (D5(v)), "The difference betweene the godly and wicked in one and the same sinne" (D5(r)), and "whereby wee may easily discerne whether we abide in the state of Nature, or the state of Grace, whether slaves to Sin and Sathan, or Servants and Heyres to Christ and his Kingdome" (C6(r)). The sheer number and variety of these "infallible" tokens of election illustrate the anxiety felt over the stated uncertainty of the doctrine. It was this side of Calvinism, this oppressive and uncertain fear of the judgment of God, which Hill argues Milton rejected in the 1640s when he rejected predestination.

But what must have remained a potent ideology for Milton from his early days as a Calvinist was the social policy of exclusion which the puritans of his era developed and implemented in response to (or excused by) this oppressive fear of an arbitrary, judgmental God.[25] William Hunt, Keith Wrightson, and David Levine have all argued that this spiritual ideology and anxiety fed into the social fears and policies of a class faced with the "growth of a 'superfluous' population of marginal laborers, squatters, and drifters" (Hunt, p. 125), prompting efforts to assure oneself of one's own salvation by distinguishing oneself theologically from the burdensome and socially disruptive vagrant poor.[26] Although some historical accounts do not give sufficient weight to the puritans' emphasis on humility and interest in caring for the poor, and although Arminianism was plainly a doctrine capable of its own forms of elitism, in puritan sermons there is clearly a frequent assertion of a "correlation between poverty of goods and [poverty of] grace" (Hunt, p. 139).[27] Dent refers to "all the prophane multitude" who are not among the elect (p. 259), and explains that penury can be a sign that God has cursed a person's "goods" because of sin (p. 199). Rogers also suggests repeatedly that poverty is a sign of

God's displeasure. Another preacher declares that poverty "might well be avoided, if sin were taken heed of and resisted, and by labor and watchfulness the unruly heart subdued" (Hunt, p. 139).

Historians have argued then that in these local puritan oligarchies' diatribes (and the legislation which followed) against the drunken peasantry, the vagrant poor, "those at the bottom of the social scale [who had become] not simply poor, but culturally different" (Wrightson, p. 2), we see the legacy of this profound Calvinist anxiety over the status of the self. As Hill suggests, the English Puritans developed a democratic vision only applicable "within the oligarchy of the elect" (p. 273). And so Calvinism supplies or supports a particular and powerful tool for social policies which exclude and condemn, including (even) Milton's divorce policy with its Arminianist language of reason and free will. Though of course the politics of gender and the politics of class have important differences, both women and the poor could be, and were, seen as other. When William Perkins describes the body of Christ he declares that "rogues, beggars [and] vagabonds . . . are as rotten legs and arms that drop from the body" (pp. 455–56).[28] For good reasons, his image bears a strong resemblance to Milton's depiction of the bad wife as "not a true limb so much . . . but an adherent, a sore, the gangrene of a limb" (p. 602). As Hill says, "for a Calvinist 'the church' meant both the whole community and the elect members of that community: when liberty was most heavily emphasized, it was natural to think most of the godly minority" (p. 252). Such an analysis well describes Puritan social policy and the tendencies in Milton's own attempts at legislative reform in *Tetrachordon*.

IX

This final divorce tract has an extremely complex and ambivalent relationship to the theologies of Milton's culture. Milton seems implicitly to demonize Calvinism as a rigid, deterministic, judgmental, and graceless doctrine by insisting in good Arminianist fashion that God's reasonable grace provides for both the joining and the separating of spouses. He even repeatedly pleads for the freedom that divorce gives to innocent women as well as to innocent men. But it is impossible simply to accept Milton's privileging of an Arminianist ideology, for that vision of human liberty which seems so attractive to modern readers conceals and also depends upon a gendered judgmentalism. The tract also shows us a Milton who is willing to borrow Calvinist terms and label those same free and innocent women spousal reprobates when they do not make their husbands happy. In fact, the analogies to Calvinism and Arminianism in the text reveal that Milton's Arminianism depends upon Calvinism when the

question of wives arises. He keeps suggesting that *Tetrachordon* is based
on the demonstrably Arminianist notion that men are free to choose their
own liberty; however, he wants that literally to apply to "men," whose free
will he then defends by condemning bad wives in terms of the harshest of
Calvinist doctrines. Milton ends up arguing, then, that the husband's free
will is at least partly attainable by declaring the bad wife a marital reprobate. And this logic circulates throughout the tract, demonstrating Milton's strategic willingness to be inconsistent about his theological terms of
reference in order to make an argument against wives. Milton persistently
invokes the scenario of a failed Christian marriage; he uses this to argue
for God's contingency plan for deserving men, but he also uses it to
declare that some women are impossible-to-love marital reprobates *from*
whom God provides the salvation of divorce. So while Milton's peers
condemn the vagrant poor who threaten the social order, Milton con-
demns the unloveable wives who threaten men's marital peace—and he
does so by declaring that wives in unhappy marriages are, without necessarily being culpable, guilty. Even in *Tetrachordon*'s supposed free-will
argument for divorce, Milton reworks the old axiom: God "proposes," but
only "man" (not woman) "disposes."

Furman University

NOTES

1. Christopher Hill, *Milton and the English Revolution* (New York, 1977).
2. For illuminating discussions of the debates over Arminianism and Calvinism and
the role of religion in the Civil Wars, see especially Nicholas Tyacke, *Anti-Calvinists: The
Rise of English Arminianism, c. 1590–1640* (Oxford, 1989). See also Patrick Collinson's *The
Elizabethan Puritan Movement* (London, 1967) and "England and International Calvinism
1558–1640," in *International Calvinism 1541–1715,* ed. Menna Prestwich (Oxford 1985),
pp. 197–223. Peter Lake reviews the debate in *Journal of Ecclesiastical History* 42 (October
1991), p. 618–622.
3. As will become evident, both Calvinism and Arminianism assumed that the other
was profoundly unmerciful and uncharitable.
4. Jean Calvin, *Institutes of the Christian Religion,* ed. John T. McNeill and Ford
Lewis Battles, trans. (Philadelphia, 1960), vol. II; *The Confession of Faith, Agreed Upon by
the Assembly of Divines at Westminster* . . . (1647; rpt. Publications Committee of the Free
Presbyterian Church of Scotland, 1970). All citations to the *Westminster Confession* list
chapter and section number.
5. James Arminius, *The Writings of James Arminius,* trans. James Nichols and W. R.
Bagnall, 3 vols. (Grand Rapids, 1977). Citations will list volume and page number.
6. Indeed, Milton's main strategy is to defend his civil and rational arguments par-

ticularly *through* readers' requests that "the Scriptures there [in the previous divorce tract] might be discuss'd more fully" (p. 582). All quotations of the tract are from Douglas Bush in *Complete Prose Works of John Milton*, 8 vols., ed. Don M. Wolfe et al. (New Haven, 1953–82), vol. 2. Hereafter cited as YP followed by volume and page number.

7. English Arminianism in the 1640s is a discourse rather than a single definable set of principles, and Milton's relationship to the ceremonialism and royalism of many prominent Arminianists is hardly unproblematic. I will confine my discussion to Arminianism's general beliefs about the subject-relations between humans and the divine as I outline here. These central beliefs do seem to be Milton's focus in this tract.

8. For this tendency to argue from the divorce tracts to the later poetry, see Barbara K. Lewalski, Diane Kelsey McColley and Mary Nyquist as listed in notes 10 and 12; also see Janet E. Halley, "Female Autonomy in Milton's Sexual Poetics," in *Milton and the Idea of Woman*, ed. Julia M. Walker (Chicago, 1988), pp. 230–55.

9. See especially David Loewenstein and James G. Turner, eds., *Politics, Poetics and Hermeneutics in Milton's Prose* (Cambridge, 1990).

10. See Arnold Williams's preface to *Tetrachordon* in YP II, pp. 156–58. See Mary Nyquist, "The Genesis of Gendered Subjectivity in the Divorce Tracts and in *Paradise Lost*," in *Re-membering Milton: Essays on the Texts and Traditions*, ed. Mary Nyquist and Margaret Ferguson (New York, 1987), pp. 99–127, and James Grantham Turner, *One Flesh: Paradisal Marriage and Sexual Relations in the Age of Milton* (Oxford, 1987) for work which avoids this tendency.

11. Stephen M. Fallon, "The Metaphysics of Milton's Divorce Tracts," in *Politics, Poetics and Hermeneutics*, ed. Loewenstein and Turner, p. 69.

12. For versions of this view see especially C. A. Patrides, *Milton and the Christian Tradition* (Oxford, 1966), p. 186; Barbara K. Lewalski, "Milton on Women—Yet Once More," in *Milton Studies*, vol. VI, ed. James D. Simmonds (Pittsburgh, 1974), p. 11; Theodore L. Huguelet, "The Rule of Charity in Milton's Divorce Tracts," in *Milton Studies*, vol. VI, ed. James D. Simmonds (Pittsburgh, 1974), pp. 199–214; Diane Kelsey McColley, *Milton's Eve* (Urbana, 1983), p. 46.

13. See also John Illo, "The misreading of Milton," in *Radical Perspectives in the Arts*, ed. Lee Baxandall (Baltimore, 1972), pp. 178–92, and Stanley Fish, "Driving from the Letter: Truth and Indeterminacy in Milton's *Aereopagitica*," in *Re-membering Milton*, ed. Nyquist and Ferguson, pp. 234–54, for critiques of the liberal reading of Milton's political agendas.

14. Annabel Patterson, "No Meer Amatorious Novel?," in *Politics, Poetics and Hermeneutics*, ed. Loewenstein and Turner, pp. 85–101. Of course in some ways it would be surprising if the Milton who could write such bitter and condemnatory invective as we see in *Colasterion*, '*Lycidas*,' and *Sonnet XI* and *Sonnet XII*, and whose life experience had not led him to view wives with charity, would unceasingly or consistently express generous sentiments toward women or wives.

15. For this model of cultural transmission see Michel Foucault, "Nietzsche, Genealogy, History," in *Language, Counter-memory, Practice: Selected Essays and Interviews*, ed. Donald F. Bouchard and Donald Bouchard and Sherry Simon, trans. (Ithaca, 1977), pp. 139–64. John Guillory's "The Father's House: *Samson Agonistes* in Its Historical Moment," in *Re-membering Milton*, ed. Nyquist and Ferguson, pp. 148–77, is a helpful example of criticism combining these elements.

16. This is of course not only a crucial line of Milton's argument in light of his Parliamentary audience, but is also of vital importance to Puritans such as William Perkins who insist that all individual actions should "be profitable not only to the doers, but to the

154   MILTON STUDIES

commonwealth" (Perkins, p. 462). Todd emphasizes the central function of "the public good" for the Puritan work-ethic (Todd, p. 148).

17. Milton has, as Maurice Kelley points out, abandoned this view of Mosaic law by the time he writes the Arminian *De doctrina Christiana*. Maurice Kelley, *This Great Argument* (Gloucester, 1962), p. 57.

18. In the *Doctrine and Discipline of Divorce* Milton even argues that divorce is "the first and last of all [God's] visible works; [as] when by his divorcing command the world first rose out of Chaos" (p. 273).

19. See in particular Arminius's argument with Perkins over whether God predetermined human fates before or after the Fall; Arminius insists that Adam's actions did affect the mind and will of God (Arminius III, 294).

20. Calvinism is discussed in more detail in section VII.

21. Fredric Jameson, "Religion and Ideology," *1642: Literature and Power in the Seventeenth Century*, ed. Francis Barker et al. (Essex, 1981), pp. 315–36.

22. William and Malleville Hallers, "The Puritan Art of Love" in *Huntington Library Quarterly* V (1942) 235–72, note the use of Proverbs to either praise good wives or blame bad ones (243); but the Hallerses suggest a general degree of benevolence conspicuous by its absence in Milton's reading.

23. Ernest Sirluck, ed., "Introduction," in YP II, p. 149.

24. The full title of Arthur Dent's tract is revealing: *The Plaine Mans Path-way to Heaven. Wherein every man may cleerly see whether he shall be saved or damned* (London, 1610).

25. Edmund S. Morgan's *The Puritan Dilemma: The Story of John Winthrop* (Boston, 1958) discusses this crisis in puritanism. This is not to say that damning the poor was unknown before Calvin—Margo Todd in her *Christian Humanism and the Puritan Social Order* (Cambridge, 1987) makes it clear that Erasmian humanists regarded poverty with some suspicion (p. 147)—simply that a new rationale came into the discourse.

26. William Hunt, *The Puritan Moment* (Cambridge, Mass., 1983); Keith Wrightson and David Levine, *Poverty and Piety in an English Village: Terling, 1525–1700, Studies in Social Discontinuity* (New York, 1979).

27. William Hunt in particular overstates his case in his desire to draw parallels between the Puritans' philosophy and Thatcherism: "these preachers . . . assumed an explanation of poverty that has been revived in our own day" (*The Puritan Movement*, p. 139). For a further critique of this view see Todd, *Christian Humanism and the Puritan Social Order*.

28. *The Work of William Perkins*, ed. Ian Breward (Appleford, Conn., 1970).

WOOD, ALLAM, AND THE OXFORD MILTON

Nicholas von Maltzahn

MEMBERS OF OXFORD University play an essential part in shaping Milton's literary reception in the late seventeenth century. Two works in particular do much to color the understanding of Milton and *Paradise Lost* in the 1690s and after: Anthony Wood's life of Milton in his *Fasti Oxonienses* (1691) is a central document in the biographical tradition, and the Oxford assistance with the 1688 illustrated folio helped speed *Paradise Lost* toward its later status as a classic and as a commercial property of special value to the influential publisher Jacob Tonson. But the Oxford from which the biography and help for the edition emerge was a Tory stronghold, where Milton's politics were viewed with suspicion since he seemed so very much a Whig. Both Wood's "Life of Milton" and the 1688 folio reflect this Oxford prejudice: the "Life of Milton" shows the sharper animus of its origins in the time of the Exclusion Crisis, whereas the assembly of the 1688 folio signals not only a conservative appropriation of *Paradise Lost* but also the later and more conflicted Toryism characteristic of the short reign of James II.[1] The distance between these productions, however, also provides another expression of that ongoing adjustment in Oxford of changing ideals for education in the Renaissance. Wood's valuation of Milton's work grows out of the older culture of disputation that directly sustains the controversial habits of so many late seventeenth-century writers; this derived from an institutional legacy in which logic had been supreme. By contrast, the assistance with the 1688 folio arises from a more liberal humanist schooling, in which a regard for classical texts was encouraged by new standards of politeness, to be promoted especially in the cultivation of the gentry.

The argument here will turn to the folio *Paradise Lost* by way of conclusion, but first the production of Wood's "Life of Milton" bears more extended review, with reference especially to the climate of political opinion during its preparation. There is a "Third Man" among the contributors for Wood's "Life of Milton," a source half-named in John Aubrey's notes, but whose possible role has occasioned only various rumors and some unlikely theories. His contribution can now be determined, and the identification not only invites reconsideration of Wood's work,

155

but affords further insight into Milton's posthumous career in Wood's Oxford world.

I

The restored House of Stuart was again threatened in the Restoration Crisis of 1678–83, a failed revolution but one of a seriousness that recent historians have urged anew. A wider significance has been argued especially for the events associated with the Rye House Plot, for the extent of opposition to the crown, and for the enduring legacy of these stirrings in the Revolution of 1688 and beyond.[2] In Oxford, reaction to the attempted rebellion of 1683 expressed itself in *The Judgment and Decree of the University of Oxford*, which set forth new measures that summer by which the university might reassure itself and the crown of its loyalty. Authored and ushered through convocation by a Tory high-flyer, William Jane, the *Judgment and Decree* demanded a loyalist and Anglican submission in members of the university. It won the thanks of the king, who in Ormond's words thought it a bulwark "ag^t those pernitious Positions w^c have so long infested & so often involved these Nations in Civill, Barbarous, & bloody Wars & Dissentions." The measures in Oxford have been described as a "highpoint of royalist rhetoric," and may be seen also as the nadir in Milton's posthumous reputation: for Milton was cited among offending authors, and some of his works were burnt in the bonfire that had been prepared in the Schools Quadrangle that afternoon. "All and singular Readers, Tutors, Catechists and others" were enjoined to ground their students in the political doctrine of passive obedience.[3] Thus it was as part of a narrowing conformity in the university that a Whig member of Lincoln College now found himself deprived of his fellowship. James Parkinson seems to have been a troubled man in any case, and if his popularity with students injured his relation with the fellows of Lincoln, so too did his appetite for rough talk, resistance theory, and arguments for Exclusion. But of the "Articles against Mr Parkinson," Wood specifies Parkinson's commendation to his students of Milton's *Defensio*—"an excellent book & an antidote against Sr Rob: Filmer"—as "particularly" exposing him to his colleagues' censure. Wood sees this as part of the larger reaction to the "crop eared plot," of which Parkinson was held to be in some part guilty, and for which he was "for a time committed to privat custody" and bound over until the next assizes.[4]

Although George Sensabaugh has suggested Milton as the Spirit of Liberty in the 1680s, a more cautious estimate finds him enrolled chiefly on many lists of seditious works, and the more out of favor in 1683 owing to the Miltonic cast of such works as Parkinson's favorite *Julian the Apos-*

tate (by the pamphleteer Samuel Johnson, 1682) and Algernon Sidney's final self-defense later that year. The year 1683 falls in the middle of a ten-year span between the third and fourth editions of *Paradise Lost*, with chiefly lesser works published under Milton's name in these years. A further mark of the disfavor into which he had fallen may be the availability for sale in August 1683, just a month after the Oxford decree, of half the rights for *Paradise Lost*, now transferred from Brabazon Aylmer, recent publisher of *A Brief History of Moscovia* (1682), to the young Jacob Tonson, who could in later years claim his investment in Milton as the best of his ventures, and who in Sir Godfrey Kneller's portrait warmly clasps a copy of *Paradise Lost*.[5]

Loyalist politics in the early 1680s enjoyed the support of the university and especially of Anthony Wood and his correspondents. Milton's fame and his death in 1674 contributed to his place in Wood's biographical collections and commissions in the 1670s and 1680s, even though the poet had only a doubtful connection to Oxford, which was the focus of Wood's research. The poet and controversialist seems nonetheless to have proven an irresistible subject for this resentful Tory, who knew Milton to be "a great Scholar and frequent Writer" if also "a great Antimonarchist" and "a Rogue."[6] But despite some scholarly attention—this "Life of Milton" is the first published biography of Milton—the biographer's sources have remained in part obscure. Long ago William Riley Parker warned Miltonists to cite Wood "with caution on the very few occasions when it is necessary to cite him at all."[7] The "Life of Milton" will now prove to be a composite of a greater number of contributions than even Parker thought; as one of Wood's Oxford contemporaries remarked on the appearance of the *Athenae*, he had "*collected* it but not *writ* it."[8] Even so, the work may still be viewed as more than the sum of its parts. In questioning Wood's value as a reporter of "true" biographical fact Parker understated Wood's usefulness as a register of instructive biographical perceptions and as a key figure for the student of Milton's reception.

Wood is indeed doubtful on points of biographical detail owing to his heavy reliance on printed sources and others' research. Much of the latter still exists in manuscript, and review of these materials further indicates the lack of immediacy between Wood and his subject. A long list might be made of quibbles with and qualifications of scholarly conclusions that have been based on unreliable parts of his text, or on parts of the "Life of Milton" assumed to be original to Wood but that prove again to be his recycling of other texts; the trust in such authorities among Miltonists is sometimes an unguarded one, and the evidence shows how derivative even Wood's distinctively Tory opinions can be.[9] It has long been recog-

nized that for the "Life of Milton" he drew on two principal sources. Best
known is his debt to Aubrey, which is great and has been well documented. Aubrey afforded Wood not only "minutes" of Milton's life but also
arranged for Andrew Marvell to provide a biography, a contribution that
was finally made instead by Cyriack Skinner, Wood's second main source.
Here Aubrey's part in supplying not only his own work but the other main
source for Wood's biography has perhaps not found sufficient emphasis,
this in part because Helen Darbishire's *Early Lives of Milton* mistook the
identity of this second, "anonymous biographer."[10] The value of Skinner's
text to Wood is evident from any comparison of the two, as Parker has
demonstrated, and Skinner's reading of *Defensio Secunda* seems also to
have guided Wood's response to the autobiographical passage in that
work.

But if only Aubrey and Skinner's contributions had been available,
Wood himself might have needed further to explore Milton's life and
works in order to achieve as much as he does in his entry in the *Fasti*.
Other friends also made Wood's work easier, such as Thomas Blount,
Arthur Charlett, and William Joyner. Although students of Milton have
pored through the Wood letter-books (Oxford, Bodleian Library, Wood
MSS F.39–45) for perspective on his biography—if missing some significant material even here—they have quite overlooked the further volumes
of notes that Wood collected (Wood MSS F.46–49 especially), even
though these are equally important in the production of the *Athenae* and
Fasti Oxonienses. Here one correspondent in particular provides Wood
with much assistance and is the origin of his most outspoken response to
Milton in the "Life of Milton." This help has gone quite unconsidered,
despite some tantalizing references to his name by Aubrey and some
consequent but unproductive citations of these references by such Miltonists as C. G. Osgood, Helen Darbishire, William Riley Parker, Harris
Fletcher, and J. Milton French.[11] The contributor was the vice principal of
St. Edmund Hall, Oxford, the young Andrew Allam.[12]

Allam's part in Wood's collections further explains those references to
him that scholars have noted in Aubrey's communications to Wood. One
is in a letter from Aubrey to Wood: "pray remember me very kindly to Mr
Allam: I am exceedingly taken with his ingenuity, and obligeingnesse.
pray aske him where Mr J. Milton speakes of his owne life & ye pagg".[13]
This echoes an earlier request in Aubrey's "minutes" of Milton's life, in
which he asks Wood to query "Mr Allam of Edm: hall Oxon, of M^r J.
Milton's life writt by himselfe. v. pagg."[14] The later letter explains any
ambiguity in Aubrey's notes and identifies the autobiographical passage
from *Defensio Secunda* as the object of his inquiry. Moreover, Allam does

supply Wood with the reference for the London edition of *Defensio Secunda,* although Wood independently cites the Hague edition in a footnote in the "Life of Milton"—it should be noted that Wood seems to have used the Bodleian's otherwise unrecorded presentation copy of *Defensio Secunda* ("given to the lib. by yᵉ author XI June 1654"), one of those seditious works that were to have been burnt in 1660, but that were then instead stored separate from the main collection in the manuscript cupboard in the Librarian's study ("*in Musaeo*").[15] But Allam was useful not only as someone who knew where to find the autobiographical passage in Milton's *Defensio Secunda;* he also provided a coherent summary of other biographical material, a summary that Wood could on a few points then reproduce word for word in the "Life of Milton." Allam has hitherto been mistaken as *the* "anonymous biographer," although this has been corrected by French, Parker, and more lately Allan Pritchard; the last confirms the consensus "that the early life of Milton supposed to have been written by Andrew Allam is purely imaginary," and that this error originates in a misreading of Aubrey (Pritchard, "Milton in Rome," p. 96). But this goes too far: Allam deserves some consideration as *an* anonymous biographer of Milton. He did write about Milton, and Wood made much use of this information.

Allam is worthy t'have not remained so long unsung. Wood himself admits how much he owed to the younger man, who "many times lent his assisting hand to the author of this present work, especially as to the *Notitia* of certain modern writers of our nation." The contribution was also observed by the great scholar Thomas Hearne, who shared Wood's Oxford milieu and many of his prejudices: "The greatest help he found from any one person in that university was from Mr Andrew Allam, vice-principal of St Edmund's Hall." Allam helped on many fronts, but he was of special assistance with the reports on more recent authors for the *Athenae* and *Fasti Oxonienses.* He was conversant to a remarkable degree with the controversial literature of the midcentury and after, so much so that it was said of him with wonder "that nothing hardly came [out] without a name but he could immediately . . . discover its Author." It is this range as a reader and bibliographer on which Wood especially drew: as he noted, Allam "understood the controversial writings between conformists & nonconformists, protestants & papists, far beyond his years, which was advanc'd by a great and happy memory," and "nothing but years and experience were wanting, to make him a compleat walking library." Of such works Allam had made a considerable collection, of which Wood also came to avail himself.[16] Wood's relations with his Oxford contemporaries were often awkward, and it is evident that in his dealings with the younger Allam he found himself in happier company.¹⁷ Although named from the beginning as a contributor to Wood's work, Allam's part in the *Athenae* and *Fasti* has not been properly documented, in part owing to some of Wood's materials being a little late to find their way into the Bodleian Library in the nineteenth century, and then their being bound in volumes separate from the more beaten track of his letter-books (in which only a small part of Allam's contribution to Wood is represented).¹⁸

Like Wood, Allam was a loyal son of Oxford, and like Wood he has a lively Tory perspective on the writers and controversies of the day. Born in 1655, he came up to St. Edmund Hall in 1671, and remained there as "tutor, moderator, a lecturer in the chapel, and at length vice-principal of his house," until his death in 1685. He seems to have died just as he was getting under way as an author in his own right: in 1684 a few establishmentarian prefaces appear from his hand, and he supplies the "Life of Iphicrates" for the Oxford translation of Cornelius Nepos, a Tory product which scorns the "polluted spawn of [Whig] Pamphlets" as a "mixture of Villany and Madness." Allam's opinions, especially his resentment of the "Fanatical faction," are characteristic of his party. His "most zealous respect" for the Church of England led him to disparage dissenting preachers as "hotheaded zealots" given to "unmannerly libelling."¹⁹ Nor did he have any sympathy for "the *Good old Cause*," of which he held a "just abhorrence" owing to "it's destructive" and "most seditious and rankest principles," "foulest practices," and "complicated villanies of treason, murther, rebellion, and other the most dissolute immoralities." On this basis he could single out "*J. Goodwin's* and *J. Milton's* infamous vindications of the proceedings against the best of *Kings*" as characteristic pieces of "Jesuiticall Puritanicall & traiterous" subversion, and his student White Kennett learned from this mentor how to deplore "those grand Patriots of Rebellion and Confusion: *Hobbs, Milton, Hunton, Grotius* and others." William Riley Parker wishfully thought Allam "young enough to admire Milton without the usual political prejudices" but the case was just the opposite.²⁰ Allam's suspicion of Milton also colors his response to Edward Phillips's *Theatrum poetarum* (1675), as he notes the evasion in that work of the awkward subject of Phillips's uncle: "In yᵗ little wᶜʰ he saith of J Milton (John) he insinuateth his near relation to him as a reason of his not delivering his judgement of him, as otherwise he might possibly have done"—such implicit disparagement of the Phillips brothers was often made explicit, as in Wood who also insistently identifies John Phillips with Milton. Always suspicious of Whigs, Allam can regard James Tyrrell, for example, as "a man of a busie temper," and can say of some other works, which he thinks are by either Locke or Shaftesbury, only that "They are wrot as well, as ye bad subject of y^m would bear."[21] Allam was of a younger generation but still loyal to older Oxford institutions and not quite capable of the suppler humanism of such Tories as Bishop Fell, or especially Henry Aldrich and the younger Francis Atterbury.

Wood drew heavily on Allam's biographical and bibliographical summaries, as well as on his Tory opinions, and adopts much of Allam's material word for word. Evident on many slips from Allam are Wood's characteristic red underlining and frequent indexing of names cited, with the latter annotation usually on the reverse of a page or letter with further symbols for Wood's system of cross-references. For Milton, the two passages on which Wood drew most come from a parenthetic entry in Allam's description of John Phillips. Phillips was trained in his "London years under y^t villanous leading Incendiarie John Milton his Unckle by Mother's side," and on this basis Allam ventures forth into a more extended response to Milton and his works. Wood applies this material both to the "Life of Milton" and to a digressive note on John Phillips in the life of Edward Phillips in the *Athenae*. Thus for the "Life of Milton" Wood makes the most of his source:

(and Milton, as we may take notice of by y^e by, was born in London, who after he had commenc'd M.A at Camb: Travell'd for some time into forraign Countrys, & but upon his return home about ye beginning of our late troubles became in his first writings *a most sharp & violent opposer of Prelacy, & ye establish'd Ecclesiastial discipline,* ~~broachd~~ *set on foot & maintain'd very odd & novel positions concerning divorce,* wrot for an unbounded liberty of ye press, & *at last arriv'd to y^t monstrous & unparralel'd heigth of profligate impudence as in print to justifie that most execrable murther of the best of Kings.* (Wood MS F.47, f. 626^r; the italics here mark words used by Wood.)

Wood's "Life of Milton" holds that Milton was

a most sharp and violent opposer of Prelacy, the established ecclesiastical Discipline and the orthodox Clergy. (14) That shortly after he did set on foot and maintained very odd and novel Positions concerning Divorce, and then taking part with the Independents, he became a great Antimonarchist, a bitter Enemy to K. *Ch.* I and at length arrived to that monstrous and unparallel'd height of profligate impudence, as in print to justifie the most execrable Murder of him the best of Kings. (*Athenae*, 1691, p. 881)

Where Wood seems to depart from his source, in earlier describing John Phillips as "principl'd as his Uncle," for example, or here further describing Milton among the "Independents" and as an "Antimonarchist," he proves still to be recycling terms introduced by Allam, who had noted Milton's adherence to "ye Independant interest" and "Philips having by this means very early imbibed [in] a most plentifull manner ye rankest Anti-monarchical principle." Wood uses the rest of this passage about John Phillips in a digression in his life of Edward Phillips.[22]

More central still in Wood's "Life of Milton" is his summary judgment on Milton, which also proves to be of Allam's formulation. Describing Milton's public career in the Commonwealth, Allam observes that he

> became Latin Secretarie to Oliver in Forraign matters, to w^m he proved very serviceable, w^n by him employ'd in business of weight & moment, a person of wonderful parts, a very sharp, biting, & satyrical wit, a good Philosopher, & Historian, an excellent Poet & Latinist, so rarely endow'd by nature, y^t had he been but honestly principled, he might have been highly useful to y^t party, ag^{st} wch he all a long appear'd wth so much malice & bitterness. (Wood MS F.47, f. 626^r; the italics here mark words used by Wood.)

Wood introduces the same passage with a caustic note of his own, but then proceeds to pass judgment in Allam's words:

> when Oliver ascended the Throne, [Milton] became Latin Secretary, and proved to him very serviceable when employed in business of weight and moment, and did great matters to obtain a name and wealth. To conclude, he was a person of wonderful parts, of a very sharp, biting and satyrical wit. He was a good Philosopher and Historian, an excellent Poet, Latinist, Grecian and Hebritian, a good Mathematician and Musitian, and so rarely endowed by nature, that had he been but honestly principled, he might have been highly useful to that party, against which he all along appeared with much malice and bitterness. (*Athenae*, p. 881)[23]

On other lesser points Allam was also influential: thus in a rather skewed bibliographic account of Milton's *Animadversions* and *Apology*, Wood follows into error not Skinner but Allam, who was also working from the autobiographical passage from *Defensio Secunda*.[24] Where the "Life of Milton" touches on Peter Du Moulin's authorship of the *Regii Sanguinis Clamor*, Wood consults Allam's further notes about John Phillips and Milton in which the references for Du Moulin's successive claims to the *Clamor* are cited.[25]

Although some of Allam's contributions may not have survived, his assistance with the "Life of Milton" seems unlikely to have been much more extensive.[26] This is difficult to judge because the Wood collections are in some disarray, and in the notebooks especially the distribution of the biographical entries registered by Wood is random for the most part. With letters, Wood kept some series in chronological order, at least from single correspondents, but it looks as if even here he gathered his bundles in no very systematic way.[27] Allam's possible further contributions to the "Life of Milton" might be inferred only if there were any more materials conspicuously unaccounted for in that text, but the "Life of Milton" shows little else not attributable to the extant sources, whether Allam, Aubrey, Skinner, *Defensio Secunda*, or other incidental communications to Wood. Nor is there much else about Milton in Allam's many other letters and notes.

The discovery of Allam's contribution sheds light on another unresolved puzzle: the question of Milton's Oxford M.A. and whether Wood should even have given Milton an entry in *Fasti Oxonienses* (as incorporated in 1635).[28] This has long drawn doubting comment, whether from Edward Phillips, who denied Milton's connection to the university, or more recently from William Riley Parker. The case against Milton's Oxford M.A. can here be further restated. The evidence now precludes J. Milton French's suggestion that it might have been Allam who heard of Milton's incorporation from Milton's "own mouth."[29] (This was most doubtful in any case owing to Allam's youth and residence in Oxford.) On the contrary, Allam instead suggested that Wood intrude a life of Milton under the name of some alumnus of Oxford with whom Milton might have a connection (Wood often interpolates extra lives in this way). Allam suggests, for example, that "An account of *Milton* may be brought into Dᵒʳ Griffith (Matthew)"; otherwise, he proposes, Milton may be discussed with reference to John Phillips "in Magd. hall."[30] As noted above, it is in reviewing Phillips elsewhere that he introduces "by yᵉ by" his most significant entry about Milton (Wood MS F.47, f. 626ʳ). As late as the early 1680s, then, he does not understand that Milton might simply be entered under the *Fasti* owing to his incorporation in the university, undocumented as it is. He was in frequent communication with Wood, and his suggestions about where to fit Milton into the *Athenae* point to a problem for which Wood as yet had no answer. Wood himself, when reviewing his notes of Oxford events, can observe of "Miltons + Goodwins books [being] called in + Burnt" (16 June 1660) that "Neither of these [are] of Oxon." His decision to give Milton a "life" of his own in the *Fasti* comes very late. Thus Milton appears in Wood's list of figures who are not alumni of Oxford but who are to be introduced secondarily under other entries; this was a feature of the *Athenae* designed to enhance its appeal. He plans to include Milton under James Harrington or Sir Walter Raleigh, and checking on his almanac entry for Milton's death Wood adds the marginal reference "See Sir Walter Raleigh."[31]

This confirms Parker's skeptical argument that Milton had no true Oxford connection. Perhaps Aubrey later told Wood about Milton's incorporation at the university, but in any case Aubrey soon questioned this when the information proved unreliable. Thus he writes Wood to report

Phillips's assertion that Milton "was never of Oxford" (29 June 1689), even though Wood then attributes his knowledge of Milton's incorporation to "my friend [who can only be Aubrey], who was well acquainted with, and had from him, and from his Relations after his death, most of this account of his life and writings following."[32] Phillips's doubts about Milton's Oxford connection were evidently more telling than any previous opinion Aubrey may have held, and Allam and Wood alike had, at an earlier date, wondered about the best way to include Milton in the *Athenae*. In sum, Wood seems to have shoehorned Milton into his work—perhaps on the strength of doubtful information from Aubrey—and then not only refused to change his text when Aubrey changed his mind but still attributed the information to his unnamed friend. That Wood may have been pleased to take such a liberty also follows from his sometimes low opinion of his loyal source: Aubrey and Wood were capable of intermittent bitterness toward each other, and if Aubrey's erratic personality seems to have helped him become a friend of Wood, it also left him vulnerable to Wood's special capacity for ingratitude.[33]

II

The description of Milton in Wood's "Life of Milton" was shaped by the politics of the Exclusion Crisis in particular: this was when Wood's collections were being amassed and when opinions such as Allam's were formulated. But between the collection and the publication of this material, history intervened in an extraordinary way first to threaten Wood's and Oxford's Tory and Anglican position, and then to leave them out of power and in opposition to the new political order under William III. The mid to late 1680s and the early 1690s show political allegiances under much strain, especially in the abandonment of the Anglican ascendancy by James II, and then in its abandonment of him in the Revolution of 1688–89. Such confusion presented difficulties not least to Oxford Tories of Wood's stripe, who often begrudged the Catholic impositions of James II, but then proved reluctant to accommodate the Whig tendencies, especially in religion, of the usurper. It is in this climate of political change that Milton was also redefined in the direction of the classic poet who emerges in the 1688 folio *Paradise Lost*. His English Protestant voice may have seemed the more valuable during the fateful succession of events in the reign of James II, as suspicions of the aims of that Catholic monarch were compounded by news of the revocation of Edict of Nantes in October 1685, by the prorogation of the Commons in November, and then by James's betrayal in promoting Catholics and toleration the next summer.

Wood's view of Milton had already been formed, but if Milton's poetry seems never to have engaged his interest, or that of his correspondents Allam and Fulman, it was finding new support among some of their contemporaries. At Christ Church especially, whether under John Fell or Henry Aldrich, a wider humanism was being promoted for students of more aristocratic background, quite different from the traditional offering to candidates for holy orders. In contrast to Wood and Allam's intellectual character, the distinctive humanism of the Christ Church men, especially those from Westminster School, again shows that at Oxford there was only an uncertain and long drawn-out expression of the Renaissance shift in education, from those arts dominated by logic and explored through debate in academic exercises, to a humanist cultivation in grammar and rhetoric, as in the *literae humaniores*, with emphasis on the classics but also history and modern languages. It was at Christ Church that Jacob Tonson found the special assistance that was to transform his new edition of *Paradise Lost*. Even as Wood prepared his *Athenae* and *Fasti*, his contemporaries were engaged in literary labors that would transform Milton's reputation as a poet and contribute to that wider embrace of his poetry evident in the 1690s and after. In this context, Wood's lack of any special response to Milton as a poet, and to *Paradise Lost* in particular, reflects not just his Oxford Tory preoccupations but an earlier stage in the reception of Milton.[34] Tonson had bought his rights to *Paradise Lost* at the ebb of Milton's posthumous fortunes, when his political prose had been again marked for condemnation. But *Paradise Lost* needed no longer to appear as an expression of republicanism and dissent. To use a metaphor of that day, comprehension rather than toleration was now to bring Milton within the English and Protestant literary *church*: he was to be included as a communicant, rather than accepted as a separate but equal member of another congregation.

Milton appears in the fourth edition of *Paradise Lost* as a literary figure of a standing beyond earlier factional contests, in which he and then his name had played such a part. The new edition in large folio, elegant type, and beautified with an illustration for each book of the poem, grew in part from patriotic pride in Milton's supreme poetic achievement. It also represents some literary reconciliation of Whig and Tory: this fourth edition has traditionally been associated with John Somers, later Lord Somers, but is more particularly connected to that Oxford circle at Christ Church, in which the versatile Aldrich plays a central part, and in which the young Francis Atterbury was to distinguish himself. The cultured Toryism of Aldrich and his associates should be seen as characteristic of the conservatism of its university setting, which viewed the threat of Roman Catholicism with dismay, even as it refused to give ground to

Dissent.[35] Especially after the intrusion under James II of a Roman Catholic as dean of Christ Church, the crisis in nation seemed but a reflection of the crisis in the House. Aldrich "became the centre of resistance to the Roman Catholic campaign in Oxford," and here Atterbury served him as an eager acolyte, following Aldrich's example in bravely controverting Catholic tracts in 1687.[36] At the same time, Aldrich and Atterbury helped change the format of *Paradise Lost*, and thus changed its very meaning for their contemporaries.

Although Atterbury would later claim to have originated the 1688 folio, it is John Dryden who seems more likely to have initiated with Tonson this chapter in Milton's reception. Dryden provided Tonson with a connection between literary London and academic Oxford, especially Christ Church, in the 1680s. Both his guidance of Tonson elsewhere—Dryden is distinctive for his close work with booksellers—and his particular interest in *Paradise Lost* suggest that he at least confirmed the publisher's early interest in Milton and in the commercial opportunities in his poetry.[37] By contrast, an originating role seems precocious on Atterbury's part and he probably only supported the venture, although his precocity as an undergraduate is not in question, and he may be presumed from his earlier translation *Absalon et Achitophel* (Oxford, 1682) already to have had some acquaintance with Dryden or Tonson or both. Dryden was eager to promote such connections at Oxford: he had flattered his Oxford audience in his prologues and epilogues for the King's Company; in 1684 he adds to "The Prologue at Oxford, 1680" what looks like an insider's joke at the expense of "the Author of the *Oxford Bells*," who may well be Aldrich; and he later attempts to gain some place at the university. That he came near success appears in his near-election as warden of All Souls'. His closer relation to Christ Church in particular may be assumed first of all from his being a product of Westminster School, and thus sharing an intimate connection with a number of dominant figures at Christ Church, not least the younger Aldrich, protégé of Dean Fell, and now sponsor in turn of the much younger Atterbury. In 1685, moreover, Dryden was seeking to facilitate his son's progress from Westminster to Christ Church.[38] Once more in the story of Milton's reception, the evidence points to Dryden's part in defining Milton's laureate role, even as the later poet advanced his own literary claims, and remained at the centre of Tonson's active publication of poetry and translations in the 1680s and after.[39]

Other works from Tonson's list show signs that he and his authors wished to promote his new property in the epic. Such preparations for publication appear, for example, in the second edition of the earl of Roscommon's *Essay on Translated Verse*. That this should in praise of

Milton now feature an additional "Essay on blanc verse" seems not unrelated to Tonson's acquisition of rights to *Paradise Lost.* In particular, this essay tries to clear Milton of the stigma of having failed to rhyme his poem, and helped with the readier acceptance of his blank verse in years to come.[40] The success of this promotion of Milton's blank verse may be reflected in Thomas Rymer's failure to publish his promised attack on the versification of *Paradise Lost*—Rymer had a part in a number of Tonson's publications.[41] Such promotion of Milton would continue into the 1690s: thus the young Addison could enter into the literary arena by supplying a Dryden-Tonson miscellany with a poem in part celebratory of Milton's distinction as a poet, and this in terms that suggest the mediating influence of Dryden's *State of Innocence*, even as Addison still apologizes for Milton's politics.[42]

But the Oxford contribution was significant, especially in the refinement of the book's production and in its reflection of the vexed political circumstances in which it was produced. The new folio edition is distinguished especially by its engravings, and these have a special interest owing to the political cartooning that has been discovered in their illustration of Satan. With reference to contemporary representations of James II, Estella Schoenberg has plausibly claimed that the spectacular plate for Book I depicts James as Satan, although she mistakenly attributes this to the Whig leanings of the illustrators—that James should suffer such treatment at the hands of Aldrich or Atterbury follows instead from their resentment of his religious politics and his interference in Christ Church and university affairs. More doubtfully, Schoenberg further proposes that the second plate satirizes Charles II in a comparable way. In view of the illustrators' allegiances, they seem less likely thus to have attacked Charles, in life or in death, and on this point Schoenberg's evidence is less conclusive in any case. The second plate therefore also seems likely to represent James, as its elongation of Satan's nose and chin suggests: the king's "hatchet-face" was distinctive. Moreover, Schoenberg's claims about the political dimension of book illustration can be strengthened with reference to Aldrich's cartooning elsewhere; this is a recognized feature of his university almanacs, in which he similarly combines topical allusion and more traditional iconography for political purposes.[43] The sequence in which the illustrations for the folio were executed remains uncertain, but the satirical cast of Aldrich's contribution points to a date of mid-1686 or later for his work, and "the last Cutt" was about to be completed by mid-November 1687, according to a letter from Atterbury to Tonson. This letter also indicates the climate of opinion in which such criticism might flourish: Atterbury here inquires after Dryden's latest

satire, even as he tells Tonson of a boldly anti-Catholic Gunpowder sermon of the week before by Thomas Creech, who seems to be helping with
the edition.[44]

Hence the Oxford contribution reflects not the Whig politics often
attributed to the 1688 edition, but the Tory resentment of James that
would make possible the Revolution later that year. Among the Tories in
question, Aldrich and Atterbury's roles in supervising the engravings is
difficult to distinguish owing to their cooperation in such matters and to
the possible involvement of other Oxford figures such as Creech. Although Aldrich seems to have contributed the illustrations for Books I, II,
and XII, the degree to which he relied on Atterbury's consultation in
directing Michael Burghers's execution of the other engravings remains
uncertain.[45] But their experience at the university with expensive academic publications seems to have contributed to the prestige of the 1688
folio, and it is through their cultural and social attainments that the subscription volume appears in a style much grander than Tonson's other folio
publications to this date, with large paper pressings for distribution by the
booksellers.[46] Atterbury's assistance in the preparation of the fourth edition appears from his efforts to gather subscribers, although his list of
contributors reflects only part of the Oxford support for the volume.[47] His
fuller involvement might be supposed in any case from his lifelong fascination with the poem, his annotated copy of which reflects an extraordinary
attention to Milton's work.[48] That Atterbury and Dryden enjoyed continuing and cordial relations is suggested not only by Atterbury's puff for
Dryden—"the living *Glory* of our English Poetry"—in his preface to an
edition of Waller (1690), but also by their later cooperation when Dryden
sought subscriptions for this translation of Virgil (1695). Atterbury would
continue to applaud Milton's poetry and his blank verse in particular.[49]
Years later, in what is either a rich irony or some more pointed gesture,
Defoe could liken the Tories, and Atterbury in particular, both to Milton's
Satan and to the very illustration of Sin that Aldrich and perhaps
Atterbury had devised in earlier days.[50]

The 1688 edition of *Paradise Lost* developed in a milieu in which an
Anglican conservatism was galvanized into new undertakings by the renewed threat of popery. This publication is noteworthy for its role in
accommodating Milton to the wider, less partisan audience that would
find Tonson's classic texts so much to their liking in the decades to come.
A comparison of the folio *Paradise Lost* (1688) to the octavo *Paradise Lost*
(1674, 1678), and especially to the quarto of 1667–69, vividly shows the
establishment of Milton as the national poet, not least in the addition of
such features as Robert White's classicist portrait and Dryden's reassuring

epigram for the frontispiece. The illustrations, especially those to Books I, II, and XII, also lend an obviously classical dimension to the text. If Somers helped organize the subscriptions to meet Tonson's costs, his contributions to the Exclusion controversy had also left him a sufficiently moderate Whig later to serve as Lord Chancellor.[51] He may be seen as part of a loose social and literary grouping from which Tonson drew much support for this folio and for other works. Moreover, many Whigs might have agreed with the Tories at Christ Church that Milton the poet needed redeeming from Milton the controversialist, that the English classic needed reclaiming from its republican but also apparently Puritan author.

For this consensus Tonson would provide a series of influential editions of Milton in the years to come, and these contributed to his development of a literary canon that has proven influential to this day. A fuller review of the subscription list points to more than "the Names of the Nobility and Gentry That Encourag'd, by Subscription, The Printing this Edition of Milton's *Paradise Lost.*" In brief, the gathering suggests a number of groups, often overlapping, which in outline suggest the cultural rapprochement intended by such associations as Roscommon's "Academy," in which the literary interests of divergent parties might lead to some nonpartisan destination. But the evidence of the subscription list also argues that in time this community of literary interest came to supply one of the means toward that agreement of Whig and Anglican Tory that shapes the Revolution of 1688. Beyond the core of Westminster and Christ Church men, and not just of Atterbury's but also of previous generations, the subscribers include many of the figures we associate with Tonson and Dryden's other literary projects of the 1680s, especially the contributors to Dryden's *Miscellany Poems* (London, 1684) and the successive volumes of *Plutarch's Lives.* The gathering may be seen as looking back to the formation and development of the Royal Society, and forward to that of the Kit-Cat Club. But the list extends far beyond this. On one hand it includes many more and less radical Whigs, of a kind we can associate with Somers and his friends, some of whom had already played significant parts in preparing the way for William of Orange, and many of whom would welcome the new king to England in the year to come. On the other hand, the list includes many churchmen and Tories of a more conservative stripe, including a number closely connected to James II himself (and loyal Jacobites in the decade to come), and extends even to Catholics such as the preaching William Hall, who graced the Catholic chapel now set up in Christ Church. There are some conspicuous omissions from the list: Anthony Wood is missing as are some other prominent Oxford figures such as Richard Bathurst, John Wallis, and Wood's friend

Arthur Charlett, nor do we find other students of Milton such as Aubrey (often impecunious), or Edward Phillips. That at least some potential subscribers were put off by the thought of supporting the work of Milton appears in a letter by the bookseller Richard Bentley to his frequent client John Evelyn.[52]

The political and cultural interests of the Christ Church group point to a new valuation of Milton's poetic art and to the wish to distinguish his and the nation's achievement on this front from the scandal of his sedition in the political prose. Although the folio *Paradise Lost* appeared a few years before Wood's entry for Milton in the *Fasti*, it bespeaks an admiration for the poet less constrained by the political preoccupations of a previous generation. In 1683, after the failure of a Whig attempt at revolution, Milton's prose works were burnt. In 1688, before the success of a revolution initially both Whig and Tory, Milton's poetry was published with acclaim. The Toryism of the Exclusion Crisis was giving way to a politics of increasing consensus, in which the gathering force of moderation was to play a significant part in political realignments and in the emergence of Milton into the English literary canon.

University of Ottawa

NOTES

My thanks to John Shawcross for helpful comment on this essay and for the abiding usefulness of his *Milton: A Bibliography for the Years 1624–1700* (Binghamton, N.Y., 1984). All manuscripts (MSS) cited are from Oxford, Bodleian Library, unless otherwise stated. Anthony Wood's (red) underlining in Andrew Allam's manuscripts is here represented by double underline.

1. A more general picture of Tory views of Milton may be traced in George Sensabaugh, *That Grand Whig, Milton* (Stanford, 1952); in John T. Shawcross, *Milton: The Critical Heritage*, 2 vols. (London, 1970–72); and in Dustin Griffin, *Regaining Paradise: Milton and the Eighteenth Century* (Cambridge, 1986), pp. 11–16.

2. Richard Ashcraft, *Revolutionary Politics and Locke's Two Treatises of Government* (Princeton, 1986); Jonathan Scott, *Algernon Sidney and the Restoration Crisis, 1677–1683* (Cambridge, 1991).

3. William Jane was the Regius Professor of Divinity and son of Joseph Jane, controverter of Milton in *Eikon Aklastos*, 1650 (Ballard MS 12, f. 65ʳ); William Jane, *The Judgment and Decree of the University of Oxford Past in Their Convocation July 21, 1683* (Oxford, 1683), pp. 3, 7, 8–9; A. Clark ed., *Life and Times of Anthony Wood* (Oxford, 1891–1900), vol. III, pp. 62–64; G. V. Bennett, "Loyalist Oxford and the Revolution," in *The History of University of Oxford, V. The Eighteenth Century*, ed. L. S. Sutherland and L. G. Mitchell

(Oxford, 1986), pp. 10–11; Oxford, Corpus Christi College, MS CCCI, f. 184, 185 (28 July, 4 August 1683); *Observator* 382 (1 August 1683); David Masson, *Life of Milton* (London, 1859–94), vol. VI, pp. 813–14; Sensabaugh, *That Grand Whig, Milton*, pp. 111–12.

4. Some held James Parkinson to be "a person of a very sober life, of a strict conversation," but the evidence points to his being not just "a great whig" but of an "unpeaceable" character: "Han't the king bum-fodder enough yet?" is his reported response to news of some earlier loyal addresses. He had previously been forced from Corpus Christi College, apparently owing to some disrespect for the nepotism of its president. Thomas Fowler, *The History of Corpus Christi College* (Oxford, 1893), p. 233; V.H.H. Green, *The Commonwealth of Lincoln College, 1427–1977* (Oxford, 1979), pp. 284–88; Wood, *Life and Times*, vol. III, pp. 68–72; Oxford, Corpus Christi College, MS CCCIX, f. 155, Anthony Wood to William Fulman, 4 and 25 August 1683; Corpus Christi College MS CCCX, f. 39, 40; Fulman to Wood, 5 September 1683 (Wood MS F.41, f. 360); John Wallis letter, 19 September 1683 (Bodleian, Add. MS D. 105, f. 79); James Parkinson, *An Account of Mr. Parkinson's Expulsion from the University of Oxford . . . In Vindication of Him* (1689).

5. J. Milton French, *Life Records of John Milton* (New Brunswick, N.J., 1949–58), vol. V, pp. 264–65; Harry Geduld, *Prince of Publishers: A Study of the Work and Career of Jacob Tonson* (Bloomington, 1969), pp. 116–20; Kathleen Lynch, *Jacob Tonson, Kit-Cat Publisher* (University of Tennessee, 1971), frontispiece, pp. 126–27.

6. Anthony Wood, "Life of Milton" in *Early Lives of Milton*, ed. Helen Darbishire (London, 1932), pp. 39, 47; Wood's note in his copy (Oxford, Bodleian Library, shelfmark Wood 88) of Edward Phillips, *Theatrum poetarum* (London, 1675), p. 114.

7. William Riley Parker, "Wood's Life of Milton: Its Sources and Significance," *PBSA* LII (1958), 3–4, but compare French to whom Wood seems "unusually dependable for a biographer of his time," "Reliability of Anthony Wood," p. 30.

8. Wood, *Life and Times*, vol. III, p. 365. Thomas Hearne similarly testifies that "Anthony was a meer Rhapsodist, throwing together whatever was sent him . . . and that, too, in the very words of the Writers, concealing their names." *Remarks and Collections*, ed. C. E. Doble, D. W. Rannie, and H. E. Salter (Oxford, 1885–1921), vol. VIII, p. 255; so too William Nicolson, "a Medly of Notes and such Informations . . . without being digested," *The English Historical Library* (London, 1696–99), vol. II, pp. 231–32.

9. Among the offenders on this point, I have made much of Wood's observation that "Miltons Hist. has onely the reputation of putting oᵣ old Authors neatly together in a connect'd story, not abstainyng from som lashes at the ignorance or I know not what of those times" (Nicholas von Maltzahn, *Milton's History of Britain*, [Oxford, 1991], pp. 27, 73, 132, 222; Wood, *Early Lives*, ed. Darbishire, p. 46): this passage proves to originate in Wood's source Thomas Blount (10 Nov. 1670, Wood MS F.40, f. 82ʳ), who would soon refer to Milton more generously as "a late ingenious Historian," *Animadversions upon Sr Richard Baker's Chronicle* (London, 1672), p. 98. Similarly, Wood's malice in observing that Milton's *Character of the Long Parliament* is "a notable account of their Ignorance, Treachery, and Hypocrisie" originates with Wood's "crony" Arthur Charlett (Wood MS F.49, f. 189ʳ; von Maltzahn, *Milton's History*, p. 18; Wood, *Early Lives*, ed. Darbishire, p. 47), although Wood did not choose to include Charlett's ill-founded report of Milton's being finally "reputed a Papist," a frequent allegation after some doubtful evidence thrown up by the Popish Plot. Charlett's hand is distinctive, cf. Lister MS 37, f. 72–73, 83, 88–89, 99, 133, 152; his politics and association with Wood are noted by Wood, in *Life and Times*, vol. III. p. 245 and V, pp. 36–37; and Thomas Hearne, in Wood, *Athenae Oxonienses . . . to which are added the Fasti*, 3rd ed., ed. Philip Bliss (London, 1813–20), vol. I, p. 11.

10. *Early Lives of Milton*, ed. Darbishire, pp. xvi–xxvii; cf. William Riley Parker, *Mil-*

ton: a Biography (Oxford, 1968), pp. xiii–xv, and Peter Beal, *Index of English Literary Manuscripts, Volume II 1625–1700* (London, 1987–93), part 2, pp. 85–86. Note how Allan Pritchard, for example, signally fails to acknowledge John Aubrey's role in bringing Cyriack Skinner into the biographer's fold, "Milton in Rome: According to Wood," *MQ* XIV (1980), 93–94.

11. C. G. Osgood, "[Review of] *The Earliest Life of Milton*. Edited by Edward S. Parsons," *JEGP* 6 (1906–67), 133–39; William Riley Parker, *Milton's Contemporary Reputation* (Columbus, Ohio, 1940), p. 6 n., and *Milton: a Biography* (Oxford, 1968), p. 1168; Harris Fletcher, *The Intellectual Development of John Milton* (Urbana, Ill., 1956–61), vol. I, pp. 2–3; French, *Life Records*, vol. III, p. 378 and vol. V, pp. 146, 276–77.

12. Date of baptism 23 April 1655, Wood, *Life and Times*, vol. II, p. 509; date of death (smallpox) 17 June 1685, Wood MS Diaries 29 (1685), f. 35ᵛ; Wood, *Athenae . . . Fasti*, ed. Bliss, vol. IV, pp. 174–76; *DNB*.

13. Ballard MS 14, f. 134ʳ (20 Dec. 1681); Aubrey soon cites Allam again, f. 136ᵛ. J. Milton French's confusion over Aubrey's pseudonym "Jo. Gregorius" is noted in Pritchard, "Milton in Rome," 96: for further examples of this usage compare Wood MS F. 39, f. 318, 321, 327, 328, 343, 368, 369, and 312 ("Jo. Baptista Gregorius Albericus"—Aubrey's birth on St. Gregory's day explains the usage, Aubrey MS 7, f. 3; Anthony Powell, ed. *John Aubrey and His Friends* (1948; rpt. London, 1988), pp. 21, 30).

14. Aubrey MS 8, f. 66ᵛ; John Aubrey, *Brief Lives*, ed. A. Clark (Oxford, 1898), vol. II, p. 72; Wood, *Early Lives*, ed. Darbishire, p. 15. These notes were in Wood's hands by September 1680 (Wood, *Early Lives*, ed. Darbishire, p. xi). Parker, *Milton*, p. 1168: "An ambiguous note by Aubrey for a time prompted several students to speculate as to the existence of a lost autobiography, or possibly a lost biography by Andrew Allam. I once fell into this trap myself."

15. Wood MS F.47, f. 626ᵛ, 689bᵛ; Wood MS F.51, f. 34ᵛ; Anthony Wood, *Athenae Oxonienses*, p. 880 (*Athenae . . . Fasti*, ed. Bliss, vol. II, p. 480); Wood, *Life and Times*, vol. I, p. 319; R. W. Hunt, *A Summary Catalogue of Western Manuscripts in the Bodleian Library*, vol. I (Oxford, 1953), p. xiv; Ian Philip, *The Bodleian Library* (Oxford, 1983), pp. 62, 64. Wood appears not to have owned a copy of *Defensio Secunda* himself, but he noted the place of the autobiographical passage in both editions and observed these and other works by Milton on the special shelves in the Librarian's study (Wood MS F.51, f. 34ᵛ), of which the *Defensio Secunda* seems later to have been lost. Here Wood further records a presentation copy of *Pro Se Defensio* (also now missing and also not noted by French or Parker, though the latter again guesses correctly that Milton would have sent these to the Bodleian, Parker, *Milton*, pp. 477, 1046), as well as the presentation copies of *Defensio* and the *Tenure* (given 11 June 1656 and still in the collection). In an article that obscures and confuses the matter, Leo Miller claims that these volumes remained "unknown to Anthony à Wood" and fails to understand the arrangements "in musaeo," nor does he allow for the ease with which books could be borrowed from the library in this period. Leo Miller, "The Burning of Milton's Books in 1660: Two Mysteries," *ELR* XVIII (1988), 424–37.

16. Wood, *Athenae . . . Fasti*, ed. Bliss, vol. I, p. cxxx and vol. IV, pp. 174–76. Hearne, *Remarks and Collections*, vol. III, p. 35, vol. VIII, p. 255, and vol. X, p. 447. Wood also lists Allam's books and further copies some of Allam's notes, Wood MS E.2(69), pp. 94, 122, 163, 180, 191, 198, 232; Wood MS 205, f. 2 shows Allam's flyleaf annotation of his ownership of a book, of the price and place of purchase, and his extended comment on its author(s). Wood, *Life and Times*, vol. I, p. 385, vol. II, p. 435, and vol. IV, p. 235. William Fulman too drew on Allam as a useful source (Wood MS F.41, f. 341: Fulman to Wood, 11 August 1681), and Allam's students could benefit from his extended tutorial bibliographies (British Library, Lansdowne MS 960).

17. The same may be said of his relation with the young White Kennett, who had been taught by Allam (Wood, *Athenae . . . Fasti*, ed. Bliss, vol. IV, p. 792) and who later writes to Wood (26 Nov. 1688) with reference to "the death of our excellent Freind Mr Allam," Wood MS F.42, f. 333.

18. Both as a writer and a receiver of letters, Allam already appears in Wood's letter-books (Wood MS F.39, f. 24–46; Wood MS F.40, f. 242–97), and his name often comes up in Wood's papers, for example "see my answer to Mr. Sprigg's letter on my shelf under my picture among Mr. Allam's letters." The assembler of Wood's *Life and Times* long ago cited Allam's voluminous notes for the *Athenae*, and gave an example of Allam's distinctive script. Wood, *Life and Times*, vol. I, p. 380, vol. III, p. 167, vol. IV, plate 1, and vol. V, p. 24.

19. Wood, *Athenae . . . Fasti*, ed. Bliss, vol. IV, p. 174–75; George Griffith, *Some Plain Discourses on the Lord's Supper* (Oxford, 1684); Richard Cosin, *Ecclesiae Anglicana Politeia* (Oxford, 1684); Cornelius Nepos, *The Lives of Illustrious Men* (Oxford, 1684), sig. a8ʳ, *2ᵛ, pp. 99–104. In such contexts "fanatical" is of course very much a Tory word, as in the formula "false & faniticall," Andrew Allam, "To the Reader," in John Corbet, *The Epistle Congratulatory of Lysimachus Nicanor* (Oxford, 1684), p. 9; Wood MS F.47, f. 409, 708.

20. Corbet, *Epistle Congratulatory*, pp. 1–2, 8; British Library, Lansdowne MS 960, f. 34ᵛ (Allam to Kennett, 21 September 1680); White Kennett, *A Letter from a Student at Oxford to a Friend in the Country* (London, 1681), p. 14; Parker, *Milton's Contemporary Reputation*, p. 6 n.

21. Allam viewed the second Exclusion Parliament as "fiery, eager, and high-flying." Wood, *Life and Times*, vol. I, p. 13, vol. II, p. 511, and vol. III, p. 357; Wood, *Athenae . . . Fasti*, ed. Bliss, vol. III, p. 664 and vol. IV, pp. 234, 764; Wood MS F.48, f. 931; Wood MS F.47, f. 357b, 619ᵛ; Bodleian shelfmark Wood 363, f. 1ᵛ.

22. "Philips having by this means very early imbibed [in] a most plentifull manner yᵉ rankest Anti-monarchical principle prov'd in a short time so notable a proficient in his Unckles bloody Schoole of king-killing yᵗ he judged himself sufficiently qualified publickly to engage in & espouse his Master's quarrel, wᶜʰ he did in his Miltoni defensio, in wᶜʰ scurrilous peice as he acquitted himself very expertly in the art of railery, & giving imbitter'd language, ~~so did he make Bp Bramhall upon far shallower grounds~~ so he would perswade us to beleive yᵗ Bp Bramhall, wrote yᵗ Apology pro Rege & populo Anglicano agst wᶜʰ he scolds & frets so much in his defensio Miltoni tho upon far shallower grounds yⁿ his Unckle had before charg'd Alex: More to have been Author of yᵗ piece above nam'd. Some time after this having seemingly renounced his former principles he appear'd agst yᵉ Fanaticks in some few small pieces, among wᶜʰ was his Satyr agst Hypocrites printed Lond: 1680 in 3 sheets & an halfe, there are several edit: of this wᶜʰ came out before." (Wood MS F.47, f. 626ᵛ). Compare Wood, *Athenae . . . Fasti*, ed. Bliss, vol. IV, p. 764: "This Edw. Phillips hath a brother called Joh. Phillips, who having early imbib'd in a most plentiful manner the rankest antimonarchical principles, from that villanous leading incendiary Joh. Milton his uncle, but not in any university, proved in so short time so notable a proficient in his bloody school of king-killing, that he judged himself sufficiently qualified publicly to engage in and espouse his master's quarrel: and this he did in his *Miltoni Defensio*, &c. In which scurrilous piece," etc.

23. Parker noted his suspicion that this and some other nonbibliographical passages were not original to Wood, but came from William Joyner, Parker, "Wood's Life of Milton," p. 10; he was wrong about the source but characteristically shrewd about Wood's text. Parker and others have also noted Wood's use of *Mercurius Politicus*: about the burning of *Defensio* at Toulouse in 1651 the notebooks now prove that, as Parker expected, Wood noted "this in *Mercurius Politicus*, no. 56, June 26–July 3, 1651," "Wood's Life of Milton," 17 n.; Wood MS F.48, f. 1036.

24. In another passage marked by Wood, Allam observes of the Smectymnuan quarrel with Bishop Hall that "There is another short piece entitl'd Animadversions upon y^e Remonstrants defence agst Smectymnuus. Lond: 1641 4to This wrot by <u>John Milton</u>, as also an Apology agst y^e humble Remonstrant, wch came out soon after his <u>Animadversions</u>." Wood MS F.47, f. 689b^v [= p. "2"]. This corroborates Parker's suspicion that Wood never saw the *Apology.* "Wood's Life of Milton," p. 10.

25. Wood MS F.47, f. 640^r; Wood, *Athenae . . . Fasti,* ed. Bliss, vol. II, p. 484–85 and vol. IV, p. 195.

26. There may be further Allam material on Milton that has not yet been recovered or identified: Wood was searching for Allam's papers a few months after his death, but in a book list he later notes "qu. Allams papers—p 48—Joh Milton" (although this reference seems not quite to describe the pages gathered into Wood MSS F.47–49). Oxford, Corpus Christi College, MS CCCX, f. 48 (Wood to William Fulman, 27 November 1685); Wood MS E.10 p. 421 (p. 435 new pagination).

27. That much may be missing appears from Wood's filing system (summarized by Clark in Wood, *Life and Times,* vol. IV, pp. 232–36), although whether any of the gaps are specifically from Allam's contribution cannot be told. A necessarily loose estimate is that as much as a quarter of Wood's slips have gone missing—from Clark's figures about 480 entries may be inferred as missing out of the over 1300 that may once have existed (37 percent), but a truer figure with reference also to the letter books, which Clark omits from his list, seems to be around 25 percent. The proportion of missing materials again goes up, however, if indeed Wood did list papers under the further files TT–ZZ and AAA–EEE (files now missing but which Clark reasonably assumes to have once been extant), and the proportion of missing materials rises in any case if we make even a conservative allowance for likely extra entries coming at the end of many of these series. Wood MS F.46, headnote: "The papers bound in this and three similar volumes and in a cloth one lettered 'Wood papers, personal etc' were found in 1883 in a large wood box in the Wood room, in the shape of numberless small parcels each usually containing the papers of a class, such as K or QQ or such like; but there was great disorder and the sets of papers were far from complete." That Wood's bundles were small, might include only a brief sequence of letters from a longer correspondence, and were filed long after the individual letters' arrival appears, for example, in his registration of letters from Ashmole and Aubrey, Wood MS F.39, f. 63–96, pp. 116–203.

28. Parker, "Wood's Life of Milton," p. 4; Parker, *Milton,* pp. 799, 806. These doubts are answered but far from decisively by J. Milton French, "Anthony Wood and the Reliability of Milton's Oxford M.A.," *PMLA* LXXV (1960), 22–30. See also the entries for Oxford and Wood in *A Milton Encyclopedia,* ed. W. B. Hunter (Lewisburg, Pa., 1978–1980).

29. Wood MS F.39, f. 386^v; Parker, "Wood's Life of Milton," p. 4; French, "Anthony Wood," 23 n. The difficulty arises from the failure of the registrar, "a careless man (though a good scholar)," to register incorporations of Cambridge graduates, Wood, *Athenae . . . Fasti,* ed. Bliss, vol. II, p. 451; this is reflected in other Fasti, such as Corpus Christi College, MS CCCI, f. 128 (which for 1636 only lists two of three incorporations), or the list prepared by William Fulman, who advised Wood on the format for his *Fasti,* Corpus Christi College, MS CCCII, f. 72^v (nor does Fulman list Milton under "Illustres Oxonienses," f. 272^v); Wood MS F. 41, f. 339 (20 June 1681). Wood's notes on convocation registers seem to have been lost, *Life and Times,* vol. III, p. 167.

30. Wood MS F.48, f. 908^v. Wood applies this note to his entry for Matthew Griffith. Wood, *Athenae . . . Fasti,* ed. Bliss, vol. III, p. 712.

31. Tanner MS 102. f. 71^v; Wood MS F.51, f. 63^v; Wood MS Diaries 18 (1674), f. 96; Wood, *Life and Times,* vol. II, p. 297. The connection lay with Milton's publication (as

Raleigh's) of *The Cabinet-Council*, for which Wood has a double listing, Wood, *Athenae . . . Fasti*, ed. Bliss, vol. II, p. 242. Comparison may be made to the way in which Wood includes a long digression about Andrew Marvell in the entry for Samuel Parker; this practice is advertised in *Proposals for Printing Athenae Oxonienses* (London, 1691), p. 1.

32. Wood MS F.39, f. 386ᵛ; Wood, *Early Lives*, ed. Darbishire, p. 35. Here the only other "friend" who connects Wood to Milton is William Joyner, but Joyner does not provide "most of [Wood's] account," and the evidence supports Parker's doubts about the closeness of his acquaintance with Milton. Parker, *Milton*, p. 1134; Hearne, *Remarks and Collections*, vol. I, pp. 288–89.

33. Compare Aubrey's unhappy note on Wood, MS Aubrey 7, f. 2, and Wood's retrospective view of Aubrey as "a shiftless person, roving and magotie-headed, and somtimes little better than crased," Wood, *Life and Times*, vol. II, pp. 116–17.

34. No record survives of Wood's having owned any of Milton's poetry, and his name is conspicuously absent from the list of subscribers to the illustrated folio *Paradise Lost* (1688).

35. Bennett, "Loyalist Oxford and the Revolution" in *The History of Oxford*, V. pp. 9–29; Walter George Hiscock, *Henry Aldrich of Christ Church, 1648–1710* (Oxford, 1960), pp. 8–12. Of Aldrich, Bennett adds that "for a generation, down to his death in 1710, he was to represent in the university the most uncompromising form of old-fashioned Toryism." Bennett, "Against the Tide: Oxford under William III" in *History of Oxford*, V, p. 40.

36. Hiscock, *Henry Aldrich*, pp. 8–12; W. G. Hiscock, *A Christ Church Miscellany* (Oxford, 1946), pp. 17–37; Gareth V. Bennett, *The Tory Crisis in Church and State, 1688–1730: The Career of Francis Atterbury, Bishop of Rochester* (Oxford, 1975), pp. 26–28.

37. Helen Darbishire, ed., *The Manuscript of Milton's Paradise Lost Book I* (Oxford, 1931), p. xiv; M. D. Ravenhall, "Francis Atterbury and the First Illustrated Edition of *Paradise Lost*," *MQ* XVI (1982), 30–31; Francis Atterbury, *Epistolary Correspondence*, ed. J. Nichols (London, 1783–87), vol. II, pp. 303–04, 456; *The Miscellaneous Works of Bishop Atterbury*, ed. John Nichols (London, 1789–98), vol. II, p. 49; *The Correspondence of Alexander Pope*, ed. George Sherburn (Oxford, 1956), vol. II, p. 124; *The Letters of John Dryden*, ed. Charles Ward (Durham, N.C., 1942), p. 22, 152–53; Stuart Gillespie, "The Early Years of the Dryden-Tonson Partnership," *Restoration* XII (1988), 10–19; Stuart Bennett, "Jacob Tonson an Early Editor of *Paradise Lost*?" *Library* 6th ser. X (1988), 247–52; Arthur Sherbo, "The Dryden-Cambridge translation of Plutarch's Lives," *Etudes Anglaises* XXXII (1979), 177–84; Sherbo, "Dryden as a Cambridge Editor," *Studies in Bibliography* XXXVIII (1985), 251–61.

38. My thanks to Paul Hammond for guidance on this point. *Poems of John Dryden*, ed. James Kinsley (Oxford, 1958), pp. 211, 1874; Louis Bredvold, "Dryden and the University of Oxford," *MLN* XLVI (1931), 218–24; Roswell G. Ham, "Dryden and the Colleges," *MLN* XLIX (1934), 324–32; J.A.W. Bennett, "Dryden and All Souls," *MLN* LII (1937), 115–16; MS Eng hist. c 6, f. 122; Dr. William's Library, London, Morrice MS 31 Q, p. 49. "The Westminster students at Christ Church were almost a class by themselves." H. C. Beeching, *Francis Atterbury* (London, 1909), p. 4; George F. R. Barker, *Memoir of Richard Busby D. D.* (London, 1895); James Anderson Winn, *John Dryden and His World* (New Haven, Conn., 1987), pp. 61–62, 415, 610–11, 613.

39. Note also the number of publications in which John Dryden's *The State of Innocence* (1677; 4th ed. 1684) governs early references to *Paradise Lost*. These include, among others, Samuel Woodford, *A Paraphrase Upon the Canticles* (London, 1679), sig. c3ʳ; Edward Ecclestone, *Noah's Flood, or, The Destruction of the World. An Opera* (London, 1679), sig. A4ᵛ, A2ᵛ–A3ᵛ; and Nathaniel Lee, who provided a commendatory poem for *The State of Innocence*.

40. Here Dryden's remarks on epic recall one of the tributes in Milton's *Poems* (1645), sig. A2ᵛ, already echoed in Samuel Barrow's commendatory verses for *Paradise Lost* (1674) and in Nathaniel Lee's on *The State of Innocence* (1677), and anticipate Dryden's claims for Milton in the hexastich fronting the 1688 *Paradise Lost*. Wentworth Dillon, earl of Roscommon, *An Essay on Translated Verse* (London, 1st ed. 1684; 1685), sig. A2ᵛ, pp. 23–25. Roscommon had already used and recommended blank verse for translation, *Horace's Art of Poetry* (London, 1680). Dryden and Roscommon were close literary friends.

41. Rymer, *The Tragedies of the Last Age Consider'd* (London 1678); Thomas Shipman, *Henry the Third of France* (London, 1678), sig. A4ᵛ-***1ʳ.

42. "Oh had the Poet ne're prophaned his Pen, / To varnish o're the Guilt of Faithless Men." Joseph Addison, "An Account of the Greatest English Poets. To Mr. H. S.," in *The Annual Miscellany: For the Year 1694*, ed. John Dryden (London, 1694), p. 322. G. Blakemore Evans, "Addison's Early Knowledge of Milton," *JEGP* XLIX (1950), 204–07.

43. My thanks to Estella Schoenberg for promptly supplying me with copies of her work: Schoenberg, "The Face of Satan, 1688," in *Ringing the Bell Backward: The Proceedings of the First International Milton Symposium*, ed. Ronald G. Shafer (Indiana, Pa., 1982), pp. 46–59; Schoenberg, "Seventeenth-Century Propaganda in Book Illustration," *Mosaic* XXV (1992), 1–24. Hiscock, *Henry Aldrich*, p. 9.

44. Letter from Atterbury to Jacob Tonson (15 Nov. 1687), Washington, Folger Shakespeare Library, MS C. c. 1 (3); Edmond Malone, ed. *The Critical and Miscellaneous Prose Works of John Dryden* (London, 1800), vol. I, i, pp. 202–205 (this is the letter cited in *Historical Manuscripts Commission, Second Report*, 1871, p. 69, but misdated to 1681). A member of Wadham and then All Souls', Thomas Creech had already translated the lives of Solon, Pelopidas, and Cleomines for Dryden's *Plutarch's Lives* (London, 1683–86); he is on the list of subscribers for *Paradise Lost* (1688).

45. Aldrich kept proof copies of Michael Burghers's plates. Hiscock, *Henry Aldrich*, pp. 8–12; Suzanne Boorsch, "The Illustrators of the 1688 *Paradise Lost*," *Metropolitan Museum Journal* VI (1972), 133–50; J. T. Shawcross, "The First Illustrations for *Paradise Lost*," *MQ* IX (1975), 43–46; Mary D. Ravenhall, "Sources and Meaning in Dr. Aldrich's 1688 Illustrations of *Paradise Lost*," *ELN* XIX (1982), 208–18; Ravenhall, "Francis Atterbury," 34; Atterbury, *Miscellaneous Works*, I, pp. 15–16. Burghers already had engraved most of the illustrations for the Tonson-Dryden *Plutarchs Lives. Translated from the Greek by Several Hands* (London, 1683–86).

46. H. F. Fletcher, ed. *John Milton's Complete Poetical Works* (Urbana, Ill., 1943–48), vol. III, p. 20. Miles Flesher, Tonson's printer for the 1688 folio, frequently worked for Oxford booksellers and authors, Donald Wing, *Short-Title Catalogue . . . 1641–1700*, 2nd ed. (New York, 1972–88); P. G. Morrison, *Index of Printers . . . in Wing's Short-Title Catalogue* (Charlottesville, Va. 1955). Oxford was fertile ground for subscription ventures, Sarah L. C. Clapp, "The Beginnings of Subscription Publication in the Seventeenth Century," *MP* XXIX (1931), 201–02.

47. Atterbury-Tonson (15 Nov. 1687), Washington, Folger Shakespeare Library, MS C. c. 1 (3). The further Oxford contribution may be judged from a comparison of the subscription list in *Paradise Lost* (1688), pp. [345–50] with the persons index in Wood's *Life and Times*, vol. V.

48. Atterbury, *Epistolary Correspondence*, vol. I, pp. 40–41 and vol. II, pp. 303–04. Atterbury's much annotated copy of *Paradise Lost* (1678) is in the Yale University Library, James Osborn Collection, shelfmark pb9; it is to this third edition that he refers in a later letter, *Correspondence of Pope*, vol. I., p. 452. Although it fails to refer to Bennett's biography of Atterbury, Hiscock on Aldrich and Oxford engraving, or the Atterbury copy of

Paradise Lost, the best study of Atterbury's role remains Ravenhall, "Francis Atterbury," 29–36; see also J. J. Balakier, "Annotations to Paradise Lost," *MQ* XXII (1988), 128–29; John T. Shawcross, *John Milton and Influence* (Pittsburgh, 1991), pp. 39–40; Estella Schoenberg, "Picturing Satan for the 1688 *Paradise Lost*," in *Milton's Legacy in the Arts*, ed. Albert C. Labriola and Edward Sichi, Jr. (University Park, Pa., 1988), pp. 12–16.

49. Edmund Waller, *The Second Part of Mr. Waller's Poems* (London, 1690), sig. A8^{r-v}; *The Letters of John Dryden*, ed. Ward, p. 172; Winn, *John Dryden and His World*, p. 481; monument to John Philips (Westminster Abbey), Beeching, *Francis Atterbury*, pp. 226–27, 304; Atterbury, *Epistolary Correspondence*, vol. I, p. 139.

50. Daniel Defoe, *The Secret History of the White-Staff* (London, 1714), pp. 70–71; Defoe, *Memoirs of the Conduct of Her Late Majesty* (London, 1715), p. 49; Defoe, *The Secret History of State Intrigues in the Management of the Scepter* (London, 1715), p. 52; *Defoe's Review*, ed. Arthur W. Secord (New York, 1938), vol. V (14, 16 June 1708), 135, 138; vol. VI (24 November 1709) 402; vol. VII (13 January 1711), 502–03; Paula Backscheider, *Daniel Defoe His Life* (Baltimore, 1989), p. 366; Irving Rothman, "Daniel Defoe," in *A Milton Encyclopedia*.

51. John Somers, *A Brief History of the Succession* (London, 1681); Henry Maddock, *An Account of the Life and Writings of Lord Chancellor Somers* (London, 1812), vol. II, pp. 116–21; William L. Sachse, *Lord Somers: A Political Portrait* (Manchester, 1975), pp. 19–25; Lois G. Schwoerer, *The Declaration of Rights, 1689* (Baltimore, 1981), pp. 30–31, 34, 37, 47–50, *passim*.

52. "I have a book for yow to subscrip to that yow will be kinder to then yow were to Milton; but I canot tell yow it tell [= till] I se[e] you for feare of a Scandalum Mag—: yow are to take this very kindly for all the Band of Translators cowld not have got soe much as this from me on a post night." Oxford, Christ Church Library, Evelyn Collection, MS Letters 155 (4 September 1686), f. 1^v. This is not the classical scholar and later Miltonist, Richard Bentley, as claimed in Margaret Jacob, *The Newtonians and the English Revolution, 1689–1720* (Ithaca, N.Y. 1976), p. 152.

PATRICK HUME AND THE MAKING OF ADDISON'S *PARADISE LOST* PAPERS

Patrick Daly, Jr.

R UNNING AS A Saturday feature in the *Spectator* for eighteen consecutive weeks in 1712, Joseph Addison's *Paradise Lost* papers embody, among other things, the two familiar strains of neoclassical criticism,
the preceptual "rules" and the more subjective view of taste or "grace
beyond the reach of art." While the first four papers examine the poem's
fable, characters, sentiments, and language, followed by two numbers on
the faults, the latter twelve book-by-book discussions of the poem cite and
praise the finer passages, or "beauties" as they were then commonly
called. It is well known that the early papers primarily employ the pa-
tently Aristotelian formula, via Rene Le Bossu's *Traite du Poeme Epique*
(1675), to examine the formal structures of the poem. But the main source
of the latter twelve numbers has yet to be identified, except to say, as
Clarence Thorpe has, that these papers "stood as a superb example of the
positive method in criticism" which was emerging at the time.[1] As for a
specific model, Addison might have been following seventeenth-century
French editions of Greek and Roman classics, most notably those by the
Daciers which include some remarks on excellent passages. However, I
would like to submit that a more tangible source than either pre-Romantic
ideas or French editorial practices was responsible for the book-by-book
discussions, that being Patrick Hume's commentary on *Paradise Lost*,
published by Jacob Tonson in 1695.

Although the influence of Hume's commentary on eighteenth-century
editors of Milton's epic is well known, Addison's association with it has been
largely ignored. Indeed Ants Oras has noted that Addison "had probably
seen at least the first pages of Hume's commentary, which was without
competitors at the time," though this critic goes on to conclude that the
Paradise Lost papers "do not appear on the whole to bear many traces of
Hume's influence."[2] Addison's debt reaches far beyond the initial pages
and takes in the whole of Hume's commentary in a pervasive material and
structural appropriation, one which enabled him to discuss many passages
of the poem in different ways. This study will demonstrate this event. In

addition, some evidence will be presented at the conclusion of this essay which suggests that Hume deserves some notice as the earliest illustrator of certain psychological underpinnings in the poetry of Milton's epic. Although Addison (and in some cases John Dennis) has been credited with pioneering the aesthetic of the sublime in *Paradise Lost*, it was Hume who first conveyed aspects of the Miltonic sublime and other subjective notions in scattered glosses throughout his commentary.[3]

These and many other kinds of glosses were not lost on Addison, who knew the 1695 work and found a good deal of its material worthy of amplification in his *Paradise Lost* papers. In several ways it is Hume's commentary which was most responsible for extending and shaping what turned out to be the most popular literary criticism of the eighteenth century.

Little is known about Patrick Hume except for what the *Dictionary of National Biography* and *A Biographical Dictionary of Eminent Scotsmen* have uncovered about this Scot, namely that he is thought to have descended from the house of Polwarth, Berwickshire, from where he eventually made his way south to London to become a schoolmaster. Not much more can be ascertained about this obscure figure, though his one major work on *Paradise Lost* is well intact, and it can help to shed some light on the course of Milton criticism in the early eighteenth century, beginning specifically with the *Spectator* papers.

Hume's only surviving literary productions are a somewhat labored elegy on Queen Mary's death[4] and, more important, the commentary on *Paradise Lost* consisting of two separate parts: a table of beauties and an annotation, the latter consisting of a running series of glosses on each book of the poem. As one of Tonson's biographers points out, the existence of both parts of this commentary is most likely the result of the commercial instincts of the period's most famous printer and bookseller: "Following the stabilization of Milton's literary reputation [in the wake of the Glorious Revolution], Tonson decided to place a chief emphasis on the text of *Paradise Lost*, on its exposition and interpretation. . . . In addition to the commentary, Hume, probably acting on a suggestion by Tonson, compiled a 'table' [of beauties]."[5] Although Hume's effort eventually failed to gain the attention of his contemporaries, the unprecedented range of his work, especially the annotation, has not been lost on William Riley Parker, who calls the 321 page annotation "the most voluminous notes on any English poet produced before modern times, and made John Dryden's likening of Milton to Homer and Virgil seem almost unrhetorical."[6] The reference is of course to the vast erudition involved in

Hume's work, which actually treated 4,012 of the poem's 10,565 lines, covering not only literary concerns, but also philosophy, geography, astronomy, and much church history. Hume's commentary eventually became a treasury from which several eighteenth-century editors and commentators of *Paradise Lost* pilfered, such as Richard Bentley (1732), Jonathan Richardson (1734), Thomas Newton (1749), and John Callendar (1750).[7]

Despite Hume's well-known connection with these editors, it is perhaps surprising that Addison has not been more closely linked with the only sustained commentary devoted to *Paradise Lost* prior to 1712. In his edition of the *Spectator*, Donald Bond does note a few parallel passages between Addison and Hume, though the association is not pursued;[8] and, as mentioned, Oras concedes that Addison knew and used Hume—but not after the initial number. However, it is hard to imagine that Addison, an overworked journalist who wrote two to three other numbers during the week, and who wrote to a friend shortly after the *Spectator* began, "If you have any hints or subjects, pray send me up a paper full,"[9] would have used only the initial comments of Hume's commentary and then ignored the valuable assistance which this work could offer on consecutive Saturdays for some three months.

Reissued in book form in 1719, the *Paradise Lost* papers were reprinted many times throughout the eighteenth century, and this success was due, in large part, to the many passages from the poem which Addison supplied for his audience. Such an approach, as Lillian Bloom maintains, worked particularly well for the early eighteenth-century reader because it "elicited the delights of the imagination," and for a good many the series probably acted as a substitute for the poem itself.[10] This critic also notes that Addison's awareness of the average Londoner's limitations in understanding the highly literary quality of *Paradise Lost* impelled him to employ passages from the poem sparingly at first, so as not to lose any reader "reluctant not to venture too far"; as the series progressed, Addison "gradually unfolded the intricacies of fiction" and even "saved" certain passages "for the halfway point in his series," that is that point at which the book-by-book discussions begin.[11] Bloom is thus indicating, among other things, that the series was composed with much care and foresight. While not wishing to diminish the assessment of the degree to which a popular rhetoric informs the *Paradise Lost* papers, I would like to point out that the deliberation with which Addison is thought by Bloom to have planned and carried out his Milton project has been greatly overstated. In fact, what has heretofore escaped notice is that Addison originally intended

only a handful of numbers for his project, and that the latter twelve
discussions were the result of a daring and extravagant improvisation
which took place after the series was well under way, an incident which
deserves some attention.

At the end of the sixth number (no. 297), Addison wrote in the
original folio half-sheet which Londoners bought and read,

I shall in next *Saturday's* paper give an Account of the many particular Beauties in
Milton, which would have been too long to insert under those general Heads I
have already treated of, with which I *intend to conclude* this Piece of Criticism.[12]
(Emphasis mine)

Sometime during the week, however, it must have dawned on Addison
the journalist that he could get much more mileage out of Milton's epic.
So he decided, contrary to his previous announcement, to write twelve
more numbers. Fortunately for Addison, a publication of the entire *Spectator* a year later in 1713 afforded him the opportunity to delete the
glaring contradiction "next Saturday's" from the above quotation and in-
sert the more consistent "my next Papers," an emendation which has
served as the copy text since. It is important to recognize that the results
of this improvisation differ noticeably from Addison's past critical practices in a few ways.

First, the decision led to eighteen numbers, a total which exceeded
all previous literary series in the *Spectator* by thirteen.[13] In addition,
while the initial *Paradise Lost* papers, as well as his earlier literary series,
all sparingly cite beauties in a representative fashion, the latter twelve
numbers constitute Addison's first treatment of the many beauties of a
given work in a generally discursive and individual way. Of course one
might argue that Addison's initial announcement of the series in *Spectator*
no. 262, when he wrote that he would "enter into a regular Criticism upon
his *Paradise Lost*, which I shall publish every Saturday till I have given
my Thoughts upon that Poem" (II, p. 520), left open the possibility of
further papers. However, there is hardly anything in this statement that
hints at that which follows, either the unprecedented eighteen Saturdays
or the two-part structure. Rather what followed in the latter numbers was
an onslaught of commentary on many individual beauties, in which Addison either enumerated or explicated passages, the two modes which parallel the dual apparatus found in Hume's commentary.

In order to best demonstrate the nature of the appropriation, first the
debt to Hume's table will be given, followed by that to his annotation,
despite the fact that Addison mingled the two approaches in comments
throughout the series. Obviously a detailed analysis of even a handful of

borrowings is out of the question, but a treatment of few passages from both parts of Hume's commentary with those by Addison should suffice to reflect a significant dependence. (An appendix supplies several other conspicuous borrowings.)

The title page to Hume's three-page table reads "A Table of the most remarkable Parts of Milton's *Paradise Lost* Under the Three Heads of Description, Similes and Speeches. The first Number marks the Book, the following the Verse." This table, with over 140 entries, each of which supplies several beauties, might have suggested to Addison a taxonomy for the "particular" passages, especially since of his 186 enumerated beauties in the last twelve papers, 136 fall under descriptions, 38 under speeches, and 12 under similes, and over 160 of these were found on Hume's table. Though the similarity between Addison's selection and taxonomy of beauties with those of Hume might be coincidental, it is not likely, especially since Addison appears to have derived a technique in sequential enumeration from the table. A simple example of this can be found in Addison's first few sketches of Satan. Under the heading of description, Hume's entry for Satan in the first book records several beauties in chronological fashion, the first few being "Satan on the Burning Lake I. 193. his rising thence. 221."[14] Turning to Addison's treatment of Satan in Book I, he cites several beauties which are found in the table, and of special interest are the first few which call to mind Hume's entry: "his Posture on the burning lake, his rising from it" (III, p. 85). While Milton's use of "burning lake" and "they rise" in the argument to Book I are constructions which apply to all the fallen angels by Milton and do not come in succession, in Addison and Hume they describe Satan exclusively and are employed in the same enumerative arrangement.

Though this and other sketches of the fallen angels in the first book are somewhat extensive, they do not approach the panoramic view of characters in the next paper (no. 309), such as Addison's next sketch of Satan which involves his speeches in Book II:

[Satan's] opening and closing the Debate [11ff.]; his taking on himself that great Enterprize, at the Thought of which the whole Infernal Assembly trembled [431ff.]; his encountring the hideous Phantom who guarded the Gates of Hell [681ff.], and appeared to him in all his Terrors [Sin, 737ff.] . . . are Instances of that proud and daring Mind. (III, p. 114)

The same sequence and some of the language had already been used by Hume in his table under 'Speeches' by Satan: "on his Throne. 2.11. going to discover a new Created World. 2.431. to Death. 681. to Sin. 737."

These leaps, which span the entire second book, are transitions which Addison could certainly have made from memory, though it is not likely that he worked exclusively in this way, in light of the sheer number of, and distance between, the enumerated beauties. What the table of beauties offered to Addison was easy access to the vast poem, and many parallel treatments can be found throughout the papers. [15]

However, while many beauties are cited in an enumerative fashion by Addison, this effect is somewhat muted because it was often mingled with that of explication. Take, for example, the hybrid approach involved in Addison's comment on Satan's trip to the new world in the third book:

His Flight between the several Worlds . . . are set forth in all the wantonness of a luxuriant Imagination [561ff.]. His Shape, Speech, and Behaviour upon his transforming himself into an Angel of Light, are touched with exquisite Beauty [634ff.]. The Poet's Thought of directing *Satan* to the Sun, which in the Vulgar Opinion of Mankind is the most conspicuous Part of the Creation, and the placing in it an Angel, is a Circumstance very finely contriv'd, and the more adjusted to a Poetical Probability, as it was a receiv'd Doctrine among the most famous Philosophers, that every Orb has its *Intelligence*. (III, p. 147)

This passage illustrates just how deft the transition from one mode to the other can be, and we barely notice the shift in it from an appreciative enumeration of beauties to a scientific explanation (by eighteenth-century standards) of Milton's phrase, "but Nigh-hand seem'd other worlds" (III, 566). Addison might very well have begun this section by referring to the table which records Satan's "Survey of this World, 3.562. changed to an Angel of Light. 3.636" ("Angel of Light" is a phrase not used by Milton), and then went to the annotation and there found Hume's interesting gloss on the above line of Milton:

'Nigh-hand seem'd other Worlds'; Following the Opinions of divers Philosophers, who thought not only the Moon to be such an Inhabitable World as this Terrestrial of ours is, and by turns enlightened by it: But [also] the stars. . . . [The same philosophers] accounting it absurd to imagine many that so many Illustrious Bodies . . . should be made to no other end, than to dart and center there Innumerable Beams of light in this dark opaque spot of Earth. (III, p. 566 n.)

These parallel passages reveal not only a similar explanation of the accepted notion of cosmic life but also the rejection of the counter mechanistic view, suggesting that the annotation was simultaneously being used by Addison along with the table.

The title page to Hume's annotation bears four major aims, clarified in brackets:

Annotations on Milton's *Paradise Lost*. Wherein The Texts of Sacred Writ, relating to the Poem are Quoted [Biblical Reference or Allusion]; The Parallel Places and Imitations of the most Excellent Homer and Virgil, Cited and Compared [Classical Parallel]; All the Obscure Parts render'd in Phrases more Familiar [Interpretation]; The Old and Obsolete Words with their Originals, Explain'd and made Easie to the English Reader [Paraphrase].

Though it might well be argued that the subject of some of Addison's comments might coincide with at least a few of Hume's four thousand glosses, certain resemblances between the two make this doubtful: many remarks contain not only unmistakable parallels to Hume's language and syntax, but even more subtle variations on his use of the specific and general, in which classes are substituted for Hume's particulars, and vice versa.

Of the four categories, Addison is most drawn to what Hume calls the "rendering" of "obscure parts," which is essentially interpretation, and at times exegesis, there being 87 instances in the 12 papers, of which 67 are found in Hume. Addison's employment of Hume can be seen best in a simple example. Of Milton's "exordium" Hume describes it as "plain, easie, and modest" (I, p. 25 n.). Addison's adaptation being typically a combination of direct borrowing and improvisation, he uses Hume's syntactical arrangement as a kind of mold into which he pours his own verbal variation of the original: he similarly writes that Milton's exordium is "plain, simple and unadorned" (III, p. 84). Neither writer elaborates the terms chosen. Though much more difficult to detect, Addison's method is equally at work in longer, more complex passages. Of Milton's handling of God in Book III Hume writes,

Our Author has been entertaining us for 264 Lines, with a Discourse of the highest Nature, as the Mysteries of God's Mercy and Justice to Mankind; of Free-Will, of the inconceivable Incarnation of his Son, and all the nicest Points of Faith; and has acquitted himself of this great Undertaking, as well as is possible for Human Understanding to do, in things so much exceeding the Compass of our Capacities. (III, p. 342 n.)

As Hume suggests, this passage of Milton's is one of the most important in the poem because the exchange between the Father and Son provides the theological background of Adam's Fall and Christ's Redemption of mankind. There is no reason why Addison should not have chosen to comment on the poem at any point without recourse to Hume, and at first glance his comment on the same passage in Book III seems quite original:

The particular Beauty of the Speeches of the Third Book, consists in that Shortness and Perspicuity of Stile, in which the Poet has couched the greatest Mysteries of Christianity, and drawn together, in a regular Scheme, the whole Dispensation of Providence, with respect to Man. He has represented all the abstruse Doctrines of Predestination, Free-Will and Grace, as also the great Points of Incarnation and Redemption. . . . the concise and clear manner in which he has treated them, is very much to be admired, as is likewise that particular Art which he has made us of in the interspersing of all those Graces of Poetry, which the Subject was capable of receiving. (III, p. 141–42)

Using the identical structure, Addison began with a comment about this material and then remarks on Milton's handling of this problem, his explicit reference to "those Graces of Poetry" hardly concealing his debt to Hume. Addison's "Free-Will, Grace [and] Incarnation" is close but not too close to Hume's "Mercy, Free-will and Incarnation."

Addison is also quite free with Hume's other categories. In a more daring kind of appropriation concerning biblical allusion, there are instances in which Addison quotes Hume verbatim, not realizing that Hume's gloss was at times textually inadequate. For example, in explaining how Milton conflated particular images from the first (v, 6) and tenth chapter (v, 12) of Ezekiel to form the vision of the angel (XI, p. 127ff.), Hume inadvertently omits, probably having worked from memory, the middle part of Ezekiel's tenth verse which is "and the wheels that the four had" (XI, p. 129 n.); likewise, in discussing the same allusion Addison quotes the same verses and neglects the same phrase (III, p. 358). Concerning paraphrase, of Milton's "If Ancient and Prophetic fame" (II. p. 347), Hume paraphrases "If old reports in Heaven" (II, p. 347 n.), and Addison, "There is . . . something wonderfully beautiful . . . in this ancient Prophecy or Report in Heaven" (III, p. 117); of Milton's "Gliding Meteorous, as Evening Mist" (XII, p. 629), Hume paraphrases "Sliding o'er the Surface" (XII, p. 629 n.), and Addison, "[Gods] do not . . . proceed Step by Step, but slide o'er the Surface of the Earth" (III, p. 389). Addison is no less unabashed in his appropriation of several classical parallels, a few of which are illlustrated in the appendix.

During the course of the series Addison is also indebted to other writers, both ancient and modern, some of whom he acknowledges— depending on their renown. Hume's commentary, however, remained the major source to which Addison kept returning, right up to the last cited beauty in the final paper (no. 369) in which Adam and Eve are described leaving Paradise. It should be of some interest that Addison, finally having reached the end of the poem without a single criticism of Milton during the book-by-book discussions, suddenly discovers a problem with the lines which end *Paradise Lost:*

If I might presume to offer at the smallest Alteration in this Divine Work, I should think the Poem would end better with the Passage here quoted ["The world was all before them, where to choose / Their place of rest, and Providence their guide.] than with the two verses which follow:
They hand in hand, with wandering steps and slow
Through Eden took their solitary way.
These two Verses . . . renew in the Mind of the Reader that Anguish which was pretty well laid by that Consideration. (III, p. 390)

None too coincidentally, Hume's gloss also questions the same lines, yet not in criticism of Milton but of Henry Aldrich, the artist responsible for the plate to Book XII: "The Angel led out our parents, loath to depart from their beloved seat, in each hand, which the Designer of our Copper Plate has not well exprest, representing him shoving them out, as we say, by Head and Shoulders" (XII, p. 637 n.).[16] Hume's objection here is far more aggressive than Addison's modest suggestion ("If I might presume to offer at the smallest Alteration"). It might be pointed out that these lines of Milton ("They hand in hand with wandering steps and slow / Through Eden took their solitary way.") went on to haunt writers of the eighteenth century attempting to come to terms with fallen man, since the scene, as Dustin Griffin remarks, is "fraught with an unresolved terror and woe, as well as regret and terror."[17] However, Addison comes too early in the century for the pervasive melancholy to be found in the poetry of the following decades, and his object here seems to be a rather basic concern with plot. Because this was the first negative criticism of Milton since beginning the book-by-book discussions, it strains credulity to think that this position of Addison's, that the poem should have ended with our first parents in a more progressive state of mind, was not sparked by a similar censor by Hume of the artist's representation of Adam and Eve leaving in a state of distress.

Certainly most Londoners in 1712 were not familiar with Hume's work. And even if some had stumbled upon it, surely very few would have waded through the "voluminous notes" in it. But a shrewd annotator of *Paradise Lost*—such as Addison turns out to be in the Milton series, with a keen commercial interest in mingling the emerging Longinian notions with the accepted standards of Aristotle, would have welcomed Hume's work with open arms, using bits and pieces along the way, and without much fear of being detected. In the final paragraph of the series, however, Addison does at least admit to the clumsy improvisation which took place in it, though his explanation is conveyed in martyr-like terms:

Had I thought, at my first engaging in this Design, that it would have led me to so great a length, I believe I should never have entered upon it; but the kind Reception which it has met with among those whose Judgments I have a Value for, as well as the uncommon Demands which my Bookseller tells me has been made for these particular Discourses, give me no Reason to repent of the Pains I have been at in composing them. (III, p. 392)

And so Addison protracted the series for twelve more Saturdays, he explains without blushing, on account of his readers and not the quarry found in the earlier commentary.

    Addison's "peculiar service to aesthetics and criticism," Thorpe writes, "was not to utilize the old . . . but to accept and adapt and transmit the new"; Addison did so by "proposing a theory of literature based on the psychological rather than formalistic, rhetorical principle."[18] Of course Thorpe is considering here the watershed papers on the pleasures of the imagination in which Addison first addresses, in anticipation of Kant, the new sensational psychology, in which "natural response"—and not reason—accounts for poetic stimulus.[19] But Thorpe and several other critics have also remarked that many of the key ideas in the papers on the imagination were first broached in the *Paradise Lost* papers in an undeveloped fashion. What needs some clarification is that these ideas did not appear until the book-by-book discussions, and we should not be taken aback if some of these notions were first conveyed by Hume, in spite of the less than favorable estimate of his critical powers. Edward Hooker thinks that Hume "did not, for the most part, single out specific books or passages for their artistic merit"; similarly, while Oras concedes that "some of [Hume's] critical judgments are stimulating," he nonetheless concludes that "much of it is superfluous."[20]
    To do justice to this obscure commentator, however, it needs to be recognized that Hume stocked his annotation with all kinds of notions reflecting the emerging Longinian movement, such as Milton's "Towring Fancy," his "strangely significant" expressions, and "sublime" language. Hardly theoretical, such comments nonetheless illustrate the more progressive critical concepts which would fully emerge at midcentury, and Hume constantly uses them and like concepts throughout his work to call attention to certain aspects of Milton's language, such as the power of suggestion, novelty, genius, beauty, and sublimity, the last of which is often noted for its attributes of size, energy, and terror. And while these comments do not approach the formulated aesthetic we find in Addison's later papers on the imagination, they very much resemble many of the

undeveloped aesthetic remarks found in the Milton series (several examples can be found in the appendix). Hume deserves, then, far more credit as a forerunner of "subjective" commentary on Milton.

Throughout the course of the *Paradise Lost* papers, Addison obviously makes no reference to the Hume or his work; he most likely knew that the annotation was poorly received in 1695 and that by 1712 had been forgotten, and for good reasons: not only did the vastly erudite and cumbersome nature of Hume's commentary scare off some readers, but the timing of this publication must also have been a major factor in its contemporary neglect. On the one hand, the first subscription edition in 1688, made sumptuous with plates and striking print, undoubtedly preempted some sales of the next editions in 1692 and 1695; many satisfied patrons of the 1688 edition didn't think another copy of the poem was necessary.[21] And if the 1688 edition wasn't enough to prevent any potential which Hume's work might have realized, Tonson's next editions of the poem, coming in 1705, 1707, and 1711 (the first two in octavo, the third in an inexpensive pocket duodecimo), must have superseded the previous publications of the poem.

The scene was thus set for Addison: catching the attention of many readers, the commercial barrage of Milton's epic by Tonson between 1705 and 1711 prepared the public for a discussion of *Paradise Lost* by Mr. Spectator in 1712 after some forty years of sporadic, incidental, and somewhat tempered praise of the poem. Such was possible, so the story goes, because of the knowledge of Milton's epic which the author brought to the series: "Almost every turn of thought [in Addison] seems to have found a vital illustration in *Paradise Lost*."[22] Addison's reputation as the champion of *Paradise Lost*, then, appears to have been sealed because of his seemingly intuitive samplings of the poem. This critical commonplace, however, belies an undeserved originality on Addison's part, since both his method and a number of comments were adapted, and in a manner uncharacteristic of him. Besides the rapid-fire enumeration of beauties, in itself a kind of enthusiasm, Addison also embarked on his own annotative journey, explicating many of Milton's passages along the way, despite his once writing in the *Tatler* that he had a "contempt for pedantry" which "sometimes spilled over upon genuine projects of learning, for example, upon editors, commentators, interpreters, scholiasts, and critics, and in short, all men of deep learning without common sense."[23] Of course it remains an artistic triumph that Addison was able to sustain at all a discussion that lasted eighteen Saturdays, in light of the staggering amount of minor commentary which required much seaming throughout the series.

190 MILTON STUDIES

In the following comparisons we find Addison deftly adapting Hume's annotations in both language and structure.

Hume: "[Milton] had need to invoke this Heavenly Muse . . . to inspire and assist him: And well he might, being to sing, not only of the Beauteous Universe, but all the Created Beings, but of the Creator Himself. . . . This argument might need a Divine Instructress. . . . [Of Tasso's exordium] we shall find him short of our Poet, both as to the Sublimity of his Thoughts and Argument as much as Helicon is inferiour to Horeb." (I, p. 6 n.)

Addison: "His Invocation to a Work which turns in a great measure upon the Creation of the World, is very properly made to the Muse who inspired *Moses* in those Books from whence our Author drew his Subject, and to the Holy Spirit who is therein represented as operating after a particular manner in the first Production of Nature. This whole Exordium rises very happily into noble Language and Sentiment, as I think the Transition to the Fable is exquisitely beautiful and natural." (III, p. 84)

The Difficulty of Poeticizing Scripture

Hume: "It must be acknowledged, a much harder Task to form a right Idea of that Eternal Being, which made the Universe; and to observe with all due Veneration, and Awful Respect, the great Decorum requisite in speaking of the True God; and to offend nothing against the Revelations he has been pleased to make of himself; and yet to manage all of this under the Heats and Heights of Towring Fancy; than either Homer or Virgil undertook, a task, by none but himself, attempted, (as he may justly boast) and impossible to be by any other undertaker, better performed." (I, p. 25 n.)

Addison: "If *Milton*'s Majesty forsakes him any where, it is in those Parts of his Poem, where the Divine Persons are introduced as Speakers. One may, I think, observe that the Author proceeds with a kind of Fear and Trembling, whilst he describes the Sentiments of the Almighty. He dares not give his Imagination its full play, but chuses to confine himself to such Thoughts as are drawn from the Books of the most Orthodox Divines, and to such Expressions as may be met with in Scripture." (III, p. 141)

The Characterization of Moloch

Hume: "Moloch is [like] those Heathens . . . who in cursed Imitation of their cruel Neighbours offered their Sons and Daughters to it; the Devil probably seducing and enticing them by these horrid Sacrifices." (I, p. 392 n.)

Addison: "The Part of *Moloch* is likewise in all its Circumstances full of that Fire and Fury. . . . He is described in the first Book as besmear'd with the Blood of Human Sacrifices, and delighted with the Tears of Parents, and the Cries of Children." (III, p. 114)

Hume: "Light, and the Blessings of it, were never drawn in more lively Colors, and finer Stroaks, than by these [lines]." (III, p. 54 n.)

Addison: "The particular Objects on which [God] is described to have cast his Eye, are represented in the most beautiful and lively manner." (III, p. 142)

Satan's Walk Outside Creation

Hume: "At a great distance it shewed like a round Ball, but now at his alighting on it appears a vast unbounded Country, its roundness being not very discoverable so near." (III, p. 423 n.)

Addison: "Satan's Walk upon the Outside of the Universe, which, at a Distance, appeared to him of a globular Form, but, upon his nearer Approach, looked like an unbounded Plain, is natural and noble." (III, p. 143)

Of Milton's Simile, "As when a scout . . ."

Hume: "As when one sent through dark and dismal Night, wandring through dangerous and unknown ways, at break of comfortable Day, has gain'd the top of some vast Hill." (III, p. 543 n.)

Addison: "Satan, after having long wandered upon the Surface . . . discovers at last a wide Gap in it. . . . His Sitting upon the brink of this Passage, and taking a Survey of the whole Face of Nature that appeared to him new and fresh in all its Beauties, with the Simile illustrating this Circumstance." (III, p. 146)

Satan's Troubled Thoughts

Hume: "While [Satan] made this Speech, full of sad and dismal Reflections, disquieted with Anger, Envy and Despair, each of these Passions darkened and overcast his Countenance, which spoiled his disguise, and discovered him a Cheat and Imposter." (IV, p. 114 n.)

Addison: "The Place inspires him with Thoughts more adapted to it: He reflects upon the happy Condition from whence he fell, and breaks forth into a Speech that is softned with several transient Touches of Remorse and Self-accusation: But at length he confirms himself in Impenitence, and in his design of drawing Man into his own State of Guilt and Misery. This Conflict of Passions is raised with a great deal of Art." (III, p. 171)

Decorum and Our First Parents:

Hume: "Where Adam relates the first Thoughts and Sentiments he had of himself . . . [Milton] has hit upon something so new and strange, that it cannot square with any Persons but those of our first Progenitors." (IV, p. 450 n.)

Addison: "A Poet of less Judgment and Invention than this great Author, would have found it very difficult to have filled these tender parts of the Poem with Sentiments proper for a State of Innocence." (III, p. 176)

Homeric Imitation

Hume: "Homer tells us, Paeon cured Mars, wounded in the Grecian Conflict. . . . From the wide Wound, a stream of Divine Humour issued forth in Color like to Blood such as Heav'nly Spirits may be allow'd to bleed. . . . an exact imitation of Homer." (VI, p. 331 n.]

Addison: "*Homer* tells us in the same manner, that upon *Diomedes* wounding the Gods, there flow'd from the Wound an *Ichor,* or pure kind of Blood, which was not bred from Mortal Viands . . . the Wound soon closed up and healed in those Beings who are vested with Immortality." (III, p. 232)

Power of Suggestion

Hume: " 'From off the Files of War': Satan lighted out of his Sun-bright Chariot . . . and according to the Homerick manner is now wounded. . . . Much more loose and redundant than [Milton's] Expressive Author." (VI, p. 339 n.)

Addison: "*Homer* adds, that the *Greeks* and *Trojans* . . . were terrified on each side with the bellowing of this wounded Deity [Mars]. The Reader will easily observe how *Milton* has kept all the horrour of this Image without running into the Ridicule of it." (III, p. 232)

Of the War in Heaven

Hume: " 'With Jaculation dire'; So in mid Air did Hills encounter Hills, with horrid Hurlyburly; a Nobler Idea of the Warring Angels, than any of the Poets have given us, of the Gigantic Invasion of Heaven by the Titans, they endeavour'd to make their Scalado, by heaping the Mountains one upon another. . . . And could not rear 'em, tho' less than these our angry Angels, hurl'd at one anothers Heads." (VI, p. 665 n.)

Addison: "It may, perhaps, be worth while to consider with what Judgment *Milton,* in this Narration, has avoided every thing that is mean and trivial in the Descriptions of the *Latin* and *Greek* Poets; and at the same time, improved every great Hint which he met with in their Works upon this Subject. *Homer* in that Passage . . . which *Virgil* and *Ovid* have copied after him, tells us, that the Gyants threw *Ossa* upon *Olympus.* . . . They proceed from a Wantonness of Imagination, and rather divert the Mind than astonish it. *Milton* has taken every thing that is Sublime in these several Passages. . . . We have the full Majesty of *Homer* in this short Description ['From the Foundations lossning to and fro']." (III, pp. 229–30)

Visions of the Future

Hume: "Most admirable and excellent are these Episodes, which here begin, and adorn our Author's Poem to the end, surpassing all those tedious stories, and the vain-glorious Boastings of the Homeric Heroes, and Virgil's artful Enumeration of the Roman Conquerors . . . as much as a Relation of what was to come to pass, from the beginning of the World, to Adam and all Mankind, to the end of it, and in order to a better, (taken out of Sacred Story,) must excel any particular or Humane History whatever." (XI, p. 433 n.)

Addison: "I have before observed how the Plan of *Milton's* Poem is in many Particulars greater than that of the *Iliad* or *Aeneid. Virgil's* Hero, in the last of these Poems, is entertained with a sight of all those who are to descend from him, but tho' that Episode is justly admired as one of the noblest Designs in the whole *Aeneid,* every one must allow that this of *Milton* is of a much higher Nature. *Adam's* Vision is not confined to any particular Tribe of Mankind, but extends to the whole Species." (III, pp. 361–62)

University of Illinois, Urbana—Champaign

NOTES

I owe a special thanks to Frederick Nash of the Rare Book and Special Collections Library at the University of Illinois for his assistance during my research. I am also grateful to Warren Dwyer, John Shawcross, and Jack Stillinger for reading an earlier draft of this essay and offering valuable comments.

1. Clarence D. Thorpe, "Addison's Contributions to Criticism," in *The Seventeenth Century: Studies in the History Thought and Literature from Bacon to Pope*, ed. Richard F. Jones (Stanford, 1951), p. 320.

2. Ants Oras, *Milton's Editors and Commentators from Patrick Hume to Henry John Todd (1695–1801)* (Oxford, 1931), p. 34. Oras excludes Addison from his study because the *Paradise Lost* papers "constitute a coherent treatise, and cannot be separately discussed in the present dissertation" of "editors and commentators" (p. 9); however, Addison's latter papers resemble, as will be shown, the work of "editors and commentators."

3. For discussions of Addison's contributions to early eighteenth-century aesthetics, see Thorpe's "Addison's Contributions," Lee Elioseff's *The Cultural Milieu of Addison's Literary Criticism* (Austin, 1963), and Jean Wilkinson's "Some Aspects of Addison's Philosophy of Art," in *Huntington Library Quarterly* XXVIII (1964), 31–44.

4. "A Poem Dedicated to the Immortal Memory of Her Late Majesty The Most Incomparable Q. Mary. By Mr. Hume. London Printed for Jacob Tonson, at Judge's Head, near the Inner-Temple-Gate, in Fleet-Street, 1695." The publication of this only known poem by Patrick Hume might have been the result of Tonson's gratitude to Hume for the painstaking effort involved in the commentary—both came out in the same year.

5. Harry Geduld, *Prince of Publishers: A Study of Work and Career of Jacob Tonson* (Bloomington, 1969), pp. 123, 125. Although nothing is known about Tonson's relationship to Hume, Geduld, agreeing with David Masson, thinks that Tonson had "found [Hume] out, and either set him on the work, or accepted the work from him already done privately as a labour of love" (p. 126). In what remains an unprecedented publishing event for the times, Tonson printed Hume's commentary in three different publishing ventures in 1695: not only was it included as part of the sixth edition of *Paradise Lost* and *The Poetical Works* (a composite edition), but it was also printed separately. For a full account of these three publications, see John Shawcross, *A Milton Bibliography for the Years 1624–1700* (Binghamton, 1984), and K. A. Coleridge, *A Descriptive Catalogue of the Milton Collection in the Alexander Turnbull Library, Wellington, New Zealand* (Oxford, 1980), p. 273. In *A Sale Catalogue of the Valuable Library of the Late Celebrated Right Hon. Joseph Addison* (London, 1799), which documents the auction of Addison's library following his daughter's death, only two editions of *Paradise Lost* are listed, the 1667 first edition and the 1695 *Poetical Works*.

6. William Riley Parker, *Milton: A Biography*, 2 vols. (Oxford, 1968), vol. II, p. 663. While three English annotations precede Hume (Thomas Speght's on Chaucer, 1597; E. K.'s on Spenser, 1598; and John Selden's on Drayton, 1613), these works pale in contrast to the great range and depth of Hume's commentary.

7. Richard Bentley, *Dr. Bentley's Corrections and Emendations on "Paradise Lost"* (London, 1732); Jonathan Richardson, *Explanatory Notes and Remarks on Milton's "Paradise Lost"* (London, 1734); Thomas Newton, ed., *Paradise Lost. A Poem in Twelve Books. By John Milton* (London, 1749), vol. 1; John Callendar, ed., *Milton's "Paradise Lost," Book I* (London, 1750). The first notice of plagiarism did not come until 1817, when *Blackwood's Magazine* demonstrated that many of Callendar's notes in his 1750 edition were taken from

Hume's annotations (vol. 4, pp. 658–62). The only study of Hume's work does not arrive until Oras's *Milton Editors*, which devotes a chapter to Hume's annotation as well as supplying an appendix which illustrates "unacknowledged similarities" by several eighteenth-century commentators and editors; Oras writes of one plagiarist: "A study of Hume's and Newton's notes of the first five hundred lines of Book I of P.L. would show that more than half the biblical references of Newton are already found in Hume's comment" (p. 22); ironically, it was Newton in his preface who said that Hume "laid the foundation [for Milton studies], but he laid it among heaps of rubbish." The first favorable report of Hume's work is not found until later in the century, when Thomas Warton called it a "large and very learned commentary" in the preface to his edition of *Poems Upon Several Occasions, English, Italian, and Latin, with Translations By John Milton* (London, 1785).

8. Donald Bond, ed. the *Spectator*, 5 vols. (Oxford, 1965), vol. III, p. 63, n. 1; p. 176, n. 2.

9. To Edward Wortley, July 21, 1711, in *The Letters of Joseph Addison*, ed. Walter Graham (Oxford, 1941), p. 264.

10. Lillian D. Bloom, "Addison's Popular Aesthetic: The Rhetoric of the *Paradise Lost* Papers," in *The Author in His Work: Essays on Problems in Criticism*, ed. Louis L. Martz and Aubrey Williams (New Haven, 1978), p. 266. Dr. Johnson also notes the significance of Addison's popular approach: "Had [Addison] presented *Paradise Lost* to the public with all the pomp of system and severity of science, the criticism would perhaps have been admired, and the poem still neglected" (*The Works of Samuel Johnson, LL.D.*, 9 vols. [London, 1825], vol. VII, p. 471).

11. Bloom, "Addison's Popular Aesthetic," pp. 274–75.

12. This passage is from the original folio (9 February 1712), though hereafter all quotations of Addison's are from Bond's edition of the *Spectator.*

13. None of Addison's previous literary series (on true and false wit, the ballad, English tragedy and Sappho) reached further than six numbers; the series on the imagination, comprising ten numbers, was the closest rival to the *Paradise Lost* papers, though this project came some months later.

14. All references from Hume's table and annotation are from the sixth edition of *Paradise Lost.*

15. As Addison continued, yet another sequential possibility presented itself. Despite Addison's announcement that "I shall beg leave to consider several passages of the second book," within a few paragraphs he is involved in interbook reporting, such as his comment on Belial "who is described in the first book, as the idol of the lewd and luxurious [I, p. 490]. He is in the second book, pursuant to the description, characterized as timorous and slothful [II, p. 109]; and if we look into the sixth book, we find him celebrated in the Battel of angels for nothing but that scoffing speech which he makes to Satan [VI, p. 620]" (III, p. 115). Addison's straying from his expressed intention to treat only the "passages of the second book" is derived from Hume's listings for Belial: under description, "Belial. 1.490. 2.109"; under speeches, "to Satan 6.620."

16. For information on the illustrators of *Paradise Lost*, see *A Milton Encyclopedia*, William B. Hunter, et al., (Lewisburg, 1978), vol. 4, pp. 55–78.

17. Dustin Griffin, *Regaining Paradise: Milton and the Eighteenth Century* (Cambridge, 1986), p. 102.

18. Thorpe, "Addison's Contributions," pp. 317, 320.

19. As Samuel Holt Monk remarks in *The Sublime*, "Kant's *Critique of Pure Reason* is the great document which coordinates and synthesizes the aesthetic concepts which had been current throughout the eighteenth century" (p. 4); the critical process generally began

with the *Spectator* papers on the imagination, though Monk also notes that even in this influential series Addison was not yet ready to distinguish between the beautiful (a pleasing comprehensible object) and the sublime (the effect on the mind of an incomprehensible object), a distinction which Edmund Burke and later aestheticians were able to make, and which Kant crystallized in his famous treatise.

20. Edward Hooker, *The Critical Works*, vol. 1, p. 513; Oras, *Milton's Editors*, p. 8.

21. John Shawcross points out that "it was not until the fourth edition in 1688 that Milton's reputation finally rose sharply," chiefly because it had the backing of several influential Whigs, most notably Lord Somers whose "high position was used to advance the cause of the edition" (*John Milton and Influence* [Pittsburgh, 1991], pp. 39–40).

22. John Walter Good, *Studies in the Milton Tradition*, University of Illinois Studies in Language and Literature (Urbana, 1915), vol. 1, p. 153.

23. Cited in Peter Smithers's *The Life of Joseph Addison* (Oxford, 1954), p. 17. A few critics betray some annoyance at this unrelenting exegete: "Almost with the exactness of an accountant, [Addison] records Milton's beauties" (Samuel Holt Monk, *The Sublime: A Study of Critical Theories in XVIII-Century England* [Ann Arbor, 1960], p. 16); "[Addison's] papers really amounted to a kind of commented 'Beauties of Milton'" (Bonamy Dobrée, *English Literature in the Early Eighteenth Century, 1700–1740* [Oxford, 1959], p. 114).

ON THE MARGINS OF AN UNNOTED ANNOTATOR OF MILTON: WILLIAM HAYLEY'S DIALOGUE WITH RICHARD BENTLEY

Shannon Murray and Ashraf H. A. Rushdy

If authors could have lived to adjust and authenticate their own text, a Commentator would have been a useless creature. If Dr. Bentley had found, or opined that he had found the word *Jube* where it seemed to present itself to you, and had judged the Subject worthy of his Critical Acumen, he would either have justified the corrupt reading, or have substituted some invention of his own, in defence of which he would have Exerted all his polemical abilities to have quarrelled with half the Literati in Europe; Then suppose the Writer himself . . . to interpose with a Gentle Whisper thus—If you look again Good Doctor, you will perceive that what appears to you to be Jube, is neither more nor less than the simple Monysyllable, Ink. But I wrote it in Great haste, and the want of sufficient precision in the Characters has occasioned Your mistake. You will be satisfied when you see the sense Elucidated by the Explanation. But I question whether the Doctor would quit his ground, or allow an Author to be a Competent judge in his own Cause.

—*William Cowper (1780)*[1]

Yet, could thy mortal shape revisit earth,
How would it move, great Bard! thy scornful mirth,
To hear vain Pedants to thy verse assign
Scholastic thoughts that could never be thine.

—*William Hayley (1782)*[2]

A CCORDING TO John T. Shawcross, the critical reception of Milton from 1732 to 1801 can be effectively divided into "four periods dominated by certain critics or concerns." While acknowledging that all "such divisions are specious," Shawcross nonetheless makes a compelling case for seeing how these seventy years fall into four discernible periods. The first period is "ushered in by the textual criticism of Richard Bentley in

1732," and, although marked by various charges of Milton's Arianism, the period is generally overshadowed by this "spectre of Bentley" until about 1740. The second period, from 1741 to 1751, is "dominated by charges of alleged plagiarism brought by William Lauder." In the third period, between 1752 and 1773, most critics provided appreciative analyses of the language, versification, and style of Milton's poetry rather than debating any particular issue or charge against Milton. The fourth period, running from 1774 to 1801, provides us with what Shawcross calls some "outstanding" but "little known" criticism and "close analysis of Milton's works" by writers whose sensibilities were starting to shift from those of their predecessors. One of the reasons Shawcross is careful to note that these divisions are by no means hard and fast has to do with the consistency of thought about Milton over the course of these seventy years. At the end of the century, as Shawcross concludes, "Milton is more entrenched in the position he held in 1732: he is still the exemplar of sublime thought and expression, he is widely imitated and quoted, and he is employed as authority for ideas and language or for poetic licence." A second reason has to do with the persistence of some of the debates. The Bentley controversy, for example, "was not a totally dead issue" as late as 1751. In fact, as Shawcross points out, the controversy continues to rear up in "critical asides throughout the century."[3] We have discovered an interesting and important specimen of one of these critical asides: extensive marginal annotations throughout William Cowper's copy of Bentley's *Paradise Lost*, annotations we believe were the careful work of Cowper's friend William Hayley. These annotations provide another brief chapter in the history of responses to Milton, add one more voice to the eighteenth-century debate surrounding the Bentley text, and show Hayley himself in dialogue with a critic he disdained, over a poet he revered, in a book owned by a friend he cherished.

The fast friendship of Hayley and Cowper began more than a decade after each, as the two epigraphs above indicate, had playfully imagined the resurrection of dead authors and the ensuing correction of vain pedants. The two were brought together by their dedication to the same dead poet, John Milton, and their meeting was a story that Hayley loved to tell. While engaged in his biography of Milton, he had been "represented in a news-paper, as an antagonist of Cowper," and as a result he initiated their correspondence; Cowper's gracious response contained both assurances that he did not intend a biography and an invitation to visit him in Weston and aid him in his true task of annotation. Thus, as Hayley wrote in his *Life and Posthumous Writings of William Cowper,* it is "to Milton that I am in great measure indebted for what I must ever regard as a signal blessing, the friendship of Cowper." Moreover, as Hayley suggested in his preface to Cowper's translation of Milton's Italian and Latin poems, that poet proved to be the fulcrum on which they based their future friendship: "As Milton was to each of us an object of constant admiration, and at this time of immediate study, for different purposes, we mutually took pleasure in animating each other to the prosecution of our respective works."[4]

It was indeed a productive friendship. Describing Hayley's second visit to Weston, Cowper writes that his "Homer finds work for Hayley, and his Life of Milton work for me." Also at this time, Cowper had begun his commentary on *Paradise Lost*, which "Miltonic labours" he thanked Hayley for taking an interest in, hoping one day that it could "be made a companion for a work of Hayley's." It was also at this time, sadly, that Cowper suffered again from the severe depression that quelled his desire to work. Cowper, therefore, never completed his annotations, nor saw them printed together with his friend's biography of Milton. A number of his own translations of Milton's Latin and Italian poetry had appeared in Hayley's *Life of Milton*, but their more substantial collaboration was to occur after Cowper's death; in 1808, Hayley edited a large quarto volume of Cowper's translations of Milton's Italian and Latin poems and his fragments of commentary on *Paradise Lost*. Two years later Hayley produced the work Cowper had hoped the world would see as a testament to their friendship. It was entitled *Cowper's Milton*—a four volume work containing Milton's poetry (including the Cowper translations), Hayley's *Life of Milton*, and Cowper's fragmented commentary. These, then, are the volumes produced between 1792 and 1810 by two remarkable friends for whom Milton was, as Hayley puts it, "an object of constant admiration." Hayley and Cowper meet again, though, in one extraordinary volume, brought together both by their "object of constant admiration" and by an "object of satirical indignation": Richard Bentley.[5] That volume is Cowper's copy of Bentley's edition of *Paradise Lost*.

As Hayley describes it, when Cowper was compiling the critical library he needed to compose his commentary on *Paradise Lost*, he came to own

a copy of Bentley's Milton, containing many very severe censures, in manuscript, against the presumptious editor, written probably when the book was published in 1732. These smothered embers of ancient animosity (to borrow a metaphor which Cowper used on another occasion) he was far from wishing to rekindle; for altho' he did not scruple to join a host of eminent writers in blaming the arrogance of Bentley, (in one of his letters he alludes, with much pleasantry, to the Doctor's contentious spirit) yet he considered the bitter squabbles of literary men as a disgrace to literature; and thought it most worthy of a scholar, and a Christian, rather to suppress the hasty occasional virulence even of angry wit, than to give it new circulation.

Cowper bought this copy of the Bentley edition in 1797; his signature and that date are still on the title page. The "smothered embers of ancient animosity" are still smoldering. Unlike Cowper, and perhaps betraying the worthiness of a "scholar, and a Christian," we have chosen to give this virulence a renewed circulation. And, moreover, we are suggesting that those notes of animosity are not as ancient as Hayley leads us to believe. In fact, we agree with Dr. Henry Richards Luard's argument that this book passed from Cowper's to "Hayley's hands," and that the marginal comments are written by Hayley himself.[6]

We cannot say whether Hayley simply prevaricates about the authorship of the marginal comments in Cowper's copy of the Bentley edition, or whether Cowper owned more than one copy of that edition. In any case, Cowper's copy of the edition (whether the only one or not) ended up in Christ's College, and there is substantial evidence to suggest that Luard was correct in maintaining that Hayley "has written all the notes" in the volume. First and most convincingly, the handwriting in the margins of the volume clearly resembles Hayley's autograph. We have reprinted pictures of a page of the Bentley edition from Christ's College Old Library and a copy of a letter written by Hayley on 27 February 1797 from the collection in the Manuscript Room of the Cambridge University Library (see figures 1 and 2). As a point of comparison, and in order to show that the marginalia are not Cowper's, we also reprint a copy of a letter written by William Cowper on 11 April 1799, from the collection of the Department of Rare Books and Special Collections of the Princeton University Libraries (see figure 3). We take the difference in size and scrupulosity of print between the handwriting in Hayley's letter and the handwriting in the margins of the Bentley edition to be the difference in discursive situations. It is the difference, that is, between the fineness of marginal commentary and the abandon of epistolary freedom. Numerous individual letters are similar enough in each document to appear to belong to the same hand. The best point of comparison, though, is the phrase "own Friend Horace" on the last line of page forty-three of the Bentley edition and "old Friend Horace" on the ninth line of the Hayley letter.

Secondly, there is a prefatory poem in the volume which is not only a meditation on one of Hayley's favorite themes—the foolishness of critics— but also recalls some of Hayley's specific arguments. For example, the poem's opening line ("Ye Criticks, would your tribe deserve a Name")

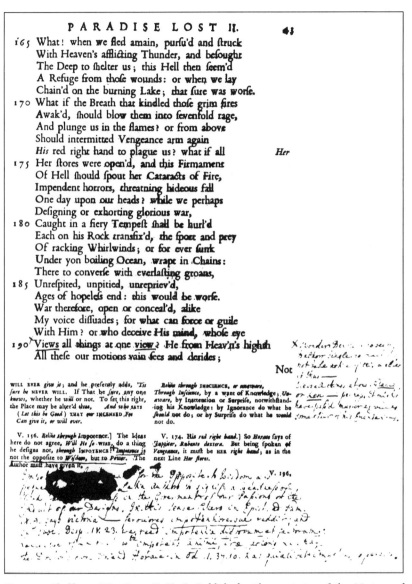

165 What! when we fled amain, pursu'd and struck
With Heaven's afflicting Thunder, and besought
The Deep to shelter us; this Hell then seem'd
A Refuge from those wounds: or when we lay
Chain'd on the burning Lake; that sure was worse.
170 What if the Breath that kindled those grim fires
Awak'd, should blow them into sevenfold rage,
And plunge us in the flames? or from above
Should intermitted Vengeance arm again
His red right hand to plague us? what if all

Her

175 Her stores were open'd, and this Firmament
Of Hell should spout her Cataracts of Fire,
Impendent horrors, threatning hideous fall
One day upon our heads? while we perhaps
Designing or exhorting glorious war,
180 Caught in a fiery Tempest shall be hurl'd
Each on his Rock transfix'd, the sport and prey
Of racking Whirlwinds; or for ever sunk
Under yon boiling Ocean, wrapt in Chains:
There to converse with everlasting groans,
185 Unrespited, unpitied, unrepriev'd,
Ages of hopeless end: this would be worse.
War therefore, open or conceal'd, alike
My voice dissuades; for what can force or guile
With Him? or who deceive His mind, whose eye
190 Views all things at one view? He from Heav'n's highth
All these our motions vain sees and derides;

Not

WILL EVER *give it*; and he presently adds, 'Tis
sure he NEVER WILL. If That he *sure*, any one
knows, whether he *will* or not. To set this right,
the Place may be alter'd thus, *And who* SAYS
(*Let this be Good*) THAT *our* INCENSED *Foe*
Can give it, or will ever.

Relics through IMPOTENCE, *or unawares,*
Through *Inscience*, by a want of Knowledge; *Unaware*, by Inattention or Surprise, notwithstanding his Knowledge: by Ignorance do what he
should not do; or by Surprise do what he *would*
not do.

V. 156. *Relics through* Impotence.] The Ideas
here do not agree, *Will He so* WISE, do a thing
he designs not, *through* IMPOTENCE? *Impotence* is
not the opposite to *Wisdom*, but to *Power*. The
Author must have given it,

V. 174. *His red right hand.*] So *Horace* says of
Jupiter, Rubente dextera. But being spoken of
Vengeance, it must be HER *right hand*, as in the
next Line *Her stores.*

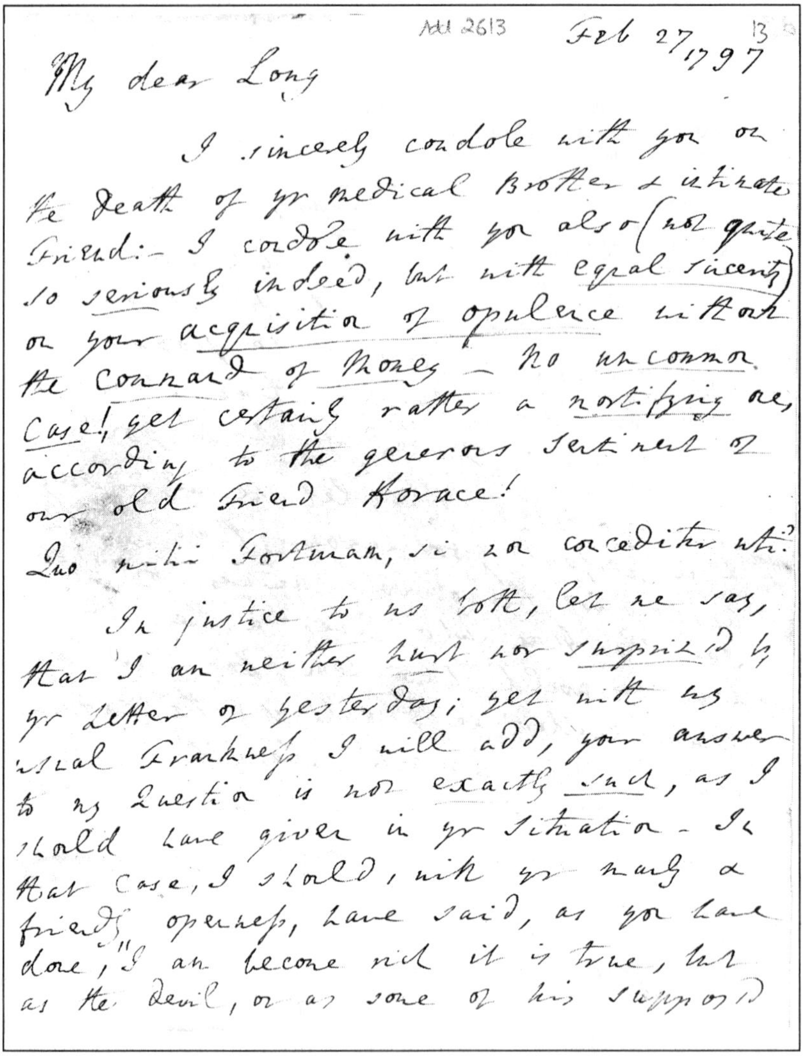

Figure 2. Shelf no. Add.2613, Manuscript Room, Cambridge University Library. Published with permission of the Syndics of Cambridge University Library.

seems to echo Hayley's sentiment in *An Essay on Epic Poetry:* "Are Critics, then, that bold, imperious tribe!" (l 265). Likewise, the prefatory poem's request for "Reason" which "guides" and "Learning, clear'd from learn'd Impertinence" echoes Hayley's request in *An Essay* for the critic's render-

> Dereham ——
> Apr: 11.1799.
>
> Dear Sir -
>
> Your last letter so long unanswer'd may, and indeed
> must, have proved sufficiently, that my state of mind is
> not now more favourable to the purpose of writing than it
> was when I received it; for had any alteration in that
> respect taken place, I should certainly have acknowledged
> it long since, or at whatsoever time the change had happen'd,
> and should not have waited for the present call
> upon me to return you my thanks at the same time for the
> letter and for the book which you have been so kind as to send
> me. Mr Johnson has read it to me. If it afforded me any
> amusement, or suggested to me any reflections, they were
> only such as served to imbitter, if possible, still more the
> present moment, by a sad retrospect to those days when
> I thought myself secure of an eternity to be spent with the
> spirits of such men as He whose life afforded the subject of it.
> But I was little aware of what I had to expect, and that a
> storm was at hand which in one terrible moment would
> darken, and in another still more terrible, blot out that
> prospect forever. —— Adieu Dear Sir, whom in those days
> I call'd Dear friend, with feelings that justified the appellation -
> I remain yours
> WmCowper.

Figure 3. Shelf no. C0199, Gen'l MSS, Cowper-Newton Correspondence vol, II, no. 141, Department of Rare Books and Special Collections. Published with permission of Princeton University Libraries.

ing "Learning's blaze an useful guide" (284). The prefatory poem celebrates critics who are "nobly useful, [and who] rise to honest fame" in the same way *An Essay* celebrates the "value" and the "useful toil" of the better sort of critic (271–72).[7]

Finally, although it is a difficult matter to assess and compare tone (and an even more problematic issue to use it as evidence of authenticity), we can say that the tone of the marginal comments agrees with the tone

Hayley was wont to assume whenever he writes of critics disagreeable to his sensibilities. For instance, Hayley did not simply offer an antidote to Dr. Johnson's biographical portrait of Milton with which he radically disagreed. He felt it necessary to refer to the author as this "unfriendly biographer," this "severe biographer," this "rough critick," and this "acrimonious biographer." Another of Hayley's targets, William Warburton, is in the *Life of Milton* referred to as a "disgusting writer, whose critical dictates form a fantastic medley of arrogance, acuteness, and absurdity." This 1794 comment regarding Warburton is actually a less pusillanimous version of Hayley's earlier comments on Warburton in the 1782 *An Essay on Epic Poetry*, in which Hayley dismissed Warburton in these harsh terms: "If I have also alluded to this famous Commentator with a contemptuous asperity, it arises from the persuasion that he has sullied the page of every Poet whom he pretended to illustrate."[8]

It is with equal gusto that Hayley takes on Bentley. His kindest suggestion is that Bentley's emendations were the product of senile dementia: "his Milton was a work of the great scholar's declining days, and seems to prove, that he was then sinking into . . . [a] most pitiable dotage." He deems Bentley deserving of the "satirical indignation" of his respondents, and he highly praises Zachary Pearce's *Review of the Text of the Twelve Books of Milton's Paradise Lost* (1733) as an adequate response to the "numerous absurdities of Bentley." It is not just Bentley's *Paradise Lost* that merited Hayley's censure; a large portion of his "Desultory Remarks on the Letters of Eminent Persons," which precedes the *Life and Posthumous Writings of William Cowper*, recounts with some relish the ridicule excited by Bentley's scholarly arguments with Charles Boyle concerning the authenticity of the Greek letters of Phalaris. In that preface, Hayley calls Bentley and his opponent "two pedantic scholars, so ungraceful in the use of their own language, that neither of them can be justly supposed competent to decide a doubtful question of this kind, by that perfect delicacy of taste, which is sometimes imagined to constitute a sort of intuitive sagacity, sufficient to detect any literary imposture."[9] Bentley, in other words, lacked sufficient taste, wit, and wisdom to be engaged in the work of literary scholarship. That, effectively, is also what Hayley's marginalia makes abundantly and exhaustively clear about Bentley's fitness to be Milton's editor.

The marginalia in Cowper's copy of Bentley's edition of *Paradise Lost* provide us with an interesting example of the critical reception of Bentley's emendations and of Milton's poetry. In praising William Empson's article on Bentley (with some qualifications about giving a central position to such an "incorrigibly eccentric" editor), Christopher Ricks has suggested that other critics today "must make full use of the . . . early editors." So too, again following Ricks's example, we should also avail ourselves of those contemporaries or near-contemporaries who responded to the early editors. The marginal commentary in Cowper's copy of Bentley's edition provides just such a rich and provocative dialogue with an early editor. Moreover, the marginal commentary in that volume is valuable to the debate surrounding Bentley's emendations because Hayley does not simply resort to what Gordon Moyles has shown to be the style of the earliest respondents to Bentley: "a cry of outrage, attended by a few witty rejoinders, satirical jibes, and clever parodies." As Moyles has shown, such writers as the anonymous author of a sixty-four page pamphlet entitled *A Friendly Letter to Dr. Bentley* (1732) responded to the emendations with a "satirical tone, a mixture of burlesque and banter, lacking in scholarly argument." Nor, though, are Hayley's comments solely concerned with detecting flaws in Bentley's "common-sense" as were the vast majority of those in Pearce's "four hundred pages of quiet, scholarly argument." Hayley was more like the author of *Milton Restor'd, and Bentley Depos'd* (1732) who also "attacked Bentley's logic" but who equally chided Bentley for his "lack of poetic sensitivity."[10] In other words, Hayley responded as both a critic and a poet.

As a critic, Hayley took up the same issues raised by other respondents to Bentley. "Bentley's critics," as Shawcross has noted, "pointed out his misinformation, his errors in reading and understanding *Paradise Lost*, his lack of knowledge of certain words or concepts, and his illogical suppositions and conclusions, as well as accusing him, by implication at least, of a nefarious purpose to reduce Milton's fame."[11] Hayley noted Bentley's misinformation and reading errors when, for example, he suggested that Bentley had "quite mistaken Milton's meaning" in the allusion to Scylla and her dogs because Milton alludes to Ovid's version of this myth rather than to Virgil's (as Bentley assumed) (no. 22). Likewise, *pace* Bentley, Hayley argues that Milton can use "impotence" as the "Opposite to Wisdom" since the word is "frequently us'd by the Latin Authors to signify a Weakness of Mind, an Unsteadiness in the Goverment of our Passions or the Conduct of our Designs." After citing examples from two of Cicero's works, Hayley triumphantly directs the reader to "the Doctor's own Friend Horace" for another instance of such usage (no. 12). Hayley also criticizes Bentley for an inability to determine the terms of a simile (no. 7) and an unwillingness to read a simile *as* a simile (no. 70). Hayley also dwells on Bentley's ignorance of key words and concepts throughout the marginalia. When Bentley changes "Shore" for "bound" in Milton's phrase "*Illimitable Ocean without* bound," Hayley scoffs that the Doctor's

"Ridiculous Trifling" "may aptly be call'd a Distinction without a Difference" since the "Shore" of the ocean is the same thing as the "Bound" of
the ocean (no. 23). He also questions Bentley's reluctance to let stand
Milton's use of "till" in describing prelapsarian gardening since the "Word
Till in common Acceptation signifies no more y^n to *cultivate*" (no. 71).
When Bentley changes "perfect" to "INDIGENT," arguing that perfection
is absolute and so Adam cannot be "*in degree* perfect," Hayley responds
by arguing that "Surely there are degrees of Perfection" and that "*Absolute* & *Comparative* Perfection ought not to be confounded" (no. 73).
Hayley, like almost all of the other respondents to Bentley, pays particular attention to Bentley's failings in logic. For instance, Hayley points out
that just because Milton had hitherto used the word "Chaos" to represent
the unbounded space on the outside of hell, it does not mean that Milton
always represents that space when he uses the same word in a more
general sense (no. 59). So, too, Hayley deflates Bentley's quite clever
reading of Adam's plaint in Book X—"*Fair Patrimony, that I must leave
you, Sons*"—by noting that the Doctor's "witty Argument seems to be
founded upon an ignorant—Blunder" (no. 82). Finally, like those critics
to whom Shawcross refers, Hayley accused Bentley of nefariously reduc-
ing Milton's fame. Responding to Bentley's comment that Milton was not
the first to have coined the word "*Imparadis'd*"—which, as Bentley
points out, is to be found in Sidney's *Arcadia* and in the Italian
language—Hayley writes: "What is this but a poor attempt to lessen the
Merit of the Author wch I cannot think at all concern'd in the Question?"
(no. 44).

Hayley also followed the practice of Bentley's critics in other more
specific ways. Like Pearce, Hayley was concerned with pointing out how
punctuation changes can aid the reader in understanding verses that appear ambiguous. Moyles has pointed out that the Richardsons (father and
son) in 1734 and Francis Peck in 1740 are mostly responsible for establish-
ing the importance of collating the first two editions of *Paradise Lost*, and
that their "comprehensive textual investigations" emerged at "Bentley's
perverse prompting." Pearce too returned to the first edition when he
wished to contest Bentley's emendations. By searching "all the first Editions," Pearce is able authoritatively to "take away the Dr's unhappy
Comma" in one particular place in Book II. Hayley is also willing to return
to the original editions to challenge Bentley's emendations. In one marginal comment, for instance, he collates the "two first Editions" in order to
demonstrate that the punctuation in the first edition dissipated what Bentley argued was verbal ambiguity (no. 6). On the other hand, it ought to be

noted that Hayley is also not above inserting his own punctuation to clarify Milton's sense (no. 37). When responding to Bentley on issues of poetics, epistemology, and theology, Hayley found himself agreeing with the much-hated Warburton. Warburton contested a certain emendation of Bentley's—based upon the Doctor's perception of the line in question as "miserably flat and creeping with wretched Accent"—by noting that the "labouring of the Verse" enacts what it is representing, which in this case is the sluggishness of Satan's "unwilling Followers." When Bentley noted that a verse describing the fall of the angels falls into a "very strange Measure," Hayley defends it because, agreeing with Pope, he believes that the "Sound sh.ᵈ seem an Echo to the Sense" (no. 63). Warburton also contests one of Bentley's emendations because the change does not attend to issues concerning Milton's representation of the faculties of sensing and thinking; so too does Hayley (no. 69). Finally, both Hayley and Warburton were concerned with some of Bentley's emendations of words and phrases that actually altered substantive ideas in Milton's Christology and his soteriology (no. 1).[12]

Like both Pearce and the anonymous critic of Bentley who wrote a letter in the *Grub-street Journal* for 2 March 1732, Hayley often found much to censure in what Moyles calls Bentley's "extreme literal-mindedness."[13] For example, when Bentley questions how God's throne could be "*mix'd* with Sulphur" unless it were first "batter'd to pieces and pounded with it," Hayley responds: "This is supposing the Throne of the Almighty to be <u>Material</u> & confining it to a sense unworthy of the Author" (no. 9). When Bentley argues that Milton uses the word "*Tast*" to talk only about eating, Hayley chides Bentley for being so literal-minded: "Is it not common to say—Such a One has no <u>tast</u> for <u>Books</u>—no <u>tast</u> for <u>Company</u>— <u>Sports</u> &c?" Milton, concludes Hayley, "plainly meant it in a larger Sense" (no. 83). While agreeing that Bentley's objection to Milton's calling an inanimate object "*Impious*" is "true in strictness," Hayley nonetheless observes that the phrasing works as a "figurative Construction" (no. 61). After all, notes Hayley, the Doctor has himself allowed the same sort of construction three lines later "to pass muster." Here, then, Hayley points to another of the faults he finds in Bentley: inconsistency. Hayley likes to counter one of Bentley's emendations by noting similar instances in Milton's poem which the Doctor "has suffer'd to stand uncensur'd" (no. 30). Bentley, Hayley concludes, is inconsistent in his editorial practice, insensitive to the nuances and play of language, perversely literal minded, and unable to recognize a poetic or figurative phrase. All these faults are noted in one exceptionally complete marginal note.

How any Man who had ever read a Classick or understood English could seriously
start such a difficulty is beyond my Conception—May not the Words—Majestick—
& Ruin—relate to <u>Face</u> as well as <u>Counsel</u>? Nay did not the Author manifestly
intend it? What is this but to charge Milton wth Nonsense (if it be Nonsense) of the
Doctors own making? And I can't see but <u>Counsel</u> may as properly be said to <u>shine
in his Face</u> as <u>Deliberation</u> & <u>Care</u> to be engrav'd on his Front—Expressions truly
Poetical & Proper—If not, how came the Doctor to pass 'em over? (no. 17).

These then are the major critical charges Hayley levels against Bentley as
a reader of Milton's poetry.

Hayley's contribution to the dialogue with Bentley becomes more
valuable when he assumes the role of poet as well as critic. Hayley's
marginal commentary is most noteworthy because it engages Bentley on
the question of "poetic manner"—an issue Moyles has shown Pearce to
mention only twice in four hundred pages.[14] Although Hayley is sometimes satirical and sometimes simply dogmatic in his assertions of Bentley's violation of "Good Sense" (no. 2), he is most often found to be
rigorously committed to asserting the right of the poet to employ poetic
and figurative language and defending those instances in the poem which
he deems "Expressions truly Poetical & Proper." Hayley brings with him
an ear for poetry which Pearce did not possess or exhibit. Hayley's concern is with what is "absonous" (no. 41), with what is "hobbling [and]
inharmonious" (no. 24), with what is "unsufferable" in sound (no. 64) and
"Wretched" in poetry—with what, in a word, is "a botch . . . against
Rules of Poetical Decorum" (no. 16). Hayley felt that Bentley's emendations concerning poetic and figurative language were particularly trou-
bling; and it is especially in the marginalia concerning "Poetical Decorum"
that Hayley sounds most confident. One of the reasons Hayley was pained
by some of Bentley's emendations is that they produced such poor poetry.
Not only is one of Bentley's alterations "nonsensical," as Hayley notes, it is
also "unpoetical" (no. 10). Hayley says he "cannot help rejecting" another
emendation "if it were only for the unsufferable affinity of the Sounds"
produced by Bentley's alteration. The line, he sniffs with disgust, "is too
grating to escape the Pen of the lowest Poetaster" (no. 64). Another of
Bentley's alterations, he mockingly suggests, demonstrates a style which
"would suit mightily well wth a Play or a Puppet Show" (no. 32).

Objecting to Milton's verse—"Ye Birds, That Singing up to Heaven
Gate ascend"—while claiming that only the sky lark "sings as she ascends"
and that the ascent to "Heaven Gate" itself would be "beyond Possibility"
because it is beyond the abilities of any bird, Bentley emends the line to
read: "*That* SOARING *up* to HEAVENWARD *ascend.*" Hayley responds by
calling the Doctor's effort "Wretched Poetry!" before dismissing Bentley's

objection about the possibility of any bird's ascending to heaven. Because the "Text is figurative & truly Sublime," Hayley argues, it ought to stand as it is. Its being "beyond possibility is a poor Objection" since "all Poetical Figures" are also liable to the same charge (no. 53). When Bentley objects to the phrase "*Ransack'd the* Center," Hayley argues that the phrase "may well pass" as a "Poetical Figure, & as such," he proclaims, it is "extremely beautifull." Indeed, he concludes, such "rigid Constructions" as Bentley's would cause the "finest Flowers both in ancient & Modern Poetry" to be lost (no. 4). When Bentley suggests a change from "*Stars, that shone*" to "*Stars, that* SHOW'D," Hayley first inquires whether "shining a Star" is not "more Poetical than showing a Star at a distance" before asserting that such "modes of Expression [are] frequent amongst the Poets" (no. 35). Rejecting Bentley's insistence that the verb "ought of right" to be in the first clause of a parallel construction, Hayley cites Virgil and Milton to show that the "Doctor's assertion is contrary to the Practice of the best Poets" (no. 19).

Hayley, then, does not simply contest Bentley's emendations as being "Wretched Poetry," however much they often do turn out to be that, but also as being essentially deleterious to the very enterprise and practice of poetry itself. Hayley's reiterated evocations of a poetic tradition in which both ancient and modern poets are licensed to produce "Poetical Figures" demonstrates his feeling that for anyone to read with Bentley's literal-mindedness and insensitivity is to endanger the liberty of poets. What Bentley's emendations ultimately suggested to Hayley is that readers, particularly a reader with Bentley's enormous influence, could insist on reading figurative language in a way that literally destroyed the poems they read and effectively revoked the poetic license necessary for the literature and language of a country to evolve. When Bentley objects to one of Milton's coinages—"I do not remember ever to have met with the word HOSTING either in Verse or Prose"—Hayley responds with an earnestness that betrays his greatest fears:

I (Doctor Bentley) never met with this before—Ergo—the Author never made use of this Expression—The Premises do by no means warrant the Conclusion—Suppose it a Word of Milton's own coining & the difficultie is remov'd—The Riches of all Languages are owing to such Liberties, wch are never denie'd to those who use them sparingly & with Judgement—Surely our Author ought to have equal Indulgence wth Spenser & Shakespear   —(no. 60)

As a poet, then, Hayley responds to Bentley's emendations with an even more serious charge than his being an inconsistent editor or an insensitive and literal-minded reader. Bentley is nothing short of a menace to the organic growth of poetry and poetic traditions. For, finally, Hayley is willing to acknowledge that Bentley was a critic with some degree of acumen; but he was willing to concede that to Bentley at the same time that he quite explicitly gave to Milton an even greater mantle. "In short," as Hayley states near the outset of his marginalia, "it must be allow'd that Bentley is a Great Critick—but Milton the better Poet" (no. 4). And in a set of marginalia that begins with a poem about critics, Hayley has made it pretty clear which mantle—critic or poet—made one a better reader of poetry.

In sum, then, Hayley's marginalia are valuable because they raise concerns that Bentley's other respondents either ignored or muted. They are also valuable because Hayley responded to Bentley in at least two distinct ways. As a critic, Hayley found Bentley's editorial practice distasteful because of Bentley's tone, inconsistency, and pedantry. As a poet, Hayley found Bentley's editorial principles dangerous because of Bentley's literal-mindedness, insensitivity, and rigidity. Because the marginalia exhibit these dual concerns, they add to the Bentley debate in new ways and trace new avenues in the kinds of response Bentley provoked. In many ways, any annotator who is writing critically of Bentley's edition at the end of the eighteenth century is in an intriguing position. He or she is, as Shawcross notes, one of a series of outstanding but little-appreciated critics writing at the end of the century. These are critics whose ambivalent positioning between eighteenth century and Romantic literary values makes them all the more valuable. Like Milton's other Romantic critics and imitators, such a critic would be revolting against the established norms and categories of eighteenth-century literary values and, therefore, discerning in *Paradise Lost* Milton's fervent literary and political revolutionary impetus. Moreover, because the annotator is writing this commentary in the margins of Bentley's edition of *Paradise Lost*, he or she is also supplementing the Romantic critique with a more refined historical knowledge of the eighteenth-century debates surrounding Milton. Therefore, this annotator is finely situated as someone whose rejection of eighteenth-century literary values is informed by his or her sense of the historical evolution of those values.

In other words, whether these annotations are Hayley's or someone else's they should nonetheless be significant to Miltonists. Of course, if the marginal commentary is Hayley's as Luard first proposed, and as we are arguing, then it would be valuable on other grounds as well. Hayley is not just a polymath, but a polymath who made Milton central to all his aesthetic theorizing. In fact, Hayley did not just write frequently about Milton. He made Milton a crucial event in anything he aspired to do.

When he set out, as an English Romantic critic arguing against French Aristotelian critics who set up systematic and rigid "Rules of Writing," he made Milton the example of the "English, self-dependant soul." He asks, what would have become of *Paradise Lost* had Milton "stoop'd to listen to a Gallic Law." When he gives advice to a painter about how best to proceed, he notes,

> Let MILTON's self, conductor of thy way,
> Lead thy congenial spirit to portray
> In Colours, like his Verse, sublimely strong,
> The scenes that blaze in his immortal song.

When he gives advice to British sculptors, he tells them to aspire to "quicken marble with Miltonic fire."[15] It was in his life of Milton that Hayley first articulated the seeds of his theory of biography—which was meant to counter Dr. Johnson's theory of biography just as his life of Milton was an antidote to Johnson's practice of biographical writing. It was also in that life of Milton that Hayley made what is probably his greatest contribution to Milton scholarship. He is the first biographer of Milton to establish what is still the regnant tripartite structure of Milton's life: early lyrical poetry (1629–1640), polemical and political prose (1640–1660), and mature epic poetry (1660–1674).[16]

Milton, then, was clearly a crucial presence in Hayley's life. As a poet himself, Hayley is avowedly influenced by Milton's style. As an aesthetic theorist, he established Milton as the standard not only for epic poetry but also for sculpture and painting. As a person, he liked to maintain that Milton was the basis of his most important friendship. As a critic of critics, he maintained that the only cure for a "subtle Pedant's more presumptive pride" was the "just Critic of congenial soul." In the end, Hayley took upon himself that role of critic to answer Bentley's pride in a copy of *Paradise Lost* owned by the friend whom Milton had given him. Cowper is said to have written to Hayley, "Every remark of yours on Milton will be highly valued by me."[17] Two centuries later, we might well echo Cowper.

Just as we cannot, with Cowper and Hayley, hope to revive an author to validate our reading, so neither should we hope in all instances to give "new circulation" to those authors who have existed on the margins of critical commentary, whether they left "smothered embers of ancient animosity" or smoldering bits of pure praise. Dr. Johnson noted that it was the "practice of many readers, to note in the margin of their books, [only] the most important passages, the strongest arguments, or the brightest sentiments." Such marginal notation is of limited use. But some manuscript marginalia, as William Slights has suggested, record a "reader talking to himself" and this spectacle is sometimes edifying because some readerly soliloquies are worth overhearing. From those readers, as Horatio tells Hamlet, we "must be edified by the margent."[18] Hayley is one of those readers and his comments in the "margent" of Cowper's copy of Bentley's edition of *Paradise Lost* form one of those occasions.

WILLIAM HAYLEY'S DIALOGUE WITH RICHARD BENTLEY

Procedure: Our additions to the text are as follows. We will number each of the eighty-three marginal comments; we will also cite on which page the marginal comments occur. We will introduce each of Bentley's contested emendations and each of Hayley's marginal annotations by naming the writer. Everything else is transcribed as closely as possible from the margins of the text. We will reproduce Hayley's notations—his x, his +, and his *—at the appropriate places. Passages that are italicized are so in Bentley's edition; passages that are underlined are so by Hayley in his hand. Where Hayley underlined words or passages which are italicized in Bentley's text, they will here be both underlined and italicized. Entry thirty-seven occurs on page 103; it is incorrectly paginated as "203" in the Bentley edition.

There are noteworthy exceptions in six of the entries. Entry thirty-six contains Hayley's insertion of a word into Bentley's note. Entry fifty has two lines which have been scribbled out beyond comprehension. In entry fifty-two, there is one Latin word which is illegible. In entry fifty-three, two Latin words are barely legible. In entry sixty, we have omitted a five-and-a-half-line Latin quotation, which follows the marginal entry. Finally, in entry seventy-eight, the word "Rouse" is barely legible.

There are thirty-one notations in the text which consist of only a "pointing hand." These are to be found at the following places: 4.491, 4.638, 5.72, 6.852, 8.190, 8.538, 8.546, 8.572, 8.588, 8.621, 9.232, 9.239, 9.267, 9.367, 9.377, 9.754, 9.824, 10.152, 10.279, 10.758, 10.899, 11.319, 11.531, 11.537, 11.561, 11.693, 11.697, 11.771, 12.69, 12.83, 12.575. There are also three passages in the text which are wholly or partially underlined. These are to be found in the following places: 3.719, 3.721 (from "rest . . . universe"), and 5.285 (from "Like . . . Son"; marginal notation: "Vide, On, IV, 252"). There are four places in the text which are wholly or partially underlined and also have a "pointing hand" in the margin. These occur at: 3.686–89, 4.91–92 (underlined from "only . . . finds"), 8.56–57 (underlined from "from . . . Her"), and 8.591 ("and" is underlined). Finally, there are four places in the book in which Hayley corrects typographical errors in Bentley's text. These occur at: 4.196

(note: "Cure"), 4.181 (note: "once" to "one"), 8.245 ("costs" to "coasts"), and 10.1072 ("collison" to "collision").

THE TEXT

Shelf no. EE.2.8, O–1K08 / 238,
The Old Library, Christ's College, Cambridge

MILTON's / PARADISE LOST. / A NEW EDITION, / By *RICHARD BENTLEY, D. D.* / *LONDON:* / Printed for JACOB TONSON; and for JOHN POULSON; and for / J. DARBY, A. BETTESWORTH, and F. CLAY, in Trust for / RICHARD, JAMES, and BETHEL WELLINGTON. / MDCCXXXII.

At the end of the preface, on page a4, verso, the following poem is written in Hayley's hand:

> Ye Criticks, would your tribe deserve a Name,
> And nobly useful, rise to honest fame:
> First from the head, a load of Lumber move,
> And from the Volume, all yourselves approve;
> For patch'd or pilfer'd Fragments, give us Sense,
> Or Learning, clear'd from learn'd Impertinence,
> Where moral meaning, or where taste presides,
> And Wit enlivens but what Reason guides:
> Great without swelling, without meaning plain,
> Serious, not simple, sportive but not vain;
> On trifles slight, on things of use profound,
> In quoting sober, and in judging sound.

Book I (pp. 1–35)

1.) (p. 12) Bentley: v. 218. *Infinite goodness.*] *Infinite goodness,* in other Places, very proper, seems here a little too high. For *Justice* and ˣ *rigid Satisfaction* was exacted for *Adam's* Sin: As the Poet sets it forth in Books III and X. Rather therefore here,

NEW PROOFS of Goodness, Grace, and Mercy shewn.

Hayley: Y Quare—how far this is consistent wᵗʰ the Christian Scheme— Vide Lib. III line 173.

> Man shall not quite be lost but saved who will:
> Yet not of will in him but Grace in Me
> <u>Freely vouchsaf'd.</u>xc—

And again—line 203.290–291.292.293. Where we find the Merit of the Son of God imputed to Man after he had forfeit'd all Title to the—Divine Favour by his Disobedience.—'Tis true the Son of God is represented as paying the Ransom—Death for Death—but without that Infinite Justice had not been satisfied wch surely 'tis very orthodox at least to suppose not to be irreconcileable wth Infinite Goodness—If I might venture then to differ from the Doctor's opinion, I sh'd think the Text ought to stand as it did before the emendment unless he can shew us that Infinite Goodness can require no satisfaction for Sin—or not so rigid a satisfaction as is here describ'd—Vide Clarke's Sermons. Vol. 8. Serm. 16. 17. 18.—where you will find a noble vindication of God's infinite Goodness in the Redemption of lost Mankind, notwithstanding the difficulties started by this Caviller—

2.) (p. 28) Bentley: v. 636. *If counsels different, or danger shun'd.*] *Counsels different* may pass with vulgar Approbation: but yet ˣ there's no hint in all the Poem, that *Satan* differs from all the Council, or acted without their Consent. I suspect the Author gave a better Word with a finer Notion thus,
      If Counsels E'ER DIFFERR'D, *or Danger shun'd.*
If *Counsels,* publickly resolv'd on, were ever *delay'd* by my Sloth, or *Dangers* shun'd by my Fear.

Hayley: ˣI don't think the Text implies that he did—This is meer Cavill— The Notion the Text would convey is this—that Satan steadily persued their Joint Counsels, & was never aw'd by Danger so that the ill Success of their Enterprize could not be justly charg'd upon Him—This is certainly very Good Sense—Away then wth his better Word & Finer Notion.

3.) (p. 29) Bentley: v. 646. *By Fraud or Guile.*] In II.188. he says, *For what can force or* guile *with Him?* And II.41. *Whether by open* war *or* covert guile. These are right: *Force* and *open War* are distinguish'd from Plot and Guile. But what difference at all betwixt Fraud and Guile? Therefore he must have given it,
      Fraud AND *Guile,* or rather, *Fraud* AND ˣ WILE.
Hayley: ˣ Guile & Wile are the same Word differently written, & I see no reason why fraud or guile may not pass as well as deceit or guile in Ninth Book. 772. & so in the first. 34. —
      NB: Guile is written and pronounc'd after the french manner, Wile after the english; as are Guarrant, Warrant—Guerre, War, & a great many others. —

4.) (p. 31) Bentley: v. 686. *Ransack'd the* Center.] Whatever is beyond Possibility does not elevate the Stile, but depress it and make it ridiculous. To ransack *as deep* as the *Center* had been bad enough; but it's still worse to ransack the ˣ *Center* it self, a single Point, whence nothing could be got. How much better, agreeably to Truth and Nature,

>Ransack'd the MOUNTAINS,

the Seat of all Metals, as *Milton* well knew: so here ᵗ. 660.

>*There stood a* HILL *stor'd with metallic Ore;*

And v. 690.

>*Open'd into the* HILL *a spacious Wound.*

Hayley: ˣ This may well pass as a——Poetical Figure, & as such is in my opinion extremely beautifull—The finest Flowers both in ancient & Modern Poetry would be lost by such rigid Constructions——In short it must be allow'd that Bentley is a Great Critick—but Milton the better Poet——

5.) (p. 31) Bentley: v. 692. Deserve *the precious Bane.*] He does not design here to accuse *Hell*, but *Riches*. And yet when he says *Deserve* the Bane; the Accusation is turn'd from *Riches* to *Hell*. Better therefore thus,

>BEFIT *the precious Bane.*
>
>*Befit, Beseen, Become.* Unless you will invert the Phrase,
>*The precious Bane may best that Soil deserve.*

Hayley: Beseem

6.) (p. 33) Bentley: v. 725. Within *her ample spaces.*] <u>*Within* makes</u> ˣan <u>Ambiguity</u>: design'd indeed for an Adverb, but looks like a Praeposition. Rather thus,

>*Discover wide*
>AND ˣ <u>HIGH</u> *her ample spaces.*

Hayley: ˣIn the two first Editions of this Poem there is a Comma put after <u>within</u>, & then the ambiguity is taken away—

   ˣ Surely <u>High</u> does not suit with what is said to be discover'd here, viz. not the <u>Roof</u>, but the ample—<u>Spaces</u> over the Pavement wᶜʰ might shew the <u>width</u> but not the <u>height</u> of the Pile.——

7.) (p. 34) Bentley: v. 762. *Though like a cover'd Field.*] Here's another Intrusion of Four spurious Lines; unworthy of admittance. The immense Hall of *Pandæmonium* compar'd to a *Saracen's* <u>Tent</u>; a first rate <u>Man of War</u> to a ˣ <u>Skuller</u>. *Won't ride in arm'd*, scurvy Accent. Put the two <u>Ends</u> together, *But chief the spacious Hall Thick swarm'd;* and they plainly shew, they were violently parted asunder by a rude Hand.

Hayley:[x] This is not the Truth of the Case: That Hall is here compar'd to a cover'd Field, and a Field may be allow'd large for the Comparison, especially when it is describ'd as containing room enough for Tilt and Tournament. The Soldan's Chair & Tent might be in that Field, & yet the whole Field was not his Tent.——

Book II (pp. 36–76)

8.) (p. 37) Bentley: v. 4. Showr's *on her* Kings *Barbaric Pearl and Gold.*] Here's farther Injustice to our blind Poet: he could not give these Words. *Showrs Pearl and Gold,* as if those dropt from the Clouds; when the one is with Labour and Danger fetch'd from the bottom of the Sea, the other from the Basis of Mountains. And what's that? *showr'd with hand?* as if any Poet ever feign'd, that the Hand was the Instrument of showring. *Showr'd Gold on her Kings:* Did no Subjects get a few Drops, the Skirts of the Golden Rain? But the *Kings* would have the worst of it; as *Tarpeia* had, when she was stifled and kill'd under the Presents of the *Roman* Soldiers. The Poet gave it thus,

[x] SOW'D *on her* CLIME Barbaric Pearl and GEM.

The best *Pearls* and *Gems* are peculiar to the *East-Indies,* Gold as common in the West. *Sow'd* well accords with *Hand,* agreeably to Use and Nature. And our Author lov'd those two Words, *Sowing* and *Clime;* as V.2.

Now Morn, her rosie Steps in th' Eastern Clime
Advancing, sow'd the Earth with Orient Pearl.

Hayley:[x] Perhaps Shew'd had been a happy Emendation if the Doctor had hit upon it as according mighty well with the hand,—agreeably to Use and Nature. The childish Conceits of this Note are below the Dignity of a true Critick——

9.) (p. 38) Bentley: v. 69. *And his Throne it self Mix'd with* Tartarean *Sulphur.*] How the *Throne* could be[x] mix'd with Sulphur, I cannot see, unless it was batter'd to pieces and pounded with it. But the Author gave it,

MARR'D *with* Tartarean *Sulphur, and strange fire.*

Marr'd, defil'd, polluted; a Word not unworthy of Heroic Stile; frequent in *Spenser,* and used here too, IV. 116. *Which* marr'd *his borrow'd Visage,* and IX. 136. *In one Day to have marr'd.* And it is prov'd from *Belial's* Reply to this Passage of *Moloch's,* v. 139. *He would on his Throne sit unpolluted.*

Hayley: This is supposing the Throne of the Almighty to be Material & confining it to a sense unworthy of the Author, who in another place describes the Chariot of the Messiah as instinct wth Spirit, vide Lib. vi. Line 752. an Idea truly Sublime! vide Line 846. Living Wheels.

10.) (p. 39) Bentley: v. 80. *With what*ˣ *laborious* flight *We sunk thus low.*] The Ideas of *Flight* and of *Sinking* do not agree well together. I suspect the Author gave it,
> *With what Compulsion and laborious* STRIFE.

Hayley: ˣ Very descriptive of the vast Height from whence they had lately fallen—Besides how could there be Strife after they were actually vanquish'd & subdued? This alteration then is not only unpoetical but nonsensical—This is Marring wth a witness, vide Note 69 . . . ——vide Note 232.

11.) (p. 43) Bentley: II.190 ˣ Views all things at one view? He from Heav'n's highth

Hayley: ˣ I wonder Bentley who seems to abhorr Jingle so much did not take notice of this & alter it thus—
> Views all things at one Glance or Ken—
perhaps it might have pass'd muster as well as some other of his Emendations.

12.) (p. 43) Bentley: v. 156. *Belike through* Impotence.] The Ideas here do not agree, *Will He so* WISE, do a thing he designs not, *through* IMPOTENCE? ˣ *Impotence* is not the opposite to *Wisdom*, but to *Power.* The Author must have given it,
> *Belike through* INSCIENCE, *or unaware,*
Through Inscience, by a want of Knowledge; *Unaware,* by Inattention or Surprise, notwithstanding his Knowledge: by Ignorance do what he *should* not do; or by Surprise do what he *would* not do.

Hayley: ˣ Impotence is here meant for the Opposite to Wisdom, & is frequently us'd by the Latin Authors to signify a Weakness of Mind, an Unsteadiness in the Government of our Passions or the Conduct of our Designs. In this sense Cicero in Epist. ad Fam. ix.9. says victoria—ferociores impoten horesque reddit; and in Tusc.Disp. iv.23. we read impotentia dictorum et factoram: hence we often meet wth impotens animi, irae, dolons &c. Nay the Doctor's own Friend Horace in Od. 1.39.10 has quidlibet impotens sperare.

13.) (p. 44) Bentley: v. 204. *Who at the Spear are bold.*] If ARE *bold* be allow'd here; here will want a Particle, BUT *if that fail them.* So that the Author must have given it,

> *I laugh, who at the Spear* SO *bold*
> *And vent'rous, if that fail them, shrink and fear,*

ˣ *So bold* implies a Boldness extraordinary, which *Bold* alone does not.

Hayley: ˣ The Doctor is so bold wᵗʰ this Author that 'tis almost endless to follow him—Let us transpose the words & the sense will be found very entire without the Particle But wᶜʰ the Critick begs so hard for—

I laugh when those who are vent'rous & bold at the Spear shrink if that fail them—In my opinion But is so little wanted here yᵗ it would make it rank nonsense.

14.) (p. 45) Bentley: v. 232. *When Fate shall* yield

> *To fickle Chance, and* Chaos *judge the strife.*] ˣ If Fate *yields* to chance, it prevents a following *Strife.* I suspect, the Poet gave it thus,

> *When everlasting Fate shall* PLEAD
> WITH *fickle Chance, and* Chaos *judge the Strife.*

Hayley: ˣ vide ante. Note. 80. where you will find the same remark hold against the Learned Doctor—

15.) (p. 46) Bentley: v. 256. *Hard Liberty before the easy yoke Of servile Pomp.*] Though *Easy* here comes a pat Antitheton to *Hard;* yet it spoils the Thought. For the Yoke was so far from being thought *easy,* that it was *wearisom* and *unacceptable.* Were it *easy;* why not eligible*, and preferable to *hard* Liberty? 'Tis likely the Author gave it,

> *Before the* LAZIE *Yoke.*

Lazy; they being suppos'd wholy employ'd in their Harps and their Hymns.

Hayley: * Because a mark of Servility—wᶜʰ Spirits that had thrown off all allegiance could not brook—this certainly was the Sense of the Author—

16.) (p. 47) Bentley: v. 274. *Our Torments also,* &c.] This Argument *Mammon* steals from *Belial's* Speech above, *v.* 217. who pleaded on the same side of the Question; and assumes it as his own and new. But to keep just Decorum, he should ascribe it to its true Author, and say it thus,

> *Then,* * as was well observ'd, *our Torments may*
> *Become our Elements.*

Hayley: * Nothing in my mind could be worse observ'd yⁿ this whole—
passage—Such a botch as this is against Rules of Poetical Decorum.

17.) (p. 48) Bentley: v. 304. *And princely* Counsel *in his Face* &c.] * How
Counsel could *shine,* or be *Majestic,* or be in *Ruin,* is beyond my Understanding. I cannot but think, He gave it,
> And princely FEATURE *in his Face yet shone.*

Spenser V.5.12.
> *In her fair Visage void of Ornament,*
> *Bewray'd the signs of* Feature *excellent.*

And VI.7.28.
> *And praise the Feature of her goodly Face.*

The Editor, not knowing *Feature, Factura,* in the Singular, turn'd it into
Counsel.

Hayley: * How any Man who had ever read a Classick or understood
English could seriously start such a difficulty is beyond my Conception—
May not the Words—Majestick—& Ruin—relate to <u>Face</u> as well as <u>Coun-
sel</u>? Nay did not the Author manifestly intend it? What is this but to
charge Milton wᵗʰ Nonsense (if it be Nonsense) of the Doctors own making? And I can't see but <u>Counsel</u> may as properly be said to <u>shine in his
Face</u> as <u>Deliberation</u> & <u>Care</u> to be engrav'd on his Front—Expressions
truly Poetical & Proper—If not, how came the Doctor to pass 'em over?
Vide Lib. III. Line–268.

18.) (p. 53) Bentley: v. 439. *Of unessential* Night.] *Night* is well, but
better would be, * SPACE.

Hayley: * Why so—the <u>Void Profound</u> implies <u>Space</u> but <u>Space</u> cannot be
said to include <u>Night</u>—<u>Space</u> and <u>Darkness</u> are as different as <u>Light</u> &
<u>Darkness</u>—The Text then conveys two distinct Ideas. The Doctors alter-
ation of It—makes Tautology——

19.) (p. 57) Bentley: v. 556. *For Eloquence the Soul, Song charms the
Sense.*] The <u>Verb</u> ought of right to be in the ˣ <u>first *Colon* of the Sentence</u>;
better, I conceive, thus;
> *Song charms the Sense,* BUT *Eloquence the Soul.*

Hayley: ˣ The Doctor's assertion is contrary to the Practice of the best
Poets. Virgil (for instance) places the verb in the last Colon of the sentence
in the following verses, among many others that might be produc'd,

Imperia Oceano, fama qui terminat astris. An. I. 291. —
Imperia ternis, animos aquabit Olympo. Ib. VI. 782.
And Milton does the same thing in other Places of this Poem, particularly
in XI. 467.

20.) (p. 60) Bentley: v. 644. *To the* horrid *Roof.*] I believe the Author gave
it, * *the* ARCHED *Roof;* a proper significant Epithet, the other merely
General. So I. 726. *From the* arched *Roof.*

Hayley: * 'Tis my opinion Milton did not mean the Roof either as Flat or
Arch'd, & indeed what is there in that one way or t'other? No, he design'd
to raise Terror & therefore makes use of a very suitable Epithet for that
Purpose—We shrink when we read It—

21.) (p. 61) Bentley: v. 654. *A cry of Hell-hounds.*] I may be ignorant of
the Hunter's Language: but I should believe he gave it,
     * *A* CRUE *of Hell-hounds.*

Hayley: Crue seems to me more proper to describe a great Number of
Men assembled together than Dogs—for instance—a Ship's Crue. & the
latter are always—distinguish'd by the word Pack—He could not but
know this and his Pride is as conspicuous in dissembling this sort of
Knowledge as is his vain Pretence to others. He may be ignorant of the
Hunters Language—Note: There is but a bare possibility that Doctor
Bentley should be ignorant of anything—

22.) (p. 61) Bentley: v. 659. *Far less abhorr'd than these Vex'd Scylla, &c.*]
Let the Editor here too take back his intruded Comparisons, *Scylla and
her Dogs:* which [x] common Fable he has yet deprav'd in the telling: for
those Dogs were incorporate with her and always stuck fast, whether she
bath'd in the Sea, or not. And see, how he has managed the Passage of
Virgil,
     Scyllam, *quam fama secuta est,*
    Candida succinctam latrantibus inguina monstris
    Dulichias vexasse rates.
Here *Scylla* vex'd *Ulysses*'s Ship, when she devour'd six of his Seamen; +
not with her Dogs, but with her six Heads: but hence the Editor takes
VEXASSE, and makes the Dogs to *vex Scylla* herself. But much rather let
him take back his fabulous *Night-Hag,* his *Dance of* Lapland *Witches,* and
his *Smell of Infant Blood;* and not contaminate this most majestic Poem

with trash, nor convey such idle, but dangerous Stories to his young and credulous Female Readers.

Hayley. ˣ The Doctor has quite mistaken Milton's meaning here: M. alludes not to anything in Virgil but to Ovid's account of Scylla in Metam. XIV.59. where the Poet tells us, that Circe having poison'd that part of the Sea where Scylla us'd to bathe, Scylla upon her bathing there the next time found all the lower part of her Body chang'd into Dogs. So that the Circumstance of her bathing was a material one here, when M. meant to relate what happen'd to her at that bathing of hers. Ovid is a good Authority for the circumstance of the Dogs vexing Scylla herself, who says. abigitque limatque Ora proterva canum: Starque canum rabies vide ut supra.

ˣ Vide the very next verse in Virgil— . . . Nautas canibus lacerasse manris.

23.) (p. 69) Bentley: v. 892. *Illimitable Ocean without* bound.] This same *Bound* cannot be allow'd. 'Tis the very same, as *Illimitable without limit,* or *Boundless without bound.* But the Poet gave it,
        Illimitable Ocean without SHORE.*
So our Author II.1011.
        But glad that now his Sea should find a Shore.
And XI.750.
        Sea cover'd Sea, Sea *without* Shore:
borrow'd from that Passage of *Ovid;*
        Omnia pontus erat; deerant SED *litora ponto.*

Hayley: * This may aptly be call'd a Distinction without a Difference— What—is not the Shore of the Ocean the Bound of the Ocean & the same vice versâ? Ridiculous Trifling!

Book III (pp. 77–104)

24.) (p. 78) Bentley: v. 34: *So were I equal'd with them in Renown,*] O̲ ̲w̲e̲r̲e̲ ̲w̲i̲t̲h̲ ̲H̲i̲m̲ ̲I̲ ̲e̲q̲u̲a̲l̲'̲d̲ ̲i̲n̲ ̲R̲e̲n̲o̲w̲n̲!̲ *

Hayley: * What a hobbling inharmonious Line is here! rather than surely
        O were I with him equal'd in Renown!
            or thus—
        O were I equal'd wᵗʰ him in Renown!

25.) (p. 79) Bentley: v. 42. <u>of Ev'n or Morn,</u>] *dewy.*

Hayley:—Sweet the coming on of grateful Evening mild—Lib. 4.645.

26.) (p. 79) Bentley: v. 49. *Of Nature's works,* to me expung'd and ras'd;]
All Nature's Map

Hayley: <u>All</u> Natures Works &c.; This seems to be the proper Reading.—
—

27.) (p. 79) Bentley: v. 42. *Day, or the sweet approach of Ev'n or Morn.*]
This can hardly be Right. * <u>The poor Man in so many Years Blindness had</u>
<u>too much of *Evening.*</u> I believe, he gave it thus;
   Day, or the sweet approach of DEWY *Morn.*

Hayley: * What a poor Conceit is this?—What an unpardonable Jest? One
would be so far from thinking of Milton's Blindness upon reading this
Beautifull Passage y^t one might rather imagine him to have been all Eye—
But why must the <u>Evening</u> be driven out from the Text in so arbitrary a
manner? does it not serve to diversify the Picture, & has it not its Delight
as well as the <u>Morning</u>? Does <u>Evening,</u> imply <u>Darkness</u>? no surely, much
less the <u>Approach</u> of <u>Evening;</u> A Man must be blind indeed not to see the
absurdity of such Remarks.

28.) (p. 79) Bentley: v. 49. *An universal Blank* Of Nature's Works.] *A*
Blank of Works is an Expression unphilosophical: the Sense must termi-
nate in *Blank.* <u>One may as well say, * A *blank Paper of Words.*</u> Besides,
That all Nature's *Works* were not obliterated to him: he had but lost One
Sense of Five: He might taste, smell, hear and feel Her Works still.
Perhaps it may be better thus:
   Presented with an universal Blank:
   ALL *Nature's* MAP *to me expung'd and ras'd.*

Hayley: * I agree this would be direct Nonsense—but put it thus w^{ch}
comes nearer to Milton's Phrase—<u>a Paper blank of Words</u>—perhaps this
would be no improper Idiom—Vi. Supra.

29.) (p. 79) Bentley: v. 55. *That I may see and tell* Of things.] *See of things*
is a Slip by unattention. It's likely He thus gave it;
   That I may see and tell *
   Things <u>ELSE</u> *invisible to mortal Sight.*

Hayley: How so?—Are they not invisible to Mortal Sight whither they are told or no?

30.) (p. 89) Bentley: v. 301. So *easily destroy'd; and* still destroys.] I am unwilling to believe, that the Author here forgot himself, *still destroys;* not attending, that this Speech is before Adam's Fall. I rather think He gave it thus;

> So *easily destroy'd; and* ˣ WILL DESTROY.

Hayley: ˣ There are many passages in those speeches of God and Messiah, where the Fall is spoken of as a Thing Past—perhaps because all Things, even Future ones, are present in the Divine Mind. Thus we read in v. 151.

> Thy Creature <u>late</u> so lov'd—

and in v. 181

> That he may know how frail
> His <u>fall'n</u> condition is ——

and yet those two passages wᵗʰ others of the same kind, Dr. Bentley has suffer'd to stand uncensur'd—

31.) (p. 90) Bentley: v. 349. *Th'* eternal *Regions.*] * *Eternal* may be defended; but yet from the Poet it was, ETHEREAL *Regions.*

Hayley: * Ipse dixit—

32.) (p. 92) Bentley: v. 397. *Back from pursuit thy Pow'rs.*] The Poet cannot yet part with his first chosen Idea of the Angels pursuing *Satan* to Hell. See Note II.996. He must here be help'd out again, to make the whole Poem agree. But here's another Mistake too, *Thy Powers extoll'd,* spoken in the Third Person; when those very *Powers* are here the Speakers. It may be alter'd thus;

> * WE THE SPECTATORS GLAD *with loud acclaim*
> *Thee only' extoll'd.*

For on that Day the Angels were not engag'd in fight, but quietly look'd on: as VI.801.

> *Stand still in bright array, ye Saints; here stand,*
> *Ye Angels arm'd: this day from Battel rest.*
> *Numbers to this day's work is not ordain'd.*
> *Nor multitude: stand only and* behold.

Hayley: * This stile would suit mightily well wth a Play or a Puppet Show—

33.) (p. 92) Bentley: v. 413. *Matter of my Song, and my Harp.*] He * <u>has again</u> the Chorus, that says this, the whole *multitude of Angels.* Better Our *Song, and* our harps.

Hayley: ˣ <u>forgets 'ks</u>

34.) (p. 96) Bentley: v. 507. *With sparkling* orient *Gems.*] Orient Gems is proper upon Earth to say, because the best Gems come from the *East-Indies:* * <u>but in Heaven the Propriety ceases.</u> So that, I believe, the Author gave it,
    Imbellish'd: thick with sparkling ardent *Gems.*

Hayley: * This same Objection may be made to <u>Gems</u> wch every body knows to be an Earthly Commodity—strictly speaking there is no Propriety in saying there are either Diamonds or Gold in Heaven but 'tis always allow'd in Descriptions of that Place, as best suited to the Level of our Capacities wch can entertain no higher Ideas of Magnificence.

35.) (p. 98) Bentley: v. 565. *Stars, that* shone *Stars distant.*] * No doubt, the Poet gave it;
    Innumerable Stars, that show'd
    Stars distant, but nigh hand seem'd *other Worlds.*

Hayley: * How so? is not <u>shining</u> a Star more Poetical than <u>showing</u> a Star at a distance? He moves a God—she looks a Queen—are modes of Expression frequent amongst the Poets—

36.) (p. 101) Bentley: v. 657. *Through* highest *Heav'n to bring.*] Better here, *Through* widest *Heav'n.* For the Embassies are [not] thence sent upwards into infinite Space.

37.) (p. [103]) Bentley: v. 719. *And how they move.*] The Poet gave it, ˣ *And how* to *move, Each had his place.* And v. 721. *Walls:* Rather, *The rest in circuit* wall.

Hayley: ˣ Put a comma after (seest) & a semicolon after (move) the sense then will be—Thou seest that the stars are numberless & thou seest how they move: so the Doctor first makes the blunder by an alteration of the stops & then finds fault wth it—Milton speaks here of all the Stars in general—<u>Planetary</u> & those call'd <u>Fix'd</u>: whereas the Doctor seems to suppose that he is speaking here of the Planetary only; & that in the next verse by the words (the rest) M. means the <u>Fix'd Stars</u>: but the rest means the remainder of the Ethereal Quintessence wch was not us'd in the formation of the stars:—

Book IV (pp. 105–45)

38.) (p. 107) Bentley: v. 38. *From what state I fell, how* glorious *once.*] All the Words adjoining, *I fell, Above thy Sphere, Threw me down,* conspire to prove that the Author instead of GLORIOUS, gave a Word that denotes, not *Splendour,* but Place and *Elevation,*

> *I fell how* * SOARING *once above thy Sphere.*

So IV.828

> *Ye knew me once no Mate*
> *For You, there sitting where ye durst not* SOAR.

Hayley: * There are no less y^n three expressions that denote <u>Place</u> and <u>Elevation</u>—but this wont satisfie the Doctor without the <u>Word</u>—<u>Soaring</u>—be admitted instead of <u>Glorious</u>—What Room can there be for such a violent Change of a Word in order to denote what was sufficiently express'd before?

39.) (p. 114) Bentley: v. 250. Hesperian *Fables true, If true, here only.*] The Editor, whoever he was, our Author's Acquaintance, would often have a Finger in so fine a Work; and here he gives us an Insertion of *Hesperian Fables.* Fables, says he, if true, here only true. Very quaint: but pray you, Sir, * <u>how can *Fables* be true *any where*?</u> a Contradiction in the very Terms. One would think, that the Printer, as he has often injur'd the Poet, had here likewise given foul Play to the Editor; who may be suppos'd to have given it thus;

> *Hesperian* APPLES *true.*

Apples and *Fables* are not very distant in Letters; and *Hesperian Apples* are celebrated by all the Ancient Writers,

> *Tum canit* Hesperidum *miratam* mala *puellam.*

But then the same Writers every one make them solid Gold, far from eatable, or of *delicious tast.* Let the Editor then take them, whether *Fables* or *Apples;* and let us close the Verse thus;

> *Burnish'd with golden Rind*
> *Hung amiable', and of delicious taste.*

And the very pat joining of the Verse betrays the Insertion.

Hayley: * An idle Question & not worthy of an answer—The Text gives no
Room for such a Smeer—it contains this plain intelligible Proposition—
that whatever the Ancients feign'd of the Hesperian Fruit might be
deem'd true of this if of any—The warmest Imagination could paint nothing beyond It—Golden Apples—not from being of the <u>Substance</u> but the
<u>Colour</u> of <u>Gold</u>—Milton plainly took it in that Sense by saing they were <u>of</u>
<u>delicious Tast</u>.

40.) (p. 121) Bentley: v. 405. *Couches close, and changes His* couchant
watch.] Here the same Fault again, and for the same reason excusable,
Couches and *Couchant*. Besides, * <u>how can the Tiger be *rising* and
couchant at the same time?</u> Perhaps He gave it,
                    His DOUBLE *watch.*
Double, as first watching one, then the other, till he may seize them both
at once.

Hayley: * The Text don't imply such a Contradiction—Does not <u>changing</u>
<u>a Posture</u> denote a <u>difference of Posture</u>—
                    ———Then <u>rising changes</u> oft
              His <u>couchant</u> posture—
Not couchant <u>after</u> he was upon his Legs but <u>before</u>—What Pretense for
any other Construction?

41.) (p. 123) Bentley: v. 472. He, Whose Image *thou art.*] This Accent is
so absonous; that our Author, well skill'd in Music, could not be guilty of
it. He must give it thus;
              Thy coming and thy soft embrace: * <u>he whose</u>
              Image thóu árt; HE WHOM *thou shalt enjoy.*

Hayley: * What can be more absonous than this?

42.) (p. 123) Bentley: v. 474. *Multitudes like* thy self.] What? all her
Progeny to be Female? no doubt he gave it,
              Multitudes like YOUR SELVS. *

Hayley: * Adam is here talking to Eve in the Singular Number—How
comes she to be thus multiplied all of a sudden? Perhaps <u>Ourselves</u> had
not been quite so improper if there had been occasion for any—alteration
at all—Her Progeny were to resemble both as Male or Female,
              —To Him (Thou) shalt bear
              Multitudes like <u>Yourselves</u>—

Is such a preposterous Jumble of Plural and Singular as cannot be admitted—

43.) (p. 124) Bentley: v. 509. Where.] Where's.

Hayley: Vide: Lib. 8.621
                    —and without Love no Happiness
          Is subintelligitur—so in this place.

44.) (p. 125) Bentley: v. 506. *Imparadis'd.*] This has been remark'd, as a Word first coin'd by *Milton.* But Sir *Philip Sidney* has it in *Arcadia,* p. 109. *So this* imparadis'd *Neighborhood made* Zelmane's *Soul cleave unto her.* And the * Italians had prior Possession, *Imparadisato.*

Hayley: * What is this but a poor attempt to lessen the Merit of the Author wch I cannot think at all concern'd in the Question?

45.) (p. 126) Bentley: v. 555. Uriel, *gliding through the* Ev'n.] I never heard but here, that the *Evening* was a Place or Space to *glide* through. *Evening* implies Time, and he might with equal propriety say, *Came gliding though Six a clock.* But it's the Printer's Language: the Author gave it,
          Thither came Uriel, *gliding through the* HEAV'N.

Hayley: through

46.) (p. 129) Bentley: v. 614. *And the* timely *dew of Sleep.*] * *Timely* is appropriated to the Courses of Nature, which are constant and regular. *Sleep* is not so fix'd to Time; as *Adam* himself says, VII.106.
          Sleep listning to *Thee will watch,*
     Or we can *bid his Absence.*
Therefore I believe the Author gave it, *The* KINDLY *dew of Sleep; Kindly,* courteous Sleep, as appointed or conscious to relieve the necessities of Animal Nature: our best Poets often use the Word.

Hayley: * Timely (i.e.) seasonable—What Epithet more proper—Is not Night appropriate to Sleep? Is it not the only regular Time for It? The Words Courteous or Kindly does not imply this wch the Author no doubt w.^d intimate by this Expression. Meanwhile as Nature Wills, Night bids us rest Line. 633.

47.) (p. 131) Bentley: v. 667. *In Nature and* all thíngs.] This is too low to
suit with the rest of the Poem, both for Accent and Sense. ˣ All *Things* had
not Life; and therefore in Them Life could not be *extinguish'd*. It may be
many ways adjusted: take this for one;

> And *extinguish Life*
> And LIGHT *in Nature's* REALM.

Hayley: ˣ Suppose only a Comma instead of a semicolon after Things, by wᶜʰ
means the Words All Things will be qualified & restrain'd by the words wᶜʰ
follow—The Sense of the Passage is plainly this—Lest total Darkness sh.ᵈ
extinguish Life in All Things, wᶜʰ these soft Fires not only enlighten, but
foment and warm.——Away then wᵗʰ—Light in Nature's Realm———

48.) (p. 132) Bentley: v. 689. *Hand in hand* alone *they pass'd.*] 'Tis no
great Discovery to tell us, they were *alone;* unless we could suppose, that
the Beasts accompanied them, who were already gone to roost. But the
Poet gave it,

> *Thus talking, hand in hand* ˣ ALONG *they pass'd.*

Hayley: ˣ Milton in v. 340. speaks after this manner—Alone as they——

49.) (p. 137) Bentley: v. 815. *Of nitrous Powder laid, Fit for the* Tun.] * I
presume, they do not barrel up Gunpowder in such large Vessels as *Tuns;*
but in smaller, and more expedite for Service. If the Fact be so; no doubt
the Poet gave it,

> *Fit for the* GUN.

Nay *Gun*, being the final Use of Powder, seems to be the fitter Word,
though Powder may be in some Cases even *Tun'd* up, and not Barrel'd.

Hayley: * A notable disquisition truly—I don't dispute & even the Doctor
allows yᵗ the Expression is—proper either way—Much may be said on
both sides—Though in this place I am rather inclin'd to favour the Word
Tun from the Preceding sentence & that wᶜʰ follows—

> —As when a spark
> Lights on a heap of nitrous Powder laid,
> Fit for the Tun, some Magazine to store
> Against a rumor'd War;

Now a little quantity of Powder is as fit for a Gun as a large one—but here
the use wᶜʰ is to be made on't, viz, that of storing a Magazine against a War
necessarily implys great Quantities wᶜʰ the Word Tun very properly
signifies——

50.) (p. 140) Bentley: v. 879. *The bounds prescrib'd* <u>To thy</u> Transgressions.] Poor Poet; in subjection to a saucy Editor, and an ignorant Printer! Thou never thought'st, that any bounds could be set to * Satan's <u>Transgressions</u>. He, though bounded never so, transgress'd in his own Mind and Thoughts, every moment of his Being; *non vitiosus, sed vitium ipsum.* But the true Reading is easily retriev'd,
<blockquote>Broke the bounds prescrib'd To thy Transcursions.</blockquote>
Hell was his Prison, which he was not to go out of, *Transcurrere,* as the Almighty says, III.81.
<blockquote>*Our Adversary, whom* no Bounds
Prescrib'd *no Bars of Hell can hold.*</blockquote>
And take notice, that <u>*Transgress* in its right meaning comes again in the very next Line; a plain Proof, that *Transgressions* is wrong here.</u>

Hayley: * Potius sic—<u>For</u> thy Transgressions—Here is an end of the Doctor's smart objection at once—& seems to me to be a more natural alteration than the other
[two lines are here scribbled out beyond comprehension]

51.) (p. 143) Bentley: v. 971. Proud *Limitary Cherub.*] If *Limitary* be, as it is, a diminishing Word, implying that he had no Royal Provinces assign'd him, but some Offices inferiour; and so the Word *Cherub* spoken in Contempt; (for *Gabriel* was a *Seraph* of the highest Order) it would be a fitter Expression, as the Author seems to have given it,
<blockquote>*Poor Limitary Cherub.*</blockquote>

Hayley: * Why so? <u>Limitary</u> is no doubt a diminutive Expression & savours of the utmost <u>Contempt</u> wch is still heighten'd by the Word <u>Proud</u>— Satan reproaches Gabriel wth being <u>Servile</u>—fitter to <u>Cringe</u> than <u>Fight</u>— Vide Ante L. <u>944–945</u>. Vide Post L. <u>974–5</u>. and means to charge him with being Proud of an office below the Dignity of an Immortal Spirit—The Word <u>Poor</u> by no means answers this Intention.

52.) (p. 144) Bentley: v. 987. *Like* Teneriff *or* Atlas, unremov'd.] So *Æneas* in *Virgil* is compar'd to the greatest Mountains:
<blockquote>*Quantus* Athos, *aut quantus* Eryx, *aut ipse nivali*
Vertice se attollens pater Apenninus *ad auras.*</blockquote>
But what is that *Unremov'd?* If it refers to *Satan,* it should be *Unmov'd,* not terrified: if to *Atlas* or *Teneriff;* <u>who ever suppos'd, that they were sometimes *Remov'd?*</u> I suspect, the Poet gave it,

> *Collecting all his might dilated stood,*
> *Like* Teneriff *or* Atlas, * UNDISMAY'D.

Hayley: * The best way of answering the above Question is to ask another—Who ever suppos'd that <u>Atlas</u> or <u>Teneriff</u> were sometimes <u>dismay'd</u>?
<u>Risum</u> Ireatis[?] <u>Amici</u>?
If I might presume to offer an <u>Emendation</u> the Line sh.ᵈ run thus—Like <u>Teneriff or Atlas Mount</u>, unmov'd:

Book V (pp. 146–80)

53.) (p. 153) Bentley: v. 198. *Ye Birds, That* singing *up* to Heaven Gate *ascend.*] The *Sky Lark* sings as she ascends; perhaps no other Bird. But *to ascend to Heaven Gate*, which *Milton* always places above the Sphere of Fix'd Stars, is outstretch'd beyond Possibility. He gave it thus;
> *That* SOARING *up* to * <u>HEAVENWARD</u> *ascend.*

Fairfax in *Tasso*, XIV.9
> *But to increase thy Love and great desire*
> *To Heavenward, this blessed Place to behold.*

Hayley: * Wretched Poetry! The Text is figurative & truly sublime—Its being beyond possibility is a poor Objection—so are all Poetical Figures—
> Hanc venia petimus[?] damusque vicissum[?]—

'Tis as impossible to ascend to the Fix'd Stars as it is to Heaven—May not this pass as well as—
> ——Sublimi finiam sidera vertice?

54.) (p. 154) Bentley: v. 210. ˣ <u>Recover'd</u> *soon and wonted calm.*] Rather thus, continuing the Sentence;
> *Firm peace* RECOV'RING *soon and wonted calm,*
> *On to their Morning's rural work they haste.*

Hayley: ˣ Recover'd is a Participle of the Ablative Case & therefore the Sentence sh.ᵈ be printed as above—

55.) (p. 160) Bentley: v. 367. *Possess This spacious* ground.] * *Ground* is too low a Word, and <u>implies that they were to dig and delve in Paradise</u>, as afterwards they did in <u>common Earth</u>. The Author gave it,
> *By sov'rain gift possess This spacious* ROUND.

As it is describ'd, VIII.304.
> *A Circuit wide, inclos'd with goodliest Trees.*

Or GROVE; as VII.537.

> *He brought thee into this delicious* Grove.

Hayley: * Why so? I am at a loss to find out the necessity of such Implication—Vide. Lib. IV. Line. 214.

> ——In this pleasant Soil
> His far more pleasant Garden God ordain'd:
> Out of the fertil Ground, he caus'd to grow.

The same Word there had been equally liable to this Objection, if it imports digging & delving.

56.) (p. 161) Bentley: v. 389. Shall fill the World more numerous with thy Sons,] *Race*,

Hayley: Vide. Lib. II. 248. The Word may include Males as well as Females———

57.) (p. 171) Bentley: v. 674. *Thy eye-lids?* and *remembrest.*] The Author design'd it, ˣ WHO remembrest.

Hayley: ˣ The Parenthesis as above sets all right— [He has placed parenthetical brackets at 5.673–74, from "what . . . lids?"]

58.) (p. 172) Bentley: v. 700. Now ere dim Night ˣ *had disincumber'd* Heaven,] *shall disincumber*

Hayley: This Narration is after the Facts had happen'd & therefore the Word (shall) would be downright Nonsense.

Book VI (pp. 181–215)

59.) (p. 182–83) Bentley: v. 55. *His fiery* Chaos *to receive their fall.*] This could not procede from the Poet: * He always represents *Chaos*, as an unbounded Space on the Outside of Hell and of this World. *Tartarus* had no *Chaos;* and *Chaos* could not be call'd *Fiery, Where, Hot, Cold, Moist, and Dry, four Champions fierce* are every moment fighting for the Mastery. The Poet design'd it thus:

> *Opens wide*
> ITS *fiery* JAWS; WIDE *to receive* THEM ALL.

So VI.875.

> *Hell at last* Yawning *receiv'd* them whole.

Its, not *His;* as 'tis in Line before *Which*, not *Who*.

Hayley: * Not always—for here is one Exception to the Contrary—'Tis true 'tis usual both here & elsewhere to figure Chaos <u>as a Confusion of all the Elements</u> as D^r. Bentley by restraining the Word to that Sense has very ingeniously endeavour'd to make it pass for Nonsense as it stands appli'd in this Place—but here it signifies only a <u>deep wide Place</u>—in this Sense <u>Tartarus</u> was a <u>Chaos</u>—a X & W—hic—<u>quod esset vastus hiatus</u>. / * Besides the marvoellous want of the Sublime in this Emendation (wch I think is as low as is possible) it may be ask'd—what occasion for this Repetition?

—<u>Wide</u> to receive them <u>All</u>

Had there been as many more we might have taken it for granted that Hell was large enough to contain them————

60.) (p. 184) Bentley: v. 93. *And in fierce* Hosting *meet.*] * <u>I do not remember ever to have met with the word</u> HOSTING <u>either in Verse or Prose</u>. The Author gave it,

And in fierce JOUSTING meet.

Hayley: * I (Doctor Bentley) never met with this before—Ergo—the Author never made use of this Expression—The Premises do by no means warrant the Conclusion—Suppose it a Word of Milton's own coining & the difficultie is remov'd—The Riches of all Languages are owing to such Liberties, wch are never denie'd to those who use them sparingly & with Judgement—Surely our Author ought to have equal Indulgence wth Spenser & Shakespear—

61.) (p. 188) Bentley: v. 188. *This greeting on thy impious* Crest *receive.*] *Satan,* as he was arm'd with a Helmet, must need receive the Blow on his *Crest:* but yet to call the *Crest,* an inanimate Metal, * *Impious* <u>is something irregular.</u> 'Tis probable the Author gave it,

This greeting on thy impious HEAD *receive.*

Hayley: * I think the Doctors objection true in strictness—but a Thing <u>inanimate</u> may as well be call'd <u>Impious</u> as <u>Proud</u> wch is tack'd to the same Word within three Lines after & is allow'd to pass muster—Both are right perhaps in a figurative Construction ——

62.) (p. 201) Bentley: v. 528. *Others from the* dawning *Hills Look'd round.*] *Dawning Morn, Dawning Light* are standing Words in Poetry; but ^x *Dawning Hills* are great Rarities; Luminous, such as do not receive the Dawn, but make it. But the Poet dictated it,

> *Others from the* DOWNS AND *Hills.*
Or perhaps, CLIMBING *Hills,* as III.346.
> *Obtains the brow of some* high-climbing Hill.

Hayley: * Dawning—signifies beginning to appear, & the Epithet in this Sense will suit well w^(th) the Tops of the Hills: for as soon as they were visible, the Angels were able to look round them & descry the Foe at a distance, if he was coming.

63.) (p. 212) Bentley: v. 866. *Burnt after them* to the bottomless *Pit.*] This is very strange Measure; * unless he affected to make his Verse *bottomless* too, to express the Idea. But that Whim pursued, would produce strange Monsters in Verse. This may be one way of changing it;
> *Burnt after them,* DOOM'D TO TH'INFERNAL *Pit.*

Hayley: * This has never wanted its admirers for the very reason w^(ch) has given our squeamish Doctor a distast for it—'Tis exactly agreeable to Mr Popes Rule in his Essay on Criticism, where he says—The Sound sh.^d seem an Echo to the Sense—Homer & Virgil abound w^(th) such strange Monsters.

64.) (p. 213) Bentley: v. 867. *Hell heard* th'unsufferable noise.] There could no great Noise caus'd by Spirits falling through next to a *Vacuum;* especially when *Moloch* says, they fell very slowly, as against their natural Levity, II.80.
> *With what compulsion and laborious strife*
> *They sunk so low.*
'Twas not the Noise of the Fall, but the Clamour of those that were falling. And *Unsufferable* fills the Verse, more than it does the Sense. Rather thus;
> * *Hell* heard the HIDEOUS CRIES AND YELLS; *Hell saw.*

Hayley: * I cannot help rejecting this alteration if it were only for the unsufferable affinity of the Sounds; Hell Yells & Hell in the same Line is too grating to escape the Pen of the lowest Poetaster——

Book VII (pp. 216–41)

65.) (p. 218) Bentley: v. 51. *And* was *fill'd.*] He gave it, *And* * WERE *fill'd.* Adam *with his Consort:* as presently, *To* their *thought.*

Hayley: * If we admit <u>were</u> instead of <u>was</u> I think the Word <u>both</u> sh^d precede it in the place of <u>and</u>—
              —<u>Both were fill'd</u> &c.

66.) (p. 219) Bentley: v. 56. With such *confusion; but the Evil soon.*] When he says, *The Evil,* and not *The Danger, the Mischief;* <u>some Word</u> <u>should have preceded,</u> implying the said *Evil.* I suspect therefore he gave it,
              * WICKED *confusion;* but *the Evil soon.*

Hayley: * Do not the Words—<u>Hate in Heaven</u>—War—with <u>such Confu-</u> <u>sion</u> necessarily imply all degrees of <u>Wickedness</u>? The Evil then of this Uproar redounded upon the Authors of It Satan & his Adherents—

Book VIII (pp. 242–65)

67.) (p. 242) Bentley: v. 17. *This Earth* a Spot, *a Grain, An Atom.*] We have it again within six Lines, *Earth this punctal Spot.* So that here it would be better, as I suppose He gave it,
              This Earth a * MOTE, *a Grain.*

Hayley: * With Doctor Bentley's leave I take <u>Mote</u> & an <u>Atom</u> to be synonymous Terms & consequently admitting it here would make Tautology & destroy the beautifull Gradation—a <u>Spot</u>, a <u>Grain</u> an <u>Atom</u>——a Thing so small that it cannot be divided——

68.) (p. 245) Bentley: v. 108. *Swiftness*——Though numberless.] We cannot allow him ^x *Numberless swiftness;* though he hit it off right before, *v.* 38.
              Speed, to describe whose Swiftness number *fails.*
It may be alter'd this way, among others;
              The swiftness of those Circles attribute,
              SWIFTER THAN THOUGHT, *to His Omnipotence.*

Hayley: ^x Suppose Numberless be understood of the Circles—What then? 'Tis God's omnipotence wch gives to the Circles, tho' so numberless, such a degree of Swiftness.

69.) (p. 246) Bentley: v. 120. *That earthly* Sight, *If it presume, might err.*] How can *Sight presume,* or *Sight err?* * *Sensus non decipiuntur.* No doubt he gave it,
              That earthly THOUGHT, *if it presume, might err.*

Hayley: * This is certainly true in some Sense—by means of our Senses we are put in possession of Corporeal Objects, and without the danger of being deceiv'd we do (as the necessities of Life require) distinguish Objects & know that what we see is as it appears, an <u>Horse</u>, a <u>Tree</u>, a <u>Man</u>, &c. but we know nothing of the <u>Nature</u>, <u>Constitution</u>, & <u>first Principles</u> of them; Much less then can our penetration extend so far as to bring us acquainted wth the Nature of the <u>Heavenly Bodies</u> that (as Milton here intimates) are remov'd to such distances from Us.

> ——Heaven is for Thee too high
> To know what passes there; Line. 172.

Besides if the <u>Sight could not err</u> we sh.^d have nothing to do (in order to become compleat Philosophers) but to fix our Eyes upon the Universe and register all that we there observe—If thy Eye is infallible——whence Microscopes & Telescopes? Are they not calculated to supply the Imperfection & Weakness of that Sense?

70.) (p. 247) Bentley: v. 145. *Her* Spots *thou seest* As Clouds.] We have had to do with these *Spots* before, V. 419.

> *Whence in her Visage round those* Spots *unpurg'd.*

And as he has manag'd them, they are a Spot upon the Face of his Poem. Those of the Moon are permanent, and have appear'd the same since the first Memorial of them; and <u>therefore * cannot be Clouds</u>. To make the Passage more tolerable, we may put it thus;

> Her FACE *thou seest*
> LOOK CLOUDY', *and clouds may rain.*

Raphael might say this This to *Adam;* though he well knew, that such Cloudiness sometimes in the Moon's Visage is not to be charg'd on her, as if she did not keep her Face clean; but is caus'd by our Atmosphere, and reaches no farther.

Hayley: * Not Clouds in <u>reality</u> but so in <u>Appearance</u>—to Us at this distance.

> ——Her Spots thou seest
> <u>As</u> Clouds——

Can any Sense be plainer?

71.) (p. 253) Bentley: v. 320. *To* <u>till</u> *and keep.*] Paradise was not to^x be *till'd,* but the common Earth after the Fall. The Author design'd it, *To* DRESS *and keep.* So *Genesis* ii. 15. *And God put the man into the garden of* Eden, *to dress it and to keep it.*

Hayley: ˣ The Word <u>Till</u> in common Acceptation signifies no more yⁿ <u>to cultivate</u>; Our English Translators perhaps chose to use <u>dress</u> here, as imagining it more applicable to a Garden—I suppose it may be otherwise in the ancient versions & the Original, wᶜʰ the Author no doubt had read & understood as well as Dʳ. Bentley——

72.) (p. 254) Bentley: v. 370. *With various living Creatures and the Air.*] This Composition is loose and gaping. Rather thus;

> *Is not the Earth*
> *And Air with various living Creatures* FAIR. *
> *Replenish'd?*

Fair here seems a proper Quality to induce *Adam* to like them. So *v.* 276.
> *And ye that live and move,* fair Creatures, *tell.*

Hayley: * The same sound returns too soon & is very disagreeable—Besides what follows, viz;
> ——All these at thy Command
> To come & play before thee &c.;
was inducement enough to make Adam like them—so that the Reason of the Objection fails.

73.) (p. 256) Bentley: v. 417. *Not so is Man But* in degree.] See the Series of this Sentence. <u>Thou art perfect, not so is Man but *in degree* perfect.</u> What rare Sense is this, *Perfect in some degree,* perfect but imperfect? 'Tis a vile Misprint; the Author thus gave it;

> *Not so is Man,*
> *But* INDIGENT; *the cause of his desire*
> *To help or solace his* Defects.

Hayley: Vi. supra! * (i.e.) in regard to other Creatures yᵗ were indow'd with Excellencies of an Inferior Nature—When we call a Man—<u>Wise</u>—or <u>Good</u>—or <u>Happy</u> we do not mean he is either <u>absolutely</u> but in <u>Comparison</u> only.—they are mere relative Terms—consider'd thus I think the Text may be well vindicated—Adam may be said to have been perfect in respect to all other Creatures but very short of Perfection when compar'd wᵗʰ the Almighty—Surely there are degrees of Perfection—<u>Absolute</u> & <u>Comparative</u> Perfection ought not to be confounded——

74.) (p. 258) Bentley: v. 467. And *Life-blood* streaming *fresh.*] 'Twas certainly too much Expense, to have <u>Life-blood stream away and be lost.</u> * The Author gave it,

A Rib

WITH *Life-blood* STEAMING *fresh.*

Hayley: * Not if we consider what follows
————Wide was the Wound
But <u>suddenly</u> wth flesh fill'd up & <u>heal'd</u>:

75.) (p. 262) Bentley: v. 591. *In Reason:* and is judicious, is *the scale.*]
Here's a strange Verse both for * <u>Measure, Elegance,</u> and <u>Sense.</u> *Reason*
must be shrunk into one <u>Syllable</u>, or else the <u>Line</u> is too long. Great
Beauty in *Is judicious, Is the scale.* And <u>what has *Judicious Love* to do</u>
<u>here?</u> *Adam* had not two Mistresses, <u>that he might make a discreet</u>
<u>Choice.</u> 'Tis a horrible Fault of the Press; for the Author gave it thus;
Love hath his seat
In Reason: UNLIBIDINOUS *is the scale*
By which to Heav'nly Love thou may'st ascend.
No Man of Judgment and Taste can doubt of this Restitution; and to
convince the others I'll produce *Milton* himself, V. 448.
But in those Hearts Love unlibidinous *reign'd.*

Hayley: * When the Measure is alter'd as I think it may easily be by
throwing out the Word (and) wch is not necessary, the Elegance & Sense of
the Lines will be indisputable; The Critick asks—<u>What has judicious</u>
<u>Love to do here?</u> The Angel instructs us in this particular when he says in
the Lines preceding—
What <u>higher</u> in her Society thou find'st
<u>Attractive, human, rational,</u> love still.
In <u>loving</u> thou dost well, in passion not,
Wherein <u>true Love consists not.</u>—
Adam then was to exercise his Judgement in distinguishing rightly between a <u>Rational affection</u> & a mere <u>Brutal Passion.</u> Herein he is directed
to make a discreet Choice————What will become of the Grave Doc-
tor's merry Conceit about two Mistresses?

Book IX (pp. 266–307)

76.) (p. 276) Bentley: v. 250. *And short retirement* urges sweet *return.*]
<u>Urges sweet</u> are Words that seem to fail the Author's Intention. *Long*
retirement more *urges* return, than *short.* Perhaps better thus;
And short retirement SWEETENS * <u>NEXT</u> *return.*

Hayley: If <u>urges</u> be an improper word here I sh.ᵈ choose to substitute <u>our</u> in the room of <u>next</u>—<u>Return</u>.

77.) (p. 279) Bentley: v. 346 [Bentley has emended "Of" to "In" in the margin]

Hayley: [Hayley has underlined "Of" in line 347]ˣ If <u>In</u> is so necessary in the Verse preceding it ought to be continued here.

78.) (p. 282) Bentley: v. 436. Then voluble and *bold, now hid, now seen.*] How *voluble* and *bold* come together, or what Affinity there is between them, is hard to conceive. I despair of making good Sense of it, and therefore offer this in its room;
　　　　* Now CAUTIOUS, NOW *bold; now hid, now seen.*

Hayley: * If this Word sh.ᵈ be admitted there would be a Foot wanting in the Measure wᶜʰ in the course of these Notes the Doctor has usually taken nice care of—To give but one example amongst a thousand others—Were Ye, Ye Fair, but cautious whom ye trust &c.; Rouse[?]—Fair Penitent— where the Word in scanning makes but two Syllables—but waving this I think the Text requires no alteration—
　　　　Then <u>voluble & bold</u>, now <u>hid</u>, now <u>seen</u>
i.e. one while the Serpent rolls himself before her wᵗʰ greater boldness and Freedom—now he conceals himself from her—& anon he appears before her, uncertain as yet when & in what manner he sh.ᵈ address himself to her——

79.) (p. 298) Bentley: v. 909. <u>Thy love so dearly * joyn'd.</u>] He gave it, JOY'D. So IX, 1166,
　　　　Who might hav liv'd, and joy'd *immortal Bliss.*

Hayley: * Not <u>Love</u> so dearly join'd—This rather seems to be the true Sense of the Author—How can I so dearly join'd & united to Thee forego thy sweet Converse & live without Thee?

Book X (pp. 308–47)

80.) (p. 329) Bentley: v. 601. *To stuff this Maw, this vast unhide-bound Corps.*] The Author seems here to have forgot himself: he represents *Death* as a *vast corpulent* Monster, whose capacious Maw can never be cram'd, whom lately, v. 264, he had call'd, *The meagre,* the lean, *Shadow;* and in his Second Book he describes him a mere Shape, or scarce such,

without Substance; as the Vulgar paint him a bare Skeleton. <u>Take there-</u>
<u>fore the contrary Idea; a *hide-bound*, thin-gutted Canibal, always devour-</u>
ing, and yet always mere Skin and Bones;

> *Which here, though plenteous, all* IS YET TOO SMALL
> *To stuff this Maw,* * <u>THAT'S EMPTIED, WHILE ITS FILL'D.</u>

Hayley: * I would here offer another very obvious alteration, & such as—
exactly conveys the Idea that the Doctor contends for—

> all is yet too small
> To stuff this Maw, this meagre hide-bound Corps.

For my own part I can form no Idea of a Thing—

> —that's <u>emptied while</u> its <u>fill'd.</u>

81.) (p. 337) Bentley: v. 800. *Which to God himself Impossible* is held.]
Here *bonus Homerus dormitabat*, our Poet forgot himself. Which *is held*
impossible? Yes, it's one of the Axioms of the Schools. But *who held it*,
when the Sole of Human Kind was *Adam* and *Eve?* Give the Passage thus;

> FLAT *Contradiction: which to God himself*
> *Impossible* MUST BE.

* *Flat* rather than *strange*, for <u>several Reasons.</u>

Hayley: * I think it strange the Doctor would not vouchsafe to give us one
of them—Besides (strange) is a Word of more Force & Spirit y^n (flat) &
must fitter for an Expostulation of so much Energy——

82.) (p. 339) Bentley: v. 818. *Fair Patrimony, that I must leave you, Sons.*]
Our Editor, much conceited of his Dozen Lines inserted above, v. 731,
would give us a few more in the same Key; *Adam's* Presages about his
Posterity's *Curses*. The Author had given it thus:

> *Nor I on my part Single; in Me all*
> *Posterity' is cursed. Ah why should all Mankind*
> *For one man's fault thus guiltless be condemn'd?*

Here we see *Adam* deeply and closely reasoning in Speculation abstruse.
Our Editor will interrupt him, and employ him in Quibbles and Points.
Fair Patrimony, Sons, says he: *would I could spend it all my self, and leave*
you none. Is not this quaint and pretty? The greatest Fortune I could
leave you, would be to leave you quite Beggars. * Ay, but <u>this *Beggary* is</u>
<u>understood of not being *Begot*, of Nonexistence.</u> How could then our
stupid Editor add the next Verse?

> *So disinherited how would ye bless*
> <u>*Me now your Curse!*</u>

If they were disinherited of Birth, if they never existed at all; they would bless him. Absurdity monstrous. And, ˣ *whom now you curse*. What *now*, already, before they existed? Go thy ways, the Flour and Quintessence of all Editors.

Hayley: * This witty Argument seems to be founded upon an ignorant— Blunder—'Tis not the Beggary of not being begot—but that of not being curs'd for his Transgression—this is the Patrimony he would leave his Posterity if he could—In this Light let us consider the whole Passage & what can be more Pathetic & Beautifull?

> ——In Me all
> Posterity stands curs'd. Fair Patrimony,
> That I must leave you, Sons: O were I able
> To wast it all myself & leave you none!

Or in other Words—

> —O could I exhaust the Divine
> Vengeance upon Myself & by that Means leave
> You in possession of that Happiness wᶜʰ I have forfeited!

On Me, Me only, as the Source &c. Vi. Line 131.

ˣ Another mistake—

> Me now your Curse—

(i.e.) Me whom according to the present sad state of Things you'll load wᵗʰ Curses hereafter—Not now—before they were born—The words cannot fairly be taken in such a Construction. ——

Book XI (pp. 348–78)

83.) (p. 366) Bentley: v. 542. *All tast forgo To what thou hast.*] When *Tast* is nam'd, who can doubt but the Poet gave it,

> *To what thou* EAT'ST. *

Hayley: * Surely the Doctor loves Good Eating—Is it not common to say—Such a One has no tast for Books—no tast for Company—Sports &c. Why then must this be confin'd to the sole Pleasure of Eating—as if That were the Summum Bonum? The Author plainly meant it in a larger Sense—meaning that Old Age so blunts the Senses that a Man may outlive his Tast for every Pleasure. ——

Book XII (pp. 379–99)

There are no marginal comments in the twelfth book.

University of Prince Edward Island
Wesleyan University

NOTES

We would like to take this opportunity to thank Mrs. Courtney, the librarian of the Old Library, Christ's College, Cambridge, for her various kindnesses in aiding our research. We would also like to express our gratitude to Gordon Moyles who taught us both the (relative) excitement of bibliographical research. Finally, we would like to thank the Social Science and Humanties Research Council of Canada for the financial support which enabled the preliminary research for this project.

1. William Cowper, letter to John Newton (10 May 1780), *The Letters and Prose Writings of William Cowper*, 5 vols., ed. James King and Charles Ryskamp (Oxford, 1979–1986), vol. I, p. 341. In the version of this letter printed in *The Life and Posthumous Writings of William Cowper, Esqr.*, ed. William Hayley (London, 1806), vol. I, pp. 180–81, the word in question is "tube" instead of "Jube." The modern editors do not mention this variation, probably more sensible than we are of how inappropriate such an act of pedantry would appear in the present context.

2. William Hayley, *An Essay on Epic Poetry; in Five Epistles*, in *The Poetical Works of William Hayley*, 3 vols. (Dublin, 1785), vol. II, p. 36, ep. II, ll. 21–24.

3. John T. Shawcross, ed., introduction, to *Milton 1732–1801: The Critical Heritage*, ed. John T. Shawcross (London, 1972), pp. 19, 26, 30, 31, 33, 22.

4. Cowper, letter to William Hayley, Esqr. (6 April, 1792), *Life and Posthumous Writings* vol. III, p. 379. Hayley's letter to Cowper (of 7 February 1792) is to be found in William Hayley, *Memoirs of the Life and Writings of William Hayley, Esq.*, 2 vols., ed. John Johnson (London, 1823), vol. I, pp. 425–27. Hayley, preface to William Cowper, *Latin and Italian Poems of Milton Translated into English Verse, and a Fragment of a Commentary on "Paradise Lost," by the Late William Cowper, Esq.* (London, 1808), p. xiv. Hayley, *Life and Posthumous Writings*, vol. III, p. 330. Hayley, preface to *Latin and Italian Poems of Milton*, p. xv. Cf. Hayley, *The Life of Milton in Three Parts by William Hayley*, in *The Poetical Works of John Milton with A Life of the Author by William Hayley*, 3 vols. (London, 1794–1797), vol. I, pp. iv–v: "I am indebted to Milton for a friendship, which I regard as honourable in the highest degree."

5. Cowper, letter to Mrs. Courtenay (4 November 1793), *Life and Posthumous Writings* vol. IV, p. 113. Cowper, letter to William Hayley, Esqr. (23 November 1792), *Life and Posthumous Writings* vol. IV, p. 30. Cowper, letter to Samuel Rose, Esqr. (29 November 1793), *Life and Posthumous Writings* vol. IV, p. 124. We have cited the 1808 volume above (note 3). *Cowper's Milton, in Four Volumes* (London, 1810); for full bibliographical information of this volume, see Norma Russell, *A Bibliography of William Cowper* (Oxford, 1963), pp. 182–83. Hayley, preface to *Latin and Italian Poems of Milton*, p. xx.

6. Hayley, preface to *Latin and Italian Poems of Milton*, p. xix. The volume was eventually purchased by Dr. Henry Richards Luard on 19 July 1887 at the sale of a Mr. Meyren's books at Sotheby's. Dr. Luard's signature and the date of purchase are still on the half-title page, as is his brief narrative history of the volume up to his purchasing it. On 16 November 1891 it was in turn purchased by John Willis Clark at the Sotheby's sale of Dr. Luard's books. Mr. Clark presented the book to Christ's College, Cambridge, in 1908 at the Milton tercentenary. Cowper's copy of Bentley's edition of *Paradise Lost* is still intact and housed in Christ's College, Cambridge.

7. Hayley, *An Essay on Epic Poetry* in *Poetical Works;* all quotations come from the first epistle.

8. Hayley, *Life of Milton*, pp. lx, lxi, lxxv, cxi; cxxvi. Hayley, *An Essay on Epic Poetry* in *Poetical Works*, vol. II, p. 116. Hayley, *Life of Milton*, p. xv. To be fair to him, Hayley was also one not simply to carp (however well he did it); when he admired a critic, he plainly said

so. In the first edition of *Life of Milton*, he refers to Richard Thyer as "one of the most intelligent and liberal of English commentators" (p. xv); and in the second edition, his praise of Joseph Warton is fulsome to a fault. See Hayley, *The Life of Milton, In Three Parts. To Which are Added Conjectures on the Origin of "Paradise Lost "* (London, 1796), pp. v–xxiii.

9. Hayley, preface to *Latin and Italian Poems of Milton*, p. xx. Hayley, "Desultory Remarks on the Letters of Eminent Persons," in *Life and Posthumous Writings* vol. I, p. xxvii.

10. Christopher Ricks, *Milton's Grand Style* (Oxford, 1963), pp. 9–10. See William Empson, "Milton and Bentley: The Pastoral of Innocence of Man and Nature," in *Milton: "Paradise Lost": A Collection of Critical Essays*, ed. Louis L. Martz (Englewood Cliffs, N.J., 1966), pp. 19–39; this essay is a corrected version of the chapter which first appeared in Empson's *Some Versions of Pastoral* (London, 1935). R. G. Moyles, *The Text of "Paradise Lost": A Study in Editorial Procedure* (Toronto, 1985), pp. 69, 68. *Milton Restor'd, and Bentley Depos'd* was attributed to Dean Swift; see Moyles, *Text of "Paradise Lost,"* pp. 68, 162n18, 182.

11. Shawcross, introduction to *Milton 1732–1801*, p. 22.

12. Moyles, *Text of "Paradise Lost,"* p. 71. Zachary Pearce, *A Review of the Text of the Twelve Books of Milton's "Paradise Lost,"* in Shawcross, ed., *Milton 1732–1801*, p. 71. William Warburton, "Remarks on Milton's *Paradise Lost*," in Shawcross, ed. *Milton 1732–1801*, pp. 109–10.

13. A. Z., letter, *Grub-street Journal*, no. 113 (2 March 1732), in Shawcross, ed. *Milton 1732–1801*, p. 58. Pearce, *Review of the Text* in Shawcross, ed., *Milton 1732–1801*, p. 80. Moyles, *Text of "Paradise Lost,"* p. 66.

14. Moyles, *Text of "Paradise Lost,"* pp. 67–70.

15. Hayley, *An Essay on Epic Poetry*, ep. 1, ll. 261, 354–58. Hayley, *A Poetical Epistle to an Eminent Painter* (London, 1778), p. 44, part II, ll. 451–55. Hayley, *An Essay on Sculpture: In a Series of Epistles* (London, 1800), p. 35; ep. II, l. 194. Hayley did also criticize Milton on certain, rare occasions. When he advises historians to avoid dwelling on the meaner parts of a nation's history, he notes how Milton, despite his "splendid mind," failed in this respect. See Hayley, *An Essay on History in Three Epistles* (London, 1780), p. 76; ep. III, ll. 303–16.

16. For an informative sketch of Hayley's significance to Milton studies, see Joseph A. Wittreich, Jr., "William Hayley," in *A Milton Encyclopedia*, 8 vols., ed. William B. Hunter, Jr., et al. (Lewisburg and London, 1978), vol. III, pp. 159–60. On Dr. Johnson's biographical theory, see *Rambler* 60 (13 October 1750), in *"The Rambler," The Yale Edition of the Works of Samuel Johnson*, ed. W. J. Bate and Albrecht B. Strauss (New Haven, 1969), vol. III, pp. 318–23; and *Idler* 84 (24 November 1759), in *"The Idler" and "The Adventurer," The Yale Edition of the Works of Samuel Johnson*, ed. W. J. Bate, John M. Bullitt, and L. F. Powell (New Haven, 1963), vol. II, pp. 261–64; and *Boswell's Life of Johnson*, ed. George Birbeck Hill and L. F. Powell, 6 vols. (Oxford, 1934), vol. IV, p. 53.

17. Hayley, *An Essay on Epic Poetry*, ep. I, ll. 242, 12. Hayley, preface to *Latin and Italian Poems of Milton*, p. xiv.

18. Johnson, *The Idler* 74 (15 September 1759), in *"The Idler" and "The Adventurer"* vol. II, p. 231. William W. E. Slights, "The Edifying Margins of Renaissance English Books" (unpublished manuscript), p. 2. A shorter version of this paper was delivered by William Slights on 17 March 1989 at the Pacific Northwest Renaissance Conference under the title "Decentering Renaissance Texts: A Littoral Reading." We would like to thank Professor Slights for kindly providing us with the complete manuscript version of the paper, and also for reminding us of Horatio's comment in *Hamlet*. The quotation is taken from Willard Farnham's edition of *Hamlet*, in *William Shakespeare: The Complete Works*, gen. ed. Alfred Harbage (New York, 1969), V, ii, 151.